D1417427

Dave Duffey
Trains Gun Dogs

Dave Duffey Trains Gun Dogs

By

Dave Duffey

1974

Sporting Dog Specialties, Inc.

Spencerport, New York 14559

© 1974 by David Michael Duffey
All rights reserved.
Printed in the United States of America
No part of this publication may be reproduced,
stored in a retrieval system, or transmitted, in any form
or by any means, electronic, mechanical, photocopying, recording, or
otherwise, without the prior written permission of the publisher.

Library of Congress Catalog Card Number: 74–75116

ISBN: 0–88376–052–5

This book was typeset by University Graphics,
and printed by Flower City Printing.
Design and Production were by Pat French.

3 4 5 6 7 8 9 10 11 12 13 14 15 16 17 18 19 20

1st Printing August 1974
2nd Printing October 1974
3rd Printing June 1975

To my son, Michael Kevin, and my grandson, Kevin Patrick in the hope that there will be other dogs and other guns to aid in molding Kevin into the kind of man Mike can be as proud of as I am of him.

Contents

Introduction

ONCE in our land there was space and game enough and the living style of our people was such that a dog could be trained for hunting in a natural way. Some very wonderful dogs learned their craft simply by doing. The opportunity was there.

For a long time whatever formal or informal training gun dogs received was offered them by their owners. Paying another man to train and develop a hunting dog was virtually unheard of. When professional trainers did appear on the scene about the last quarter of the 19th century most of them dealt with "bird dogs", the pointers and setters. The sportsmen who loved to bird hunt, but found they lacked the time or talent to train their own gun dogs properly, found the services of a professional trainer a most worthwhile investment.

The Ruffed Grouse and Woodcock coverts of the east hadn't been gobbled up by industrial and metropolitan sprawl, flights of Prairie Chicken and Sharptailed Grouse peppered the sky over the mid-western and western prairie lands and occupied the cut-over and burned openings in the timber country. In the south quail flourished on the over-grown plantation lands. There was country and game for bird dogs.

Following World War I, some wealthy eastern sportsmen "discovered" two types of dogs popular in the British Isles, the flushing dogs (spaniels) and the retrievers. Neither ranged out and pointed coveys of birds. The spaniels worked restricted coverts within range of a shotgun, flushing the birds and fetching them when they were shot. Retrievers were specialists, performing the task from which they derive their name, fetching downed birds.

1

At first the Labrador, Golden, Flat-coated and Curly-coated Retrievers coming from the British Isles were considered chiefly as "duck dogs", joining the U.S. developed Chesapeake Bay Retrievers and American Water Spaniels, along with the earlier accepted Irish Water Spaniels, as waterfowlers' companions. Sometime after World War II came the general recognition that with proper introduction and training many of the retrievers could be utilized as flushing dogs to produce upland game for the gun as well as do the picking up after the shot.

With the introduction of spaniels, mostly English Springers and a few Cockers, followed by the retriever breeds, the trickle of popularity in the 1920's became a steady stream in the 1930's. Spaniels and retrievers were well established by the end of World War II in 1945.

That period marked the start of another wave of popularity for a different kind of gun dog. U.S. hunters, particularly in those areas that contained several species of game, became fascinated by the idea of a multi-purpose or "all-around" dog. Many thought the answer lay in the Continental pointing breeds, starting with the German Shorthaired Pointer and the Brittany Spaniel; then the Weimaraner and eventually such breeds as the German Wirehaired Pointer, Vizsla, Wirehaired Pointing Griffon and Pudelpointer.

These so-called versatile pointing breeds have established themselves with thousands of U.S. sportsmen, or are in the process of doing so, and there are other European breeds that may eventually attract attention, become a fad, and eventually be generally accepted.

As the "new breeds" from the British Isles and the Continent won themselves places alongside the long established Pointers, Irish, English and Gordon Setters in the North American gun dog ensemble, the transition was taking place in which the human emphasis on living changed from rural to urban. Huntable acres were either lost or posted against trespass and some bird species, like the Prairie Grouse, became rare. In some instances the declining species were replaced by the introduction of such exotics as Pheasant, Hungarian Partridge and Chukar Partridge. In other areas the decline of native species, largely through habitat destruction and human population pressures, meant a serious loss of hunting opportunity.

Despite all this, today there are more upland bird and waterfowl hunters in the U.S. than in the halcyon days. Sportsmen have labored and paid to maintain their favorite outdoor pastime through the support of state and federal wildlife management and research programs and the acceptance of paying fees to enjoy guns and gun dogs on controlled hunting areas.

Due to modern transportation, short working hours and good pay, probably 100 times as many sportsmen hunt more frequently and diligently than in the years of their grandfathers and great grandfathers. They also have an infinite variety of dog breeds from which to select the individual that best suits their needs. And, because the bags of game can not be as great as they were in the good old days, more emphasis is placed on other facets of the hunt. One of the major accessories, a virtual requirement, is a reasonably well-trained gun dog.

The man who is really serious about hunting can still hire the services of a professional trainer. There are more persons today earning a living developing gun dogs for other people than ever in our history. There are thousands of others who want a good gun dog but may feel that the comparatively infrequent hunting they do does not warrant an expenditure for professional training and they must do the job for themselves.

Added to their ranks is the canine version of the do-it-yourself craze so popular in this country, perhaps not so much for economic reasons as in satisfaction gained in the personal molding or developing of something worthwhile at a time when virtually anything can be "store bought".

Lacking facilities (land, birds, certain types of equipment) and with little or no experience in the selection, care and training of any animal, how is the city and suburban oriented hunter going to go about acquiring and training a competent canine gunning companion who will add to the hours and days of pleasure afield?

It is to those sportsmen, who may be getting their first puppy or who have been less than successful in one or more attempts with previous gun dogs, that this book is addressed. I hope the thrust and content of *Dave Duffey Trains Gun Dogs* does not rule out a reading by the experienced and successful trainer of a satisfactory gun dog or the man fortunate enough to have sufficient land and game available to develop the abilities of a well-bred dog simply by hunting him. There are many fine books on training dogs. I, for one, have never read one that didn't provide some new or different insight into training a gun dog.

It is no criticism of trainers offering tips, or writers of training books, to assert that all too frequently they make two assumptions:

3

1.   That readers know, understand and grasp more than they actually do or will admit they do.

2.   That the would-be trainer of dogs will somehow find himself adequate facilities, chiefly free access hunting lands, and game birds which will permit him to develop his dog both in and out of the open hunting seasons specified in the law.

My hope is that I will not "put down" any readers by recounting explicitly the basic steps in training. By recognizing that there are artificial devices and mechanical means that will aid in "getting through" to a gun dog, between us we may be able to get your dog well-started with a minimum of hard-to-come-by birds and acreages. Then, it can be expected that a season or two of hard hunting will contribute to both your pleasure and the development of a gun dog to be proud of.

No man can expect to own a great, good or even fair gun dog until that dog has had experience on birds. And the more game, both wild and artificially propagated, and that is shot over the dog the better he will be. There is no substitute for feathers for a gun dog to find, point, flush or fetch, or for natural habitat for a dog to negotiate and learn how and where to hunt.

But we must recognize that our opportunities and situations have changed both gradually and abruptly. If for no more cogent reason than necessity we may be forced to alter our approach to achieving a goal. Our goal is training a gun dog and as dog trainers we would be remiss in our efforts if we did not utilize artificial and mechanical devices and perhaps unorthodox or novel techniques to compensate for loss of the opportunity to accomplish this goal by the tried and true, natural way.

It is not expected that this modern book on dog training will win widespread acclaim from the traditionalist and old timer. And because I am a traditionalist, with a penchant for admiring things as they used to be and a reluctance to project myself into the future, I undertake the writing of this book with some trepidation.

But I'm also a fatalist. It's my belief a man must accept what life deals him and live with it if he cannot change it. It is in recognition of the situation as it exists for a very large segment of our upland bird and waterfowl hunting population that stimulated the writing of this book, based on more than thirty-five years of hunting with and training my own gun dogs, almost a decade of taking pay for training dogs for other sportsmen and, for the past fifteen years, attempting to answer thousands of letters about dogs and their training sent by sportsmen to the dog editor of *Outdoor Life* magazine.

Describe it as you will, "a primer", "a treatise", "backyard training for gun dogs", "starting your hunting dog", "the mechanics of dog training" or "a heap of damn foolishness". But *Dave Duffey Trains Gun Dogs* is intended to help all hunters and all hunting dogs who may need assistance in coping with the development and maintenance of a modern day sporting dog. When you've tried it, I can only hope you'll like it and it will help to enhance the appreciation of the grand sport of shotgunning with a good dog.

David Michael Duffey
Wild Rose, Wisconsin
March, 1974

How To Use This Book

Every dog trainer likes to think his methods are the most effective and every writer likes to think his book is so enthralling that it will be read from cover to cover. I'm no exception.

But, there are many ways to remove the pelt of a feline and more than one way to train a canine. Furthermore, the techniques I use, while tried and proven personally, will not work on every dog or will not be properly applied by every trainer who tries them.

It must also be recognized that an "instruction book" too often smacks of the school days that many people are glad are long behind them. And, the man or woman who is all wrapped up in one type' or breed of dog may find what's written about others less than interesting.

Because I would like everyone who buys the book to read the whole book I have tried to make it as readable as possible while clearly showing the how and why of selecting, training, caring for and appreciating a good gun dog. Because it might be disasterous to try a certain training approach on one type of dog that works well on another, the book is compartmentalized and chapters deal with specific things. Yet, some methods work on virtually all dogs or are interchangeable among the types of gun dogs that will be classified and discussed. So it would be beneficial to read chapters on retrievers, for example, even though the pointer breeds are your major interest, and so on.

For the person who has not yet selected a breed of dog from which to pick an individual or who may think he's made up his mind but doesn't yet own a dog, I strongly recommend that you read the whole book. You may find that another type or breed suits your needs much better and the training techniques are better suited to your particular situation. For those already committed or more knowledgeable, I can only hope that reading the entire book will broaden that knowledge and promote understanding of why different people have varying preferences in gun dogs, aiding in appreciation of gun dogs regardless of breed, size, color or specialty.

But because there will be readers who skip chapters that are not of primary concern to them, and to allow other readers who peruse the book in its entirety to go back and concentrate on the chapters most important to them, *Dave Duffey Trains Gun Dogs* has been organized so they can do so.

When you use this book I have two major requests which, if acceded to, will virtually assure you that your choice of a canine will turn into a useful, maybe even a great, gun dog.

1. When you are reading a chapter or section dealing specifically with the type or breed of your choice and you are instructed to read about a technique contained in another chapter (in the pointing dog section, for example, I may tell you to turn to the retriever section to find a method used to teach retrieving or, in the retriever section refer you to the spaniel section to learn how to teach a flushing dog to hunt before the gun) please check it out. It is for your and your dog's benefit to do so.

2. When you've read the book or any part of it don't just put it down saying, "Sounds interesting. Guess maybe I'll try it sometime." And don't put the book on a shelf to gather dust.

To successfully train a dog you must do as well as read. The purpose of this book is to stimulate your interest in getting out and working with your dog and to show you the quickest and most pleasant way of accomplishing something for your effort. Turn to it when you encounter a problem and see if perhaps I haven't anticipated your trouble and your dog's reaction and suggested a means of coping with it.

I have explained to many of the persons who have brought their dogs to me to be trained that there is no great, deep, dark secret to training gun dogs. It is largely a matter of my being paid to spend the time with the dog that the owner should but doesn't. If you do not want to devote some effort to training your own dog neither this book, nor any other, will train your dog for you. If you can't find time to work with your dog and pay attention to him for a few days out of each week but still want a trained gun dog, buy one already trained or send your young dog to a professional. It will be a better investment than this book.

Many people say, "Oh! I could never train a dog." Some of them are right. There are individuals who can not and should not undertake the training of a dog. But most sportsmen and women, with proper guidance, can do a most satisfactory job. Some with the natural flair will quickly master the art of dog training and may find it an all-consuming hobby or even a means of livelihood.

Your success or failure as a trainer of a good gun dog, or much of it, will depend largely upon your effort. But this type of effort should be pleasant and fun for both you and your dog. I hope this book will show you how to get the job done and enjoy doing it. Have at it, and good luck.

There is no accounting for individual tastes. Prejudices and extenuating circumstances must be taken into account. Therefore, no man can pick a dog for another man anymore than he can presume to select for him the young lady or type of young lady with whom to share his life.

Many would be dog owners get off on the wrong foot in the selection of dog breed or type from which they pick the individual dog who will share their hunting experiences for a decade; just as many men are dazzled by the pulchritude and personality of a party–girl when a lass of scholarly or industrious persuasion might better suit their lifestyle.

Appearance, past experience, things you have heard and read, or the availability of a pup or young dog suitable for training may have already helped you to make your decision or firmed up your choice. I won't try to persuade you to try something else. But if you have questions or doubts, or are wide open to suggestion, the observations and opinions regarding the most practical breeds of dogs to be used on different kinds of game should serve as a useful guide. Hopefully this will save the one–or–two–dog owner, who lacks the personal experience to make an objective choice, a deal of time, money and disappointment. It should also give the dogs a break by indicating that the owner may be expecting too much of a gun dog that just isn't cut out for the tasks assigned him.

9

Let's first get something straight. Judgements offered here as to which breed is good for what may be somewhat arbitrary and there will always be exceptions to the general rule. Furthermore, with luck of the draw and diligent training along with sufficient experience, there will be some wonderful dogs that will do about everything a man can ask of a hunting dog.

A few years ago a young man brought a Gordon Setter bitch into my kennel and we took her afield where she put on quite a show on Pheasant. Her owner modestly disclaimed any ability whatsoever as a trainer. "I just took her hunting and she's been doing like that since before she was a year old," he said. "And she's a darn good duck dog too."

"Guess you could say I just didn't know any better," he continued. "We do a lot of duck hunting and the only dog I ever had before her was a Labrador. I just took her along, the first couple ducks I shot fell right in the open water in front of her, she swam out, grabbed 'em and came in with 'em and now I think she's a better retriever than my brother-in-law's Labrador."

There are many hunters who would, upon watching this dog perform and hearing such a tale, rush out and put their money down on the first Gordon Setter that they could get their hands on. The truth of the matter is another Gordon like that one would be damned hard to find. Conversely, had that dog been brought to me, or to another professional, for training there is a strong likelihood we would never have discovered her duck fetching ability. Us "knowledgeable dog men" know setters aren't waterfowl oriented.

What this should point out is the fact that there are some very darling dogs among *every* breed which, given the opportunity, will virtually train themselves and will perform duties above and beyond the specialties to which they are generally relegated. Others can be trained to perform about any task the owner sets out for them, some are restricted to a single facet of upland hunting and, unfortunately, there are some dogs that never become proficient at any type of hunting, much less master a multiplicity of jobs.

While some breeds have a stronger inclination and the requisite physical characteristics to become jacks of all trades than others, the development of an individual dog into a crackerjack specialist or a useful general practitioner rests more with opportunity, experience and training plus the intelligence and ability of that individual than it does with the breed from which the selection was made.

10

1

Gun Dog

Classifications

KEEPING that in mind let's get to the business of picking the right breed for the kind of hunting you do and hope that the individual dog you wind up with will perform in the manner that can be expected from the majority of others belonging to that breed. Should you be so fortunate as to get a real natural there will be no need for you to read any further. Wonder-dog will train himself. But don't count on such a blessing. Even if you are so favored, few men today have the time and opportunity to permit a dog to develop naturally. And the actual training of such a dog by essentially artificial means will be easy, fun and good for both you and your dog.

Before we discuss the game to be hunted, you should know that there are four distinct types of gun dogs in general use on upland birds and waterfowl in North America. They are:

1. Pointing dogs, which include Pointers, English, Irish and Gordon Setters.
2. Flushing dogs, which include English Springer, English Cocker and American Water Spaniels.
3. Retrieving dogs, which include the Chesapeake Bay, Golden and Labrador Retrievers and Irish Water Spaniels.

4. Versatile pointing dogs, which include the German Shorthaired and German Wirehaired Pointers, Brittany Spaniels, Wirehaired Pointing Griffons, Pudelpointers, Vizslas and Weimaraners.

Some of the breeds included in this list you may never encounter afield, for they are relatively rare and perhaps rate no more discussion than a number of breeds which have arbitrarily been dropped from the list because of their scarcity, namely, the Curly-Coated and Flat-Coated Retrievers, the Boykin, Clumber, Cocker, Field, Sussex and Welsh Springer Spaniels.

The classifications, as given, somewhat describe what breeds in that category are expected to do afield and also reflect the kind of work that is emphasised in field trials conducted for each specialty. There is also some overlap, as in the following explanation.

Very briefly, field trial pointing dogs are required to range widely, seek and find game, point their birds and remain steady to wing and shot when the handler flushes the birds and discharges a blank shell. No birds are actually shot and no retrieving is required.

When hunting with the pointing breeds most sportsmen want and expect their dogs to find, pick up and bring in shot birds, or at least "point dead". Many want their dogs to restrict their range when seeking game (hunt closer than field trial dogs) and very few require steadiness to wing and shot.

Field trial flushing dogs are required to hunt a pattern that keeps them within range of a shotgun and upon finding and flushing a pheasant must sit and remain steady to shot, then retrieve upon command the bird that is killed. They are also given simple retrieves in water, and must always be under control.

When hunting with flushing dogs, most sportsmen allow their spaniels more independence, and in exercising less control settle for a more erratic pattern and generally do not have their dogs steady to shot. They want their shot birds retrieved and many use spaniels as waterfowl fetchers. Although too small to compete with them, American Water Spaniels are often classified with the retrievers and they and English Springers can do the duck work asked by many casual waterfowlers.

Field trial retrieving dogs do just that, retrieve out of water and on land birds which are shot so the falls can be marked and remembered by the dog or hidden so the handler can direct his dog with

A class Pointer, Blakemore's Ed Farrior, demonstrates desired high style and intensity on point.

A German Shorthaired Pointer displays an intense, but typically less lofty point on game than displayed by stylish Pointers.

Finnegan, an Irish Water Spaniel, retrieves the real thing, a Mallard Duck.

whistle and hand signals to the bird. Retrievers in trials do not hunt before the gun and produce birds.

When hunting with retrievers, some hunters use them strictly in the manner of trial dogs (non-slip retrievers), in that they sit quietly at the side of the hunter in boat or blind and fetch downed birds upon command. A few use them in conjunction with pointing dogs which do not retrieve, the retriever walking at heel until birds are shot and then being ordered in to pick up the downed birds after the pointing dog is cast on to find more live birds. Many hunters also use their retrievers in the same manner as spaniels, working out in front within gun range to produce upland game and fetching it once it is knocked down.

Thus many spaniels are used as retrievers and many retrievers as flushing dogs. This overlap in duties means that many of the training procedures applied to retrievers are also useful in the education of a spaniel, and vice-versa.

The versatile pointing breeds, which I have always referred to as "Continental Pointing dogs" because of their origins on the continent of Europe, in contrast to the British Isles origins of our other gun dog breeds, are the Johnnies-Come-Lately to the North American hunting scene. They have become popular only since World War II, as com-

14

Smokepole, one the greatest shooting dogs to compete in field trials, shows his form.

pared to the post-Civil War emergence of pointers and setters and the acceptance of the British spaniels and retrievers in the 1930s.

For years trials for the European breeds were, and still are, conducted along the lines of the field trials for pointers and setters, although the Continental dogs did not range as widely and for some of them there was a retrieving requirement.

But in recognition of the fact that these breeds were not developed in Europe to hunt in the manner of North American "bird dogs", (or at least not as pointer and setter field trial dogs are expected to perform) within the past decade an organization known as the North American Versatile Hunting Dog Association has established its own standards regarding gun dog performance.

The testing in these Natural Ability and Utility Dog trials is patterned more after the German *Pruefung*. The dogs are required to hunt for upland game, point it, remain steady to flush and shot and *retrieve* game that is knocked down. They are also required to retrieve from water, trail "wounded" game and a number of other tasks testing their versatility as hunting dogs.

The emphasis in pointing breed trials is on style, wide-ranging independent hunting effort and stamina. In versatile hunting dog

15

testing control, and the ability to perform a variety of tasks well, serving as a combination pointing, retrieving and tracking dog, are noted. It actually is a test against a standard, not a competitive trial to determine which dogs are to win and place.

When hunting with the versatile gun dogs, most hunters expect their dogs to work almost within shotgun range, point the birds and fetch them when they are shot, and to retrieve out of water when necessary. Some do not even require a stanch point, using these breeds as flushers and fetchers, since many do not reach out beyond shotgun range and provide shooting even though their work is improper. As with the other pointing breeds, steadiness to wing and shot is a nicety that is seldom seen.

Considering the fact that *most* men who hunt on foot with pointers and setters do *not* want extreme ranging in their dogs and also require them to retrieve, as in the case of the spaniels and retrievers, there is an overlap of expected performance from pointers and versatile dogs.

There also exists in the field trial world a "shoot to kill" type of pointing dog trial in which Pointers and setters are judged on their retrieving as well as finding and pointing ability. Because the range of many "meat dog" Pointers and setters is comparable to what may be considered "big-going" among the versatile breeds, there are many similarities in work that water down the classifications as I have listed them.

You must first decide whether you want a dog to flush and fetch game or one to point and fetch game. The training of a flusher/fetcher will probably be easier than the training of a pointer/fetcher, given the restrictions most hunter-dog trainers must live with today. The retriever and spaniel breeds fit the flusher/fetcher category, the pointers and versatiles the pointer/fetcher category.

Now evaluate your hunting. Do you concentrate on just one or two game species or does your hunting encompass a wide variety?

Detailed discussions of each breed of gun dog in subsequent chapters, regarding their temperaments and abilities should help you decide. But get the four general classifications straight in your mind and familiarize yourself with the names of the breeds so you know what kind of dog we're talking about before you move to the next chapter dealing with the game birds and dogs best suited to hunt them.

2

The Birds,

and Best Breeds for Them

LET'S level with each other. If you want to know what dog's best for Dusky Grouse, Franklin's Grouse, Spruce Grouse, Sooty Grouse, Ptarmigan, Desert Quail, Massina Quail, Mountain Quail, Sealed Quail, Valley Quail and maybe some others I haven't even heard of, you and I aren't on the same wave length.

If this is to be an honest book and of value to you it must be based on personal knowledge. I've never hunted the above named species. From what I've heard of some of them I doubt they are suitable for hunting with any kind of dog. That makes it unlikely I will ever hunt them or do it often enough to make any evaluations. I hunt because I enjoy the work of a good dog afield. I hope you do too. So I can only beg your forgiveness for the limitations of my knowledge and hope that the discussions about dogs suitable for work on the better known game species will be adaptable to your situation if one of the rarer species happens to be your cup of tea.

Our line-up consists of Pheasant, Bobwhite Quail, Ruffed Grouse, Prairie Grouse (Pinnated, Sharptailed and Sage), Woodcock, Chukar Partridge, Hungarian Partridge, Mourning Dove, Duck, Goose, Rail and Snipe.

Please bear in mind that this is not a book about birds. Therefore we are not going into descriptions of plumage, mating habits, feeding patterns or even how to hunt them and what size shot to use. We are

As pheasant are wont to do, this one flushes a bit early as hunters move into position and the English Setter starts to go with the bird. (Photo courtesy of Olin Mathieson Chemical Corp.)

going to discuss their reactions to dogs and their behavior when hunted with dogs, mostly in an effort to substantiate recommendations in regard to the best breeds for the job.

If in the course of this discussion *you* learn something about the game you prefer to hunt, consider it a bonus. If you already know all there is to know and disagree with my observations write me a nasty letter. It'll make you feel better and *I* might learn something.

Pheasant

This fancy-colored bird is a tough cookie for a pointing dog to handle *properly*. Therefore, you gamble every time you hunt Pheasant with a dog that points them. Maybe on one or two days out of five, particularly in inclement weather, Pheasants will hold tight under a point long enough for you to reach your dog and flush the bird in the classic manner. On such days you'll wonder why anyone would hunt Pheasant with anything but a pointing dog!

But on those *other* days the sequence may go something like this: Your pointer gets down to business, makes a nice cast to a brushy fence row and hits scent hard, locking up on point, maybe 150 yards

To make sure of a flush on a sneaky Pheasant when it is pointed, try to trap it between you and the dog as Dave Duffey and Twist are doing here.

from you. As good Pointers and setters run this is not a long way off. You hustle up there. But before you reach the dog he breaks his point and starts a cautious stalk. The bird is moving on him. From there along 40 acres of fence line it is creep and stop. Creep and stop.

Your patience wears thin. Your dog senses this and you both push a bit faster. Then 60 yards to your front, the gaudy bird, having run out of cover, lifts with a derisive cackle and you *whoa* your dog without shooting. Or, if you touch off a shot in frustration, your keyed up dog explodes and chases the untouched bird out of sight. Your stalk and the time it takes to get your dog back and settled down has consumed 15 to 20 minutes of hunting time.

Or, same situation, but your dog will hold his point until ordered to re-locate. You stomp around in front of the dog trying to flush and every second your dog's tail lowers and he loses character 'cause he knows the bird has left. You tap him on the head, sending him on. He may repeat the careful stalk and stop performance on foot scent. Or if he's a real bird dog he'll dash out high-headed looking for body scent. But the vagaries of scent are his undoing and he "bumps" the bird. You have to *whoa* him and make a split second decision to shoot

19

Springer Spaniel Saighton's Searcher demonstrates how a good spaniel forces a wily Cock Pheasant to leave the ground and afford the hunter a shot.

(because you want the bird more than you want to make sure your dog will have proper manners) or to withhold fire and reaffirm to your dog that he is not to flush and chase.

Of course, it doesn't always happen this way. You may find yourself in possession of the rare pointing dog who will make a looping cast, head off the Pheasant and pin him between you. That's beautiful work, but something only a few dogs are born knowing about or learn after long experience. All too frequently hunting Pheasant with a pointing dog is an erratic and frustrating thing.

Thus, for consistant production and performance in keeping with some standard of proper dog work, the pheasant is best hunted with a flushing dog. The spaniel bustles through the cover like a vacuum cleaner, busy and active. His accelerated tail action indicates he's hit scent. He twists, bounces, turns, pushing the pheasant hard, forcing him to dodge and double. You hustle along keeping close to your excited dog, gun on the ready. The spaniel drives in hard and 20 yards from you the bird is in the air cackling. You swing on him and drop him. Success.

Again, it doesn't always happen this way. An uncontrollable spaniel will flush everything out of range or, in some instances, will trail a bird that chooses to run down a furrow in a straight line and flush him wild. But I'm assuming an average or normal situation and a "country-broke" or fairly well trained dog in both the instances of the pointer and the spaniel. The point is that it was not lack of ability or training that fouled-up the pointer, but the actions of the bird which is beyond your's or your dog's control.

A bird that runs, skulks and hides deep down in wet places is no problem for a flushing dog. He can work properly by utilizing both foot and body scent and is more willing and adept at penetrating thick, swampy cover than the pointer. Finally, he will recover more shot birds than will all but the most unusual pointer. Flushing dogs are generally better retrievers than pointing dogs, marking falls more accurately and driving in to snatch up cripples when the pointing dogs may hesitate momentarily (or actually point) a live bird, giving it time to escape.

Much the same can be said for the other flushing classification, the retrievers. They usually give a less animated performance than do the spaniels, although in terms of proficiency there's not a great deal to choose. On cornfield drives retrievers and spaniels can be put to good use if kept at heel to pick up downed birds and occasionally be cast to flush a skulker.

If one insists on a pointing dog for Pheasants, I would give the German Shorthair, German Wirehair and Brittany the nod over Pointers and English Setters. Their slower pace, shorter range and more thorough coverage of restricted cover are all advantages in Pheasant hunting.

What it boils down to is you can expect one of the versatiles to hunt closer to the gun than can be expected of most pointers or setters. When he does it right and points a bird, because of this proximity,

21

Bobwhite Quail Cock. (Photo courtesy of Olin Mathieson Chemical Corp.)

Pheasant Rooster. (Photo courtesy of Olin Mathieson Chemical Corp.)

chances are better the Pheasant will still be there when the hunter comes up to flush. When he does it wrong and bumps a bird, chances are good the flush will be within gun range and for many hunters this is all they care about. As a result there are many Shorthairs, Wirehairs, Brittanies, etc. in use who are part time pointers of game and others that are fulltime flushers. From a dog man's standpoint this is wrong. But it's done.

Spaniels rank at the top as Pheasant dogs, retrievers second, versatiles third and pointers fourth. There will be many individual exceptions, and representatives of every group can be expected to do a fine job in given circumstances.

Bobwhite Quail

If the good Lord fashioned any bird that is ideal for hunting with a pointing dog it is the Bobwhite Quail. It inhabits range that is open enough to allow a hunter to keep track of a wide–reaching dog and, once located by the dog, quail generally lie quiet under the point for long periods of time, allowing the hunter to approach liesurely and flush the birds properly.

However, because of differences in terrain and climate it is possible to hunt quail with individual dogs from any of the four classifications. But nothing compares to doing it with a good Pointer or English Setter.

Like dog training, quail hunting should be as relaxed and Pleasant as possible for both gun dog and sportsmen.

By natural bent and to some extent by training and experience there are pointers and setters who excell as "covey-dogs" and others that do best as "singles-dogs".

Unless a hunter shoots only coveys, a normal procedure on quail is as follows:

A pointer makes casts to likely looking cover, skimming the edges in his quest for game scent and taking in a good bit of territory. Upon striking body scent the dog pinpoints it accurately and assumes the rigid pose known as a point. If a brace of dogs is being used the second dog, upon coming upon his pointing bracemate also stops, honoring the other dog's find. This is known as a back, an honor, back-pointing or back-standing. The hunter or hunters move up, walk out in front of the stationary dogs, scare up the birds and shoot. Good shots will put more than one bird on the ground out of a covey rise. When the downed birds are retrieved some hunters may send their dogs on to seek another covey.

But most will make an effort to hunt out the single birds that have scattered off from the main body, particularly if they have marked their flight and know approximately where the birds have dropped in. There are individual dogs which do not care to and do not hunt

When a pointing dog makes a find and points, a mannerly bracemate honors that find with a back, as these Pointers are doing.

Hunters move in to flush a single quail pointed by a good "singles dog" after the covey was flushed and shot at.

singles well. Others demonstrate considerable proficiency at this task. Some do both very well.

An overly-simplified description of the difference in action and attitude between the covey and the singles dogs would be to characterize the covey dog as a hard-running, far reaching independent dog which may sometimes be difficult to control. The singles dog will have a more restricted range, more deliberate and careful manner of hunting and more amenable to his handler's bidding. It might be said that a covey dog skims off the cream while the singles dog laps up the milk.

These differences in dogs will be most generally exhibited among Pointers and English Setters. The versatile dogs most often fall in the singles-dog category as do Irish and Gordon Setters. Spaniels and retrievers must, of course, operate within range of the gun.

In certain instances, the flushing dogs can be used to hunt Bobwhite Quail, although this type of hunting is by no means in a class with gunning Bobs over a dog that points. Examples would be in very thick cover or bitter cold weather when birds are holding tight and may be passed up by a pointing dog; or use at heel in conjunction with pointers to be sent to retrieve after the shooting is over; or to flush up marked singles while the pointing dogs are out seeking coveys.

The man who hunts quail off horseback shouldn't consider anything but a Pointer or English Setter, preferably of the covey-dog type. The hunter on foot, in restricted coverts, may prefer one of the versatiles, the Gordon, Irish, or a Pointer or English Setter singles-dog type. A good combination is a Pointer and one of the versatiles, if two dogs are used, the latter usually being a better retriever.

Thus, the recommendations for a dog with which to hunt quail are just reversed from those with which to hunt Pheasant. The pointing dogs are preferable, the versatiles runners-up and the flushing dogs trailing.

Keep the covey-dog, singles-dog differentiation in mind as we work our way through some of the other game bird species so you can make exceptions to the advice being given if your particular hunting circumstances seem to warrant some deviation from the expected norm.

Ruffed Grouse

The drummer of the uplands, the Ruffed Grouse, is another tough bird for a pointing dog to handle properly. Yet when an English Setter or Pointer, by a combination of natural bent and experience learns

The Brittany Spaniel is a top choice among pointing breeds for work on Ruffed Grouse and Woodcock.

how to do the job it is a beautiful and classic form of hunting. There are many good, *young* quail dogs of these breeds but few good, *young* grouse dogs. So the inveterate grouse hunter who prefers pointing dogs doesn't expect too much of a dog until he's put in three or four seasons.

Therefore, from a get-with-it-quick and practical standpoint the flushing breeds have to be rated as best bets and in most instances the versatiles ranked higher if the hunter wants his birds pointed.

Ruffed Grouse are generally at the edge of or inside dense cover where both walking and shooting may be difficult. This in itself calls for a close-working dog, for it is hard to keep track of the dog whether moving or locked up on point. There are few objectives in a grouse wood, i.e scattered cover that should hold birds if there are birds about. Ruffed Grouse may be anywhere in a block of dense cover. Furthermore, a great deal of noise disturbs the birds who will sneak off far ahead of the hunters and considerable shouting and whistling is necessary to keep a wide-ranging dog on the handling track.

Finally, a quarterback with a different game style governs the behavior of Ruffed Grouse, than the ones calling the plays for Pheasant and Bobwhite Quail.

As described previously, the Pheasant calls a running game. The quail, when in doubt, freezes "the ball". In contrast, when there is a question of what play to call, the Ruffed Grouse quarterback says "take to the air."

Thus, it is all too common for a Ruffed Grouse to fly out from under a dog's point through no fault of the dog. The hunter spots his dog pointing along the edge of an alder run, 75 yards away. As he is moving up to his dog, the bird roars up and is into a screen of cover too quickly to afford a shot.

Even with a very close-working pointing dog, almost simultaneously with the dog's snapping into a point (or within mere seconds afterward) the bird may flush. It will be hard for the hunter to tell whether the flush was caused by the dog crowding the bird or because of the wary grouse's behavior. When a pointing dog causes the flush he should not be shot over lest he get the idea that he doesn't have to point his game. Too many wrong guesses in a tricky situation can lead to a dog who is not stanch on point. That is not proper pointing dog work.

Thus, while hunting grouse with a pointing dog is the epitome of the sport it can be frustrating. There is a good chance of spoiling a young dog if the questionable shots are not passed up, and a dog requires patience and understanding on the hunter's part until he acquires the requisite experience in handling these birds.

Flushing dogs, on the other hand, will provide good Ruffed Grouse shooting at a very early age, often well before they are a year old, virtually by doing what comes naturally. Grouse will run on the ground before the noise a dog in motion makes. Flushing dogs will trail them, indicating by accelerated tail action when they are on birds, and will literally drive the bird into the air in front of their noses. The main requirement is that they confine their questing to gun range. The cover grouse frequent aids in naturally restricting their range.

While pointing dogs generally provide the hunter with easier shots, this is not necessarily the case in grouse cover. In many instances the flusher can be sent into a tangled tag alder strip or other heavy spots with the hunter staying in the clear. There he can bring his gun into play more readily than when he must fight his way into a dog on point to put the birds up properly. Finally, the spaniels and retrievers make recovery of shot birds surer than do the pointing breeds.

American Water Spaniels, like this one holding a Ruffed Grouse, are compact, natural and versatile gun dogs.

Labradors can be efficient Ruffed Grouse flushers and retrievers as Onyx demonstrates.

If a hunter insists on a dog that points Ruffed Grouse, for most a good individual from among the versatile breeds will be satisfactory sooner than will be a Pointer or English Setter. Because few of the versatiles are naturally wide-ranging dogs it is easier to put the necessary control on them to keep them close in grouse cover. They are more painstaking and deliberate in their work and more likely to work with low heads and creep with a moving grouse. The Brittany Spaniel, in particular, has the spaniel curiosity that provokes poking into every nook and cranny in which a grouse could be found rather than a tendency to "skim the edges".

The careful creeping after a point has been established is abhorrent to pointing dog purists. But it can be practical for the grouse hunter since the dog's movement and noise will keep an antsy bird on the ground longer, allowing the hunter to move up for a good shot. It is the sudden cessation of movement and noises when a pointer slams into a point and holds it that causes the grouse to flush wild.

For both practical and fun production of Ruffed Grouse the flushing dogs have to be put at the top of the list, the versatiles in the middle and the pointing breeds last.

Woodcock frequent dense cover and a high white-tipped tail and white markings help locate a Pointer like Twist when the dog locks up on birds.

Woodcock

Much the same that has been said about the suitability of different types of gun dogs for Ruffed Grouse can also be said in regard to hunting Woodcock. This long-billed migrant is most often found in the same coverts as grouse.

There is one noteworthy difference. The Woodcock holds very well under a dog's point. In this tight-sitting respect they are equal to or second only to Bobwhite Quail. So you can get classic pointing dog work on these birds. However, because they are in cover which may be even more dense than that frequented by Ruffed Grouse, the pointing dog used must be very close ranging and deliberate.

Even the flushing breeds should be more circumspect in their hunting patterns when worked on Woodcock than on other game and it is no accident that the smallest of spaniels, the Cocker, was once favored as a Woodcock dog and got its name from being called a "cocking dog."

Probably the best dog for Woodcock is one of the versatile breeds who will work *very* close, point and hold the point until ordered to flush—then jumping in and putting the bird out. This allows the hunter to assume an advantageous position in an opening or clearing

29

Sage Grouse are really too
large for a small Springer
Spaniel like Pumpkin to retrieve properly.

A Sage Grouse is a mouth-
ful but no big deal for a
large, strong Labrador retriever like Dave Duffey's
Stormy.

where he can swing his gun, rather than thrash around in a tangle.

But such a dog is not commonplace and most sportsmen will do best
with a flushing breed, particularly a small spaniel, all right with one
of the versatiles and be least likely to develop a good Woodcock dog
from among the pointing breeds.

Prairie Grouse

For brevity, under the one heading, three separate species of
Prairie Grouse will be dealt with. They are the Pinnated Grouse and
the Sharptailed Grouse, which are similar enough to crossbreed and
produce hybrids, and the more distinct Sage Grouse. As indicated
these are birds of the grasslands, although the Sharptail shows more
affinity to brushy lands than do the others. All three species are referred to as "chickens" by local hunters.

Because they are birds of big country, are seldom found in large
numbers (and then only in a relatively few localities) a man serious
about hunting them can consider only the pointing breeds, a Pointer
or English Setter of the covey dog type. If any game species requires a
pointing dog steady to wing and shot as well as stanch on point, it is
the Prairie Grouse.

Itchy, out-lying birds may leave a dog's point early. If he breaks and
chases he will flush the main body of the covey which is holding tight.
Even after the major portion of the covey has been flushed and shot at,

Flirt, a Springer Spaniel, delivers a Saskatchewan Sharptailed Grouse to her owner, Dave Duffey.

there may be one or two straggler birds that should be put out and shot before the dog moves out to retrieve so that a bird flying off doesn't distract him from the pick-up work.

Hunting Prairie Grouse with a pointing dog is usually hot, dry work with bird behavior complicated by prairie winds. It calls for an enduring, wide ranging dog. Trying to differentiate between what's desired in a good bobwhite dog and a good chicken dog would be drawing a very fine line.

However, Prairie Grouse can also be successfully hunted with a spaniel or a retriever trained to work in the manner of a flusher. Many hunters of these Prairie Grouse, particularly the sage chickens, spot their birds from automobiles and then walk them up, or hike across good country doing their own finding and flushing. They can then use a spaniel or retriever to do the picking up. Finally, when birds are sitting tight in brushy arroyos, windbreaks, bluffs and other thick cover, hunters can walk the flanks of these hideouts, sending in their flushing dogs and gunning the birds as they come out.

But the top choice in gun dog types for Prairie Grouse is the pointing dog specialist, followed by the versatile breeds, with the flushing dogs bringing up the rear. With these birds really competent retrieving is usually not a vital necessity since they are easily downed in relatively light cover and even cripples seldom get too far off, in con-

31

trast to the Pheasant which will make an escape even when loaded down with lead unless a good retriever is put in the vicinity of the fall.

Chukar Partridge

This is a tough game bird for any gun dog to hunt. In its natural habitat the climatic conditions and terrain affect a dog's ability to properly locate scent and are hard on his footpads and toenails. When shot as stocked birds on commercial hunting areas the Chukar might best be compared to Pheasant, tightsitting at times in certain cover, but willing to leg it in light stuff.

Running and flushing wild in mountainous, rocky country, Chukars can make a hunt sheer frustration for pointing dogs or versatiles. On the other hand, heat and lack of water seem to weigh more heavily on the retrievers and spaniels who work in the uplands, than on the sometimes shorter-haired, maybe thinner skinned, pointing breeds, with the versatiles falling in between.

I can't honestly recommend the best type of gun dog for Chukar hunting, but lean toward using a retriever or spaniel kept at heel to do the fetching or to be sent in to flush a marked covey once the hunters are in readiness for the flush.

Hungarian Partridge

The Hun, while attracted to agricultural lands in contrast to the Prairie Grouse's preference for wild or rangelands, is still a bird of the open country and may be present in or near the same habitat as the birds of the grasslands. While there are times when a covey will take to its heels, for the most part its behavior when hunted with dogs is similar to Bobwhite Quail. Coveys are pointed, hold, are flushed and shot.

But the coveys are in open country, they fly off much farther than quail (which will usually break for the first available and close-by cover) and there is much less singles-hunting to be done since generally a Hungarian covey will stay bunched.

If you've read this far you know by now that a medium to wide-ranging pointing dog must be far and away the recommended choice for Huns but the versatiles can do the job if you prefer close work.

32

The flushers, spaniels and retrievers, can be utilized primarily for pick-up work, although this can be important. A Hun on the ground seems to be perfectly camouflaged and is difficult to mark down exactly or to spot even in the sparsest of cover.

Besides, Huns have the disconcerting habit of flushing wild and out of range when worked by a flushing dog, although they will usually hold quite well when pointed. They will hold tighter on each subsequent flush, if the covey can be marked down, but it means a great deal of walking before dog and gun can approach within gun range.

So the picks, in order of preference, are pointing, versatile, retrieving and flushing dogs.

Dove

The discussion of a dog for Dove shooting will confine itself to the very popular Mourning Dove, although it might also generally apply to the much less common hunting of relatively rare White-wing Dove and Band-tailed Pigeon. It will also apply to the shooting of common barn pigeons which are fun to hunt but largely unrecognized as game birds.

This is work for a retriever. The birds are taken as they fly into a feeding patch or water hole. In most instances it can be compared to waterfowl hunting, except that the weather is usually mild, or even hot, and a dog physically equipped to withstand severe cold weather conditions is not required, and most falls are on land rather than in water.

For this reason, while retrieving dogs are to be preferred because of their natural inclinations, the flushers (spaniels) may edge in on this preference and one of the versatiles trained to sit quietly with the gunner and sent to pick-up the downed birds (non-slip retrieving) can prove most satisfactory.

Even a properly trained pointing dog may serve in this job. But a good Pointer or setter with the proper urges that make them the outstanding performers they are in reaching out to seek game are seldom amenable to the discipline required to develop a steady, sure retriever, differing in temperament and natural bent from the retrievers, spaniels and even the versatiles.

So the order of preference is retrieving, flushing (trained in non-slip performance) versatile (also trained in non-slip work) and point-

33

Skipper, a yellow Labrador, and his owner Jack Wilson lie in wait for Mallards to come into a cornfield.

ing. They line up this way because straight retrieving is the integral part of a retriever's training and is more easily taught to the spaniels and versatiles than to the pointing breeds.

Waterfowl

Despite the popularity of duck and goose hunting, the subject of suitable dogs for use in this sport can be very briefly dealt with. The

American Water Spaniels, like McGurk holding a Mallard Duck, were developed in Wisconsin for hunting out of duck skiffs but are also useful upland game hunters.

name of this game is *retrieving,* fetching birds knocked down (usually in marsh cover, frequently in open water and occasionally on land) under the most trying conditions. Only one type of dog is eminently and universally acceptable—one of the retriever breeds.

Possessing the necessary physical requirements and temperamental make-up, developed and normally trained in this non-slip retrieving specialty, they are head and shoulders above any other type for waterfowl work. Considerable water work may be required and should be done by a spaniel, and some can be expected of the versatile type. When dogs in the pointing classification retrieve out of water it is usually a surprise or bonus and even then seldom utilized.

The occasional duck hunter may find that the spaniels and versatiles will perform satisfactorily for him, but avid waterfowlers are usually specialists in this sport themselves and require a specialist for their needs. That's what the retrievers are, although with training their duties can be broadened to encompass producing game for the gun as well as fetching it after it is downed.

That puts dogs in the retriever category as many lengths in the lead in the sport of waterfowling as was Secretariat in the Belmont Stakes, with spaniels as possibles, versatiles as probables and pointers lost in the dust.

35

Rails

Hunting of these shore birds, even though they exist elsewhere, is largely confined to the eastern coast and rates more of a specialty or novelty sport than most of the other gunning mentioned. Again, the nod is to the retrieving breeds, almost exclusively, although the spaniels have some possibilities.

High, dense cover, tangled, mucky underfooting, that won't support a dog but impedes swimming; multiple falls of small birds that don't give off much scent and will dive when crippled; require a strong, savvy dog with a good nose and unquenchable desire to find a bird. Even among the retriever breeds a good rail fetcher is in the category of a good Ruffed Grouse dog among the pointing breeds.

Wilson's Snipe

To many, snipe hunting may bring to mind a practical joke, like sending a mechanic's helper for a left-handed monkey wrench, and it has become a somewhat esoteric sport in North America. The reason I haven't consigned it to limbo is that, in contrast to rail shooting, the Wilson's Snipe or Jacksnipe can provide some sport with all four categories of gun dogs.

There may still be some snipe shooting done over decoys, for which of course a retriever fits in best. But most sportsmen will encounter these zig-zagging migrants in the early fall in boggy meadows and along marsh edges. They will hold to a dog's point, but seldom do pointing dogs take to pointing them "naturally" as they do other game bird species.

If much Jacksnipe hunting is planned, and a dog that points is wanted, the versatiles get the nod over the pointing breeds, with the setters usually taking to the wet going better than pointers. Much fun can be had hunting snipe with flushing dogs. Spaniels and retrievers are to be highly recommended since the birds customarily bank against the wind and turn out over water when put into the air. A dog that likes water work is a must.

Since most hunter encounters with snipe are infrequent and casual and there is no call for a Jacksnipe dog, flushing dogs rate as tops. Snipe are great for training young dogs since they are easy to spot flushing in the open as they do and calling attention to their flight with their cries. They help a youngster to put together the sequence of scent, bird in the air, gunshot, downed bird to fetch.

In common with the Woodcock, the Dove and the Rail, Jacksnipe are not readily retrieved by numerous individual dogs among all the breeds. Whether it's the feather texture, smell, taste or what not, I can not tell you. Only a dog could testify. But you should know so that it comes as no surprise to you should your dog retrieve other game birds naturally or with very little training but balk at those mentioned above.

Summary

At this point you've either skipped around and read the recommendations regarding the best types of dogs to use in hunting your favorite game bird or birds or you've waded through the chapter in its entirety. Let's hope it was the latter, for you will find the comparisons worthwhile in the final decision, which rests with you, as to which of the four types of gun dog: pointer, versatile, retrieving or flushing, best suits your needs.

Before moving on to the specifics about the various breeds in each category and the training methods to bring out the best in them, a summary and explanation should put the opinions expressed in their proper perspective.

The foregoing recommendations have been based on the supposition that most readers will be acquiring a puppy. This may be as their first dog or as a replacement for another dog, or other dogs, they have hunted with, to varying degrees of satisfaction and success.

If you are obtaining a well-started or a trained dog, all bets are off. In that case, the breed or color or anything else about the dog is relatively unimportant as compared to what that individual dog does. If he does the job you want done to your satisfaction, I couldn't, and you shouldn't, care less if the dog is a Chihuahua or a St. Bernard.

There are exceptional individuals among all breeds and exceptions to all rules. Dogs are living, feeling, instinctive, even thinking animals, not machines turned out to certain specifications and tolerances and wholly predictable. My recommendations are based on percentages and what can be generally expected, based on personal experience and that of many close friends who are as deeply involved with dogs as I am. This should be kept in mind in regard to what you've already read and what you will be reading.

Some assumptions you can safely make include the conclusion that if the game you are hunting is customarily found in coveys, (more than two birds grouped together) such as quail you will be most happy with a dog that points. Birds usually found singly or in pairs, like Pheasant, are better targets for dogs that flush their game. Birds that come to the hunter, like waterfowl, give the nod to retrievers. Thus, among the pointing dogs you will find many good quail dogs but comparatively fewer good Ruffed Grouse and Pheasant dogs.

On the assumption that most hunters don't have the opportunities, cannot or will not take the time to develop a dog that handles Ruffed Grouse and Pheasant properly and wants the use of a proficient dog as quickly as possible, gun dogs of the flushing type have been touted for those birds.

As pointed out in the introduction, too few of today's sportsmen have the opportunity to develop a gun dog naturally. Many may have little talent for training a dog or if they possess this touch, lack the chance to discover what makes dogs tick and prove their ability to come up with that "once in a life-time" gun dog.

So, because the talents of most aspiring dog trainers may be either unknown or found wanting, it is paramount that some flat recommendations be made. These will increase the chances of a sportsman enjoying the work of a useful dog in return for the amount of time, too often minimal, that is spent on the dog's education.

Perhaps there are talented trainers who might make a gun dog out of a lap dog, given the time and money. But we must recognize our shortcomings and there is little point in doing things the hard way unless there is something mighty important that needs proving. So if you are driven to prove you can train a Pointer to be a better goose fetcher than a Chesapeake Bay Retriever or you insist on a Labrador retriever that will point quail coveys, have at it.

But the matching up of game birds to gun dog types has been attempted in an honest effort to make your work with your dog as easy and pleasurable as possible and the training techniques should make it possible for you to have an acceptable gun dog even though your training and actual hunting opportunities are restricted by the stresses and realities of modern day living.

With that in mind, let's get to the specifics of how to train gun dogs of the pointing, flushing, retrieving and versatile types and what you might expect from the various breeds within those categories in the forthcoming chapters.

3

The Retrievers

IF it were possible to train a good hunting dog within the confines of your own backyard chances are this dog would be one of the retrievers.

The things that are customarily asked of the retriever breeds, and the equable temperaments of the majority of these dogs, are suitable for mechanical and artificial training procedures. So it is fitting that the retrievers kick off the sections on the breeds and the methodology of training them.

But before you buy, you should know something about whatever it is you are getting. So without further ado, let's find out something about the kind of dog you'll be working with if you've selected one of the retrievers: Chesapeake Bay, Golden, or Labrador, as the answer to the kind of hunting you want to do. The fairly rare Irish Water Spaniel will be dealt with and the Flat-coated and Curly-coated retrievers, which are comparatively non-existent in North America, will be also touched upon.

Because all the retriever breeds are asked to do essentially the same thing and, if you peeled off their hides, it would be difficult to establish which specimen belonged to which breed, it is inevitable that comparisons will be made. Also there may be useful references made to, say, Golden Retrievers in the section dealing with the Labrador and so on. So, even though you may have made up your mind which breed interests you most, please take a few extra minutes to read up on the others so you miss nothing about your favorite and come to understand something about "those other dogs".

Labrador retrievers like Poncho, owned and trained by Dave Duffey, are sleek intelligent dogs easily trained as fetchers and flushers.

Labrador Retriever

The Labrador retriever needs no apologists, ranking as the most popular retriever on this continent and one of the most popular gun dogs—and with good reason.

Physically and temperamentally the Labrador is able and willing to do what millions of hunters want a gun dog to do, "bring home the bacon" whether it be waterfowl or upland birds. In addition, their great intelligence, level, sensible attitudes toward almost everything they encounter makes for a very easily trained dog that can be thoroughly enjoyed in the home during the off-season.

Physically the Labrador is a large dog, but not outsize, height running about 23 inches at the shoulder with weight on either side of 65 pounds. Their short, dense coats are water and weather resistant and generally unattractive to mud, burrs and odors. Along with the strength and power to bull through muck and bog and his stamina to swim for hours, the Labrador has the agility to negotiate, without undue strain, the upland terrain.

Love of water and natural retrieving ability are shown by these two Labrador pup littermates, one yellow, one black.

It is this sort of balance that makes the Labrador a favorite as a practical hunter and fetcher of a wide variety of game, both aquatic and terrestrial. And this balance is shown temperamentally as well as physically.

Their fire and drive is balanced by serenity, courage by common sense, eagerness by patience, and independence by docility. They leave no doubt about their enjoyment in performing their tasks and seem proud to please their trainers.

The Labrador was recognized as a distinct breed by the English Kennel Club in 1903. But from a sportsman's standpoint there is no cause to speculate about the origins of any of the retrievers coming from Great Britain except to make this observation. At one time, in both Great Britain and the U. S., dogs used to pick up and retrieve shot game were simply referred to as retrievers. In time breeds were developed from this common stock, short-coated black dogs became Labradors, long-coated black dogs became Flat-coats, long-coated yellow dogs became Golden Retrievers and so on.

The first Labrador is supposed to have arrived in the U. S. in 1917. But as recently as 1926 only three were recorded by the American

41

Kennel Club, which at that time lumped all retrievers in one category. The breakthrough in popularity began in the 1930s and the major decade of development was roughly the late 1940s to late 1950s.

Labrador, Golden, Curly-coat and Flat-coat importation was begun by wealthy sportsmen from the northeast who had become familiar with the work of non-slip retrievers during shoots in the British Isles. The latter two breeds never caught on, and it was the Labs and Goldens that supplanted the Irish Water Spaniel and the native Chesapeake Bay retriever in the waterfowl marshes of the North American continent. Some of the early retriever trainers were British Isles natives who were familiar with the requirements and training methods for non-slip retriever work. Retriever popularity spread from the east to the midwest and then to the west coast.

Sportsmen discovered, probably by accident, that a goodly percentage of Labradors took readily to hunting before the gun in the manner of spaniels, which took them out of the category of non-slip retrieving specialists and made them contenders for accolades as multi-purpose dogs. This adaptation to upland hunting by Labs and, to a lesser extent, the other retriever breeds, plus the popularity of retriever field trials, may well have saved retrievers from near oblivion when waterfowl bag limits and seasons were drastically reduced in the late 1950s. This is particularly true in the midwest and far west where both waterfowl and pheasant are gunned extensively. Ducks in the morning and pheasant in the afternoon is a most popular hunting routine. The Lab has proven a great favorite for this dual purpose work.

Labradors can be any solid color, black being by far the most prevalent, followed by yellow and chocolate. Although there is a prescribed standard, as a factual matter there is some variance in appearance from the heavy-bodied, shorter-legged "original-type" Labradors to a leaner, taller type that has developed in this country, probably in answer to performance standards desired in U. S. marshes and uplands.

Labradors are good-looking, no-nonsense gun dogs that can be highly recommended to the sportsman who is a waterfowl specialist or who hunts both waterfowl and upland game birds. They are probably the most versatile and adaptable breed among the retrievers, present few training problems and are most easily brought along by a beginner and can be most highly polished by an experienced trainer.

Chesapeake Bay Retrievers like this one are big, rugged, no-nonsense gun dogs, unbeatable for duck and goose retrieving.

Chesapeake Bay Retrievers

It is not easy to call a Chesapeake Bay retriever pretty. But their physical and mental toughness, practical and most highly prized, wins great admiration for this native American breed.

The distinctive and peculiar nature of the Chessie must be understood and coped with if he is to be handled properly. Along with the Irish Water Spaniel, the Chesapeake is least likely to progress rapidly, if at all, when trained by the mechanical means that are so successful with the Labrador and Golden Retrievers.

Chesapeakes do like to do things their own way. But they have a great degree of innate ability, stick-to-itiveness and stubborn determination. The trainer who gets through to these dogs through the combined tactics of firm discipline and acceptance of idiosyncracies will come up with a retriever that will perform amazing feats.

The Chesapeake's origins are subject to a tale regarding a pair of shipwrecked puppies who found their way to the Maryland shores and

Chesapeakes are tough, but when the trainer gets through to them, they pay attention.

myths of bitches being staked out in swamps where they were bred by otters, resulting in the water-loving qualities of the breed. It seems likely that breeds like the Otterhound and Coonhound went into a mixture with the "water dogs" that lived with the Chesapeake baymen to produce a strain of dog greatly resembling the Chessie of today that was breeding true to type shortly after the Civil War.

There is no question that this is one of the few breeds developed on the North American continent, its early development being concentrated in the Chesapeake Bay region from whence the breed is named and the popularity spreading to the Mississippi and west coast waterfowl flyways.

Physically the Chesapeake is about a 70 pound dog, between 21 and 24 inches at the shoulders. Both undersize and oversize specimens will be encountered, with the latter more likely. They exude an expression of sheer power and determination, having the physical ability and stubborn desire to accomplish the most rigorous tasks a hard hunter could ask of them.

Their coats are unique and eminently suited for a dog that can literally live in the water; dense, highly-oiled and rough to the touch,

44

with a wave that approaches a crisp curl along the back and down onto flanks and shoulders that wards water off the skin; backed by a wooly undercoat that insulates against cold. The description "dead grass in color" covers many shades of coat from a rich cocoa hue to almost cream color.

When high hindquarters are coupled to a long back, the appearance may be swaybacked which, while no handicap in the water, doesn't lend itself to the cutting and turning an upland hunting dog must do. But this old-style Chesapeake is giving way to a shorter-coupled type in an effort to produce dogs that move more efficiently on land, increasing their versatility.

For the duck and goose hunter who lives and breathes his sport there is no better choice than the Chesapeake, although individual Labradors and occassionally Goldens and Irish Water Spaniels may approach its proficiency at that game. With individual exceptions the Chessie is not at a par with the others for upland work, although he can get the job done.

In comparison Chesapeakes do not display the biddability of the Labrador, the affection of the Golden or the sense of humor of the Irish Water Spaniel. The Chesapeake is his own man, aggressive and possessive, suspicious of the motives of strangers, but devoted to those he knows and unwilling to share them or his work with other dogs.

In that light, if you are looking for a watch dog to provide protection as well as a practical gun dog you may well lean to the Chesapeake. If I drove into a yard with a dog running loose in it and the dog was a Chesapeake I'd stay in the car until the owner made an appearance; if it was an Irish Water Spaniel I'd be prepared to retreat; if it was a Labrador I'd figure he'd be reasonable and if it was a Golden I'd figure on being accepted as a buddy.

Golden Retrievers

A strikingly beautiful dog, the Golden retriever ranks as the second most popular retriever in North America, thanks to a combination of looks, temperament and ability.

As compared to the handsomeness of the Labrador, the ruggedness of the Chesapeake and the oddity of Irish Water spaniel appearance the Golden must be termed pretty. In keeping with this physical picture the Golden is extremely affectionate and loving in disposition and has feelings that are easily hurt.

A Golden Retriever "brings home the bacon" to his pro trainer, Junior Berth.

The opposite extreme from the Chesapeake's independence and toughness, the Golden is soft in temperament, responds best in training to coaxing, praise and sweet talk and they are honest and completely trusting.

Like the other retrievers they are sizeable dogs, again in the two-foot high, 65–75 pound category. What makes their appearance so striking is their long, reddish-gold colored coats. A dense undercoat which insulates against cold is most efficient, but the outer coat is a disadvantage in everything except appearance. It attracts burrs, mud and sticktights and loads up with water and requires more attention than Lab or Chessie coats.

After being brought over from England, the Golden was developed primarily in the mid-west following World War II. They are the only retriever breed other than the black Labrador, which has dominated competitive trials since their inception, to win National Championships. England officially recognized Goldens as a breed in 1910, Canada in 1927 and in the American Kennel Club recognition came in 1932.

They are highly intelligent and quick to learn. Too much pressure or discipline wrongly administered can cause Goldens to sulk. Being somewhat "spaniel-like" in temperament they can be stubborn in an ingratiating way.

They have good noses and take readily to learning to hunt before the gun in the manner of the spaniels and are agile enough to last through a day's gunning. With individual exceptions, Goldens have to be ranked behind Chesapeakes and Labradors for waterwork under the most arduous conditions.

Creditable performances can be expected on both land and water, under normal circumstances. Women who are aspiring hunting dog trainers will find the Golden temperament ideally suited and men should be more quickly able to establish control over the less rambunctious Golden than the other retriever breeds. They are hard to beat when doubling as most loveable companions and children's buddies.

Irish Water Spaniel

Circumstances and the advent of the Labrador and Golden retrievers have come close to obliterating the comical appearing and acting Irish Water Spaniel from the North American sporting scene.

Irish Water Spaniels, like Finnegan shown retrieving a dummy, are comparatively rare in the hunting field.

But it wasn't always so. From the last quarter of the 19th century to the late 1930s they shared with the Chesapeake and the American Water Spaniel the distinction of being the most popular waterfowler's dog in North America, being the first retriever imported to this country, used in the mid-west about Civil War times and being well known on the eastern seaboard and west coast by the turn of the century. In the early 1920s they led all other retrievers in the number officially registered and there were many more of pure or mixed lineage at work for sportsmen and market hunters who didn't bother with registration papers.

Today they are relatively unique dogs. But if a good one can be found they are capable workers in the marshes and uplands. They have tightly curled, ropy coats protective against the water but prone to become water-logged and matted with sticktights and burrs, impeding progress and requiring more than casual attention.

The Irish display distinctive top-knots on their heads and bare, spike-like tails which have earned them the nick-name of "rat-tailed spaniels". Their appearance and temperament strongly indicates the use of the Poodle (which itself was originally a duck retrieving breed) in the breed's make-up when it was developed in Ireland in the mid-

48

A dry Irish Water Spaniel, Finnegan, sits and stays for pro trainer, Orin Benson.

Note curls and poodle-like top-knot on this wet Irish Water Spaniel.

1800s. They are long-legged dogs, with a peculiar rolling gait, and about the same height and weight as the other retrievers. . . . up to two feet at the shoulder, 55 to 70 pounds. The color is solid liver.

They are highly intelligent but temperamental and object to being forced to do anything. If they can be shown how to do something or conned into thinking they've figured things out for themselves the results can be gratifying. They are at their best in the marsh and bogs and will do their best upland game work on birds hanging out in that type of terrain.

If you like a different kind of dog with a personality that can be both amusing and exasperating but never dull or mechanical, can laugh at yourself and your dog and enjoy training challenges that test your ingenuity, give the Irish a try.

A Pertinent Digression

Digressions are pertinent when they contribute to explaining situations and one seems in order here, offering possible reasons why breeds like the Irish Water Spaniel, American Water Spaniel and

49

Chesapeake Bay Retriever served so well for so long and then declined in popularity. For between the two World Wars a generation of waterfowlers was referring to one of these three breeds when speaking of a duck dog.

That era saw the tag-end of market hunting, most liberal bag limits, spring and fall shooting, live decoys . . . it could be termed the heyday of waterfowling. Proficient guns and ammunition, undrained wetlands and large numbers of birds for a comparatively few shooters meant more ducks down for a dog to retrieve in one day than most get a chance at in several seasons today.

Waterfowl retrievers weren't professionally or formally trained. They learned by doing. If they weren't wise enough to pick up the rudiments of what was expected of them they were discarded.

The past 30 to 40 years have seen tremendous increases in both the general and the hunting human populations, loss of wetlands, decline in waterfowl numbers and the introduction and development of the other retriever breeds.

With the substitution of field trials (first held in the U. S. in 1931) for actual hunting experience in the training and development of retrievers and the advent of numerous professional trainers to develop such dogs it eventuated that the newer retriever breeds, Labradors and Goldens, were more adaptable to the various mechanical training techniques which ingenious trainers devised to cope with the limitations of time, bird numbers and actual gunning opportunities.

Hunters no longer needed extremely rugged dogs to bring back 100 or more ducks a day, day after day during long seasons, and trainers saw little need to try to cope with balky temperaments when more biddable, and therefore easier to train, breeds had become readily available. Admiration remains for the indominantable qualities of the Chesapeake, for example, but for most hunting dog buyers who required, figuratively, a half or three-quarter-ton pick-up truck for their work, something in the Mack truck class had definite drawbacks.

But there are, and hopefully always will be, sportsmen who have a preference for "think-for-themselves, natural gun dogs." They will accept the challenge of channeling these qualities through training sessions that are costly in time and money for the professional and frustrating to the amateur. They will take pride in an unusual dog that rewards them in terms of solving field problems that would baffle easier trained but less determined dogs.

But while today's do-it-yourselfer must recognize the truth of such claims as "when conditions are so bad you'd hesitate to ask a dog to do it, you know a Chesapeake is enjoying himself" or "the Irish Water Spaniel is too smart for his own good and, when he's a mind to, can outwit his handler," a sportsman must also be aware that in terms of rapid progress during training and satisfaction in the hunting field he probably will be best served by a Labrador or Golden retriever.

Summary, Comparisons and Suggestions

No two dogs and no two men are of exactly the same temperament or physical structure. I can only make general suggestions and recommendations regarding which breed of dog you may settle on, based on personal experience . . . and prejudices . . . which you must weigh when you make your decision.

Assuming that I had decided on a retriever as the type of dog I wanted, if I were primarily an upland bird hunter with some duck hunting tossed in, I would pick in this order, Labrador, Golden, Irish and Chesapeake.

If I was primarily a waterfowler with some upland hunting on each year's agenda the pick would be Labrador, Chesapeake, Irish and Golden.

If I hunted waterfowl virtually exclusively my choice would be Chesapeake, Labrador, Irish and Golden.

If I hunted upland birds exclusively the order would be Labrador, Golden, almost at a par, with the Irish and Chesapeake trailing.

If I did considerable rail and snipe hunting or my duck hunting was mostly jump-shooting I'd give the Irish a try, although there's no reason the other three breeds might not rate equal consideration.

As a multipurpose, easy-to-train dog for the widest variety of work, most readily available from proven stock, it would be the Labrador by a wide margin, the Golden and Chesapeake in the middle and the Irish bringing up the rear.

If I was looking for a family dog and pet primarily and hoped to use the dog occassionally for hunting I would opt for the Golden and expect the Labrador to work out very well too. The Irish would be a source of amusement and the Chesapeake most protective.

If I decided I might dabble in field trials in addition to hunting with my dog there'd be no choice but the Labrador, with the runner-up

Goldens, who have the second most wins as compared to Labs; and the Chesapeakes, whose ratio of wins compared to number of dogs entered is good, trailing badly; with the Irish least likely to perform properly in trials.

If I was going to do very little training at all, just take my dog hunting and hope for the best, I'd get a Chesapeake or Irish, be hopeful about a Labrador and least optomistic about the Golden.

If I had to pick a two-word description for each breed the best I would characterize the Labrador as "sensibly pleasant", the Golden "lovingly affectionate", the Chesapeake "dourly independent" and the Irish "clownishly erratic".

The Labrador rates as the least complicated to train with the greatest ability to turn out okay despite trainer errors; a soft-spoken man with a light touch and a great deal of patience will find the Golden to his liking; the loud and rough, don't-give a-damn character will do less damage to the Chesapeake than to the others; an easy-going man with a great sense of humor will have a ball with the Irish.

There you have some personal evaluations for your consideration in picking a dog from the retriever breeds. What about the Curley-coated and Flat-coated retrievers? I can only say try one if you can obtain one and you are looking for something different have at it. But as I said at the start, to be useful to you this book must be based on honest experience. I've seen both Curley-coats and Flat-coats work, could not fault what I saw to any great degree but I have never owned, trained or hunted extensively behind one.

Now, let's get on to the training of that angel or rascal which the luck of the draw, when you picked a pup, has saddled you with for the next decade or so.

4

Training Retriever

Gun Dogs

MOST retrievers out of good hunting or field trial bloodlines come with an almost built-in fetching ability. That is, they have strong instincts to pick up objects and carry them. The trainers who take advantage of this instinct and channel it into a finished product, the picking up of a downed bird from land or water and a happy delivery of the game to hand will enjoy schooling their retrievers in their primary duties.

Fetching is the retriever's speciality, therefore the thing he should take to most readily and easily. There is no point in making a lot of unnecessary work for the trainer or unpleasantness for the dog by teaching artificially and mechanically something that should be basically natural to these breeds.

This brings us to the debate about which is better, the natural retriever or the force-trained retriever? Far too much is often made of this subject, perhaps due to misunderstanding. If I had to choose between a really natural retriever and one that has been force-broke I would choose the latter every time.

A purely natural retriever is a dog whose inclinations have led him to picking up the first thing thrown for him or the first bird shot for him and bring it back somewhere within the vicinity of his master. The trouble is with the master, who may figure that he has a wonder dog that has trained itself and no further work is required.

That man will discover, however, that, with rare exceptions, this

Retriever pups, like this black Labrador and this Golden Retriever, should demonstrate willingness to pick up and carry at an early age.

great natural will encounter some situations he doesn't like and decide not to fetch at all. In short order the dog will become a "some time" retriever, one who might or might not fetch a bird, depending upon circumstances.

At the other extreme is the dog that is force broken to fetch. He may not be at all happy about what he's doing, but he damn well does it because of the consequences he will suffer should he refuse. It is a training method that is arduous and tiresome for both man and dog. Regardless of reluctance or refusal to pick up a dummy, or a bird, the dog is forced to do this upon command and he responds reflexively to this command rather than suffer some pain that goes with a refusal.

Because there are times when a retriever crops up who has no natural "pick up and carry" ability or is just plain bullheaded, force training must be resorted to. So how to do it will be outlined. But I'm inclined to look on force breaking as a last resort and consider a retriever that won't pick up and carry instinctively about on a par with a pointer who has to be taught to stand his birds rather than point them naturally. Such a dog may be ever-so-proficient but he lacks the class and style that is imbued in a good dog who is happy about what he's doing.

A yellow Labrador puppy parades around carrying a dummy, showing natural inclination to pick up and carry, while a Springer Spaniel pup tries to figure out how to rush in and snatch it away.

Fortunately, there is a middle ground between those two extremes. For 99 out of 100 of the sportsmen who are going to train their own dogs, this is the easiest and most enjoyable method of turning out a *reliable* retriever. And as a bonus, your dog lets you know by his demeanor that he's as pleased about the whole deal as you are. Furthermore, most professional trainers take advantage of what might be termed either a coercive natural method or a permissive force method of teaching a retriever to perform properly.

You have a choice. Accepting the risk that he will be a "some-time" or "once-in-a-while" retriever just let your dog learn on his own; use the method to be described in this chapter; or, if it should prove non-applicable to your particular dog or you enjoy doing things by rote, use the force method.

Retrieving is one of the first things your retriever pup should learn, but simultaneous with his fetching lessons he should have some rudimentary instruction in his desired response to three commands.

Name

First, the pup should learn his name. This comes almost naturally. Every time you speak to the pup work his name into the conversation and make it distinctive and emphatic whether greeting, praising or scolding him. His name is a cue that there is more to come and will probably be followed by a command. In his adult years, encountering a situation familiar to him, the dog may anticipate the command and

55

come to you when his name is spoken, get into a car or kennel, sit, etc. without the additional command being given.

No!

No! Is the second easily taught command. A pup starts learning its meaning from the first time he starts doing or gets into something he shouldn't. You probably won't have any difficulty making your order sharp and emphatic. Add emphasis with a swat on the flank with your open hand or a tap on the muzzle with your forefinger. It won't hurt him but is unpleasant and along with your tone of voice will convince him to abandon whatever it is he's doing.

You, in turn, will come to recognize the value of repetition in dog training. For you will have to repeat his name and the No! command many times. But you probably will be pleased with his response and his eventual grasp of the fact that such things as chewing and nipping, for which he's chastised, are truly no-no's.

Come Here!

Teaching a pup to come when he is called involves taking advantage of the fact that pups are usually looking for something to do and will instinctively chase anything that runs from them. The command can be either "Come" or "Here" or "C'meer" or "To Me" or whatever else you dream up. The actual word itself is not important, except that it be short and clear and you settle on it as the only command you use to elicit a response. The dialog I suggest through this book will be words in most general use among trainers, with occasional personal picks.

Get your pup's attention by saying his name when he's not distracted by something extremely interesting, then move away from him clapping your hands and repeating, "Here, Duke! Here, Duke! Here, Duke!" He'll chase you. Let him catch you. When he does, fuss over him and tell him what a good puppy he is.

With a very responsive pup, you may be able to squat down and coax him to you. You can reward him with a bit of food if you want, but your voice and hands should be able to convey all the reward he needs.

When you feed the pup, which should be several times a day up to

A recalcitrant Labrador is about to be reminded that he is to respond to a command by a handy attention-getter, a slingshot loaded with a light marble.

four to five months of age, call him to you and the food. He'll learn the proper response is pleasant and rewarding. This is another basic procedure in dog training: praise and petting for doing right, displeasure and discomfort for doing wrong, administered even-handedly and consistently.

Then as the pup gets older and you move from this fun and games training to the serious stuff, when he ignores a learned command and it is necessary or politic to "get his attention," plink him with a slingshot propelled marble or splatter him with a thrown stone or snowball. He'll come to you to make the world right for him again rather than kiting off in fright.

Starting Age

We have been talking here of pups of about two to three months of age. Get your pup if possible between the ages of six to twelve weeks, taking the place of his dam and littermates and starting his training immediately. It is very important that a gun dog become people oriented, have confidence in them but also absorb the fact that there are rules he must live by.

At this tender age he is not ready for the discipline and rigors of serious training. But he is ready and able to learn and should not be allowed to stagnate by being left to his own devices whether closely confined or running wild. You can play with your pup and train him at the same time. I call this stage "play-training". The procedure will also be used to get your pup well on his way to being a trustworthy fetcher of game birds as we move on to introducing him to his prime purpose in life, retrieving.

Doubling Up

But before delving into that, let me point out that you may not have recognized that in the teaching of the "name", "no" and "come" lessons you've been accomplishing a number of other things.

For examples, the saying "No!" then the swat or tap indicate to the pup that chewing up stuff is not acceptable behavior, the petting when he does right conditions him to handling and he learns that hands can either praise or chastise, depending upon his behavior. The clapping of hands as you move away while calling him conditions him to sharp noises. Then if you should fail to properly introduce him to gunfire, or make an error, the chances of his becoming gun-shy are substantially reduced.

This is called "doubling-up" in my lexicon and there will be a great deal of it in this book, for it greatly shortens the time you must spend to develop a dog you are proud of. I point it out now because in the interests of space it will not be possible to detail multiple benefits of various training procedures. Watch for it. But even if you miss it, you will still benefit.

Another thing you should be aware of, which will make your training easier and more productive, is the importance of:

Time and Timing

When working with a puppy, two or three 10-minute sessions or even shorter periods, will accomplish more than one half-hour period. Even with an older dog, workouts daily or several times a week are much better than trying to cram it all into one day.

Pups and young dogs also develop at different paces. A knowledge-able, experienced trainer may recognize when a certain dog will be ready for each phase of his work and hold up introduction until such time. But no one can tell you how to spot "when the light goes on" in a specific dog.

However, you should be aware that every pup will catch onto some phase quickly and balk at another. When following the procedures in this book, keep plugging until the light dawns or, by sheer power of repetition, the thing you want is drilled into the dog. No matter how bright and willing, no pup is going to be trained in one session or emerge as an overnight wonder.

Puppy and dog training requires time, technique, repetition and, some say, patience, although I think persistance is more accurate.

A pup's span of attention to any one thing is short, so don't overdo one excercise. Mix 'em up, introducing each new step and including the things he's already learned as he advances. Variety is the spice of life for both gay blades and gun dogs and should be introduced before boredom or fatigue sets in. With the young pup, play-training to retrieve can provide this spice and make future serious sessions easy to absorb.

Fetch It!

An old glove or a knotted boot sock are all you need to introduce your pup to picking up and fetching. It has to be something he'll like to take hold of and can easily carry. So it shouldn't be too big, hard or slippery.

You and the pup get off by yourselves, preferably in a building, where there are few distractions and where runaway space will be limited. An aisle or hall is fine. Tease the pup with the sock by skittering it around in front of him so he'll try to grab it. Then skid it along the floor just a few feet at first. Short tosses should be saved for later. He should be able to see it slide along the floor, go after it and grab it. The distance can be increased a little each session.

When he picks it up call his name and, squatting down, coax him to you as you introduce a new command: "Here, Duke. Fetch!" and keep repeating until he comes to you with the "dummy." Eventually you will drop the "Here" command and say "Duke, Fetch!" as you slide or toss the sock, sending him to retrieve.

If you should be working the pup outside near his kennel or inside

59

near his sleeping box, always station yourself between where he picks up the sock or dummy and his "home." Almost invariably he will head for his quarters with whatever he has in his mouth, just as his ancestors toted food to their dens. You should be there to intercept him. In time, coming to you with whatever he is retrieving will become a habit. If you toss the sock toward his home base he will probably run away from you to hide out with his prize, rather than turn and bring it back to you.

When he brings the object to you or near you, firmly but gently take it from him, telling him to "Drop!" Don't play with him if he refuses to let go. Hold the sock in one hand, slide your other hand into his mouth, pressing his lower lip against his teeth, squeezing just enough so he'll open his mouth in protest, releasing the sock. Be gentle, but firm and don't engage in a tugging, prying match. Tell him what a good dog he is and fuss over him.

Repeat this performance each session for five or six times. Then quit. Do it several times a day or whenever you have time. But make it short and sweet and conclude on a note of success. It will surprise you how quickly the pup goes scrambling after the thrown object and returns to you with it. You become an integral part of this game.

When working with a very young pup always squat or kneel. It puts you nearer his level and seems to inspire confidence. When not "training", handle, fool with and talk to your pup as much as possible. You want him to have complete trust in you and think you're the greatest. Then if you make mistakes, which we all do, or something spooks him, his devotion to you will help overcome any set-backs.

It is preferable to start the retrieving training inside a garage, kitchen, basement or other confined area which the pup is familiar with and provides a minimum of distractions. Once he's doing it like he's supposed to you can do the retrieving training outside. With some pups you may be able to shortcut and start out in the yard. But the safe, sure way, is inside or if the outdoors provides too much distraction work him indoors until he gets it down pat.

Birds and Dummies

At about four months of age retriever pups should be big enough to handle a retrieving dummy. This should be substituted for the glove or sock. Forethought in saving some game bird wings from your

Dummies, like the one this Irish Water Spaniel is retrieving, are valuable aids in basic training and refresher work with all spaniels and retrievers during the off-season.

hunting trips will also pay off. They are small and you can alternate them with the glove or sock when the pup is very small. Then when you switch to dummies they can be taped onto the dummies, accustoming your pup to picking up feathers at a very early age and familiarizing him with game scent he'll be asked to work later.

Should you have a pup too small to take along when the hunting seasons are open, bring home small game birds, like Quail and Woodcock, and toss them for retrieving work a few times before you dress them as a substitute for the glove or sock he's already doing fine on. If he's doing well on those, it shouldn't take too much encouragement to get him to pick up the whole bird. Tease him a bit with it to increase his interest before you toss it. Don't use large birds like duck or Pheasant. But you can utilize their wings.

Any time after he's going out well after the tossed bird, five to ten yards is plenty far even when gradually worked up to, you can start him on something that will be a bit more difficult considering his extreme youth.

Do not throw the object so he can see it and mark it. Drop it down when he isn't looking, in plain sight, not more than five or six feet from his starting point. Tell him, "Duke, Fetch!" and make the tossing motion with your arm. He probably will go a little way looking for something to fetch. When he sees it, he'll pounce on it.

A Chesapeake in training retrieves a plastic retrieving dummy for the late Charles Morgan, noted professional.

Should he fail to find it, spin around and act confused, walk toward the object to be fetched, repeating the tossing motions and encouraging him with "Duke, Fetch!" Don't ever let him fail to bring in something once you've told him to fetch and never fake tosses. Nothing succeeds like success and trust. A dog that is fooled can't be blamed for not responding properly and if he is allowed to go about his play while you pick up the object it will set back his training and set a pattern for doing a half-hearted job and quitting when asked to make a difficult retrieve when he gets older.

By undertaking the early play training of your pup you are instill-

A yellow Labrador gets a reassuring pat of praise for learning his lessons and making a nice retrieve of a shot pigeon.

ing behavioral patterns he'll follow when he gets older. Bad patterns will be hard to correct. But the instilling of good responses can make advanced training so simple you may find yourself exclaiming, "that smart son of a bitch seems to train himself."

So even though you have to literally put the pup right on the un-tossed "hidden" object, point it out to him, guide him there and have *him* pick it up. Then trot away from him and call as you would when he retrieves a tossed object. Praise him when he picks up and when he delivers.

The Other Commandments

As soon as the pup has the general idea and responds fairly well to "Name", "No", "Here" and "Fetch" you can start to introduce six other basic commands. But in conjunction with the new things continue to work on the first four, not slacking off until you are surprised and disappointed when he *doesn't* obey, rather than just pleased when he *does*.

Your attitude when you start a pup at two months of age must be pleasure with his accomplishments, encouraging what he does right, while ignoring or indicating displeasure with his wrong-doings, yet refraining from any harsh discipline.

The other basic commands are "Drop", "Sit", "Wait" (or Stay)", "Kennel (or Get In)", "Heel" and "Hunt 'em out". Once he's got his Ten Commandments down you will be able to take him most anywhere you care to; he'll be prepared for the rigors of serious training and, after proper introduction to gunfire, ready to take afield on a real hunt. Depending upon the precocity of the pup and your diligence this may be between the ages of five to twelve months, seven to eight months being a good general average.

All at an age, when you may have been advised is the proper age to *start* training! This is not in conflict with such advice. A professional trainer usually does not have the time to coax a tiny pup along as you are doing. He wants the dog when it is physically developed enough and emotionally stable to stand up under *formal* training, for he has a limited time to produce results for the money he receives.

But play-training your own pup carries no risk and is productive time in taking advantage of a period in a puppy's development when he is ready, willing and able to learn. Once he has learned these basics he probably will be the best-behaved canine of any age in the neighborhood. It is entirely possible that if you don't choose to add the refinements that will "finish" your retriever, once he's learned these basics he will prove out as a satisfactory gun dog through field experience when actually hunting.

Drop!

The command to release a retrieved object is "Drop" which your pup has probably almost mastered because you were using it in connection with his preliminary retrieving lessons. To repeat, say "Drop" several times as you take the retrieved object from his mouth. If he won't let go, grasp the object with the left hand and the pup's lower jaw with the right, sliding your thumb into his mouth, pressing his lower lip against his teeth. He won't bite. He'll open his mouth to relieve the pressure and you can take the dummy. You want it brought to hand, not dropped on the ground. After a couple of dozen retrieves you can expect he'll be releasing on command. If not, keep at it until he does.

Sit!

To teach a dog to sit on command, place your left hand flush against and under the juncture of the pup's neck and chest, preventing his moving ahead. Straddle his hips with your right thumb and forefinger, squeeze a bit and push down, saying "Sit!" This forces him into a sitting position. Then praise him.

Let him do a little fetching or playing before you put him to this. He'll work off some of the steam that may prompt him to wiggle and cavort. If he's a little tired, so much the better. But if he's worn out he may sprawl rather than assume a sitting position. It may be a tougher task to jack him up than to plunk him down.

When he's dropping his butt well, with little resistance to hand pressure, after several sessions, try saying "Sit!" and refrain from using your hands.

By gosh! He did it!

Lay on the praise, petting and sweet talk. Which is probably an unnecessary reminder. You'd have to be some kind of a robot not to let the pup know just how pleased you are.

He didn't do it?

Don't get shook up. That's not abnormal. Just bring those hands into play again. Say "Sit" and firmly sit him down. Then praise him. He'll soon be doing it without manual aid. Just don't let him ignore the command! Always force him down if he doesn't sit voluntarily. He'll be dropping his fanny in no time, on command, without physical assistance from you if you refuse to let him get away with not doing it.

65

Signals

Your pup is now ready to learn his first *hand signal!* In conjuction with the verbal command to "Sit", thrust your arm upright, index finger poking the sky. Once he connects your gesture with the verbal command he'll start sitting on that gesture alone. He's then taken the first step toward being a dog that can be directed by hand signals. Keep at him until he responds properly each time.

Whistle signals? One sharp blast on your whistle means Sit! Proper training procedure is to say "Sit"! while simultaneously raising your arm and tooting once on the whistle. With repetition your dog will hit the ground with his butt at the proper verbal, whistle or hand signal.

When he does it without question, at your side or in a confined area, let him roam off a little and go to work on him so he'll sit on command even when he's some distance away. *Do not call him in and then make him sit.* Go to him and plop him down on the spot where he was when you signalled.

(While on the subject of whistles, a trilling or successive beeping of your whistle should indicate "Come here" to a dog. Use the whistle in this manner in conjuction with your verbal "Here!" command and in time he'll be coming to the whistle alone. A whistle is sharp and attention getting, saves your voice and is not as disturbing to game in the field as a human voice.)

Once a pup has learned to sit upon command, make maximum use of your training time (double up) by putting him at a sit alongside you each time you throw something for him to fetch.

The pup will quickly associate starting a retrieve from a sitting position. Retrieving should be what a retriever likes to do most. So sitting promptly can lead to fun, adding spice to the training routine. Training should be as enjoyable as possible for both man and dog and everyone likes an alert, happy response rather than the sulky performance of a chore.

Stay!

A dog that will remain stationary until ordered to move out is a pleasure afield and around the home and there is no end to the reasons he should learn this:

Doing away with his jumping out of boat or blind every time a shot is fired; halting the chase of a missed upland bird; stationing him at a point of vantage where he can mark falling birds; remaining in one spot when you leave him for a short while; and so on and so on.

With retrievers, keeping a dog glued to a designated spot (steadiness) is usually done with the dog in a sitting position. He can see and mark well and it takes more effort on his part to start moving (break) than if he were lying down or standing.

You can forget about this command if you choose to train your dog to sit tight and not move until further orders on a strictly Sit! order. However, I find myself ultimately using this more or less supplementary command to reinforce the Sit! and indicate I really mean business. You may choose to say "Whoa!", "Wait!" or anything else as long as it anchors your dog.

There are two ways to teach a dog to stay and both are well utilized. During fetching practice have him sit, hold him by the collar or scruff of the neck with the hand on the side at which he is positioned. Toss the dummy with the other hand.

Grab him with both hands and restrain him firmly as you command "Stay!" He'll get up as he starts toward the dummy and at first you needn't push him back into a sit. Align him in the right direction, don't restrain for more than a couple seconds at first, then say "Duke, Fetch!" and let him go.

Don't start exercising restraint until the pup is crazy about fetching and then initial restraint time should be minimal. You are teaching him a new command, not trying to convey the idea you are against fetching.

Gradually hold him longer until you can take your hands off him and he'll hesitate, waiting for the "Fetch!" command. Eventually you'll be able to say, "Sit! Stay!" and he'll stay in a sitting position until sent. As he starts catching on, you will find a short leash attached to his collar an aid in restraint, to be snapped off when you send him, or even dropped to drag along as he goes out and comes back. But just the hands work better on pups less than five months.

The alternate method of teaching staying-put runs no risk of interfering with retrieving desire and therefore may be started before the short cut method described above.

Sit your dog. Move away from him as far as you can while still keeping a restraining hand on him and repeating, "Staaay! Staaay! Staaay!" At this stage it is not a sharp command, but a soothing,

Sit! and Stay! are taught by gradually backing away from the dog or dogs while cautioning with voice and upraised hand. It can be done with more than one dog at a time as Dave Duffey demonstrates with these Chesapeakes, but for openers, trainers should concentrate on a single dog. In a short time, the cautioning can be dispensed with and the dog depended on to stay. Punish him when he disobeys.

steadying assurance. If the pup follows or moves away, plunk him back into position and sharply command "Sit! Stay!" Keep this up until you can take your hand off him or even straighten up before he moves. When he does, re-position him and repeat, "Sit! Stay!"

When you can straighten up without his moving, keep your arm upright with the cautioning finger pointing skyward, reminding him to "Stay!" if he indicates he's going to move. Then quickly release him from control with a command like "Alright!" or "Okay!" Then call him to you for praising and petting. Don't hold him too long at first. But keep prolonging the time, backing away a step or two, hand in air indicating "Sit!" and eventually he'll be staying without any spoken word.

Once he's pretty solid, turn your back, walk around him etc. tempting him to move, always ordering "Stay!" if he indicates he's going to move out. If he does leave before you say "Alright!" take him back to his post and start over. Let him know how pleased you are when he waits for the release signal. In a short time you will be able to walk around him, his head will swivel watching you and even if he shifts his position a bit he won't leave the designated spot, even when you duck out of sight for a moment or two. Then start staying out of sight for longer periods until you can leave him for several minutes and return to find him still anchored.

He's learned the most important step in being "steady" and we've doubled up again, teaching him the word that means he's released from control, "Alright!"

Heel!

I would not attempt to teach heeling before the age of four months and prefer to hold off until about six months. This will be the pup's first taste of comparatively harsh restraint because there is no efficient way to play-train a dog to heel, which means walk quietly and attentively at the handler's side until told to do something else. So the pup should be physically and mentally advanced enough to take it and have confidence in his handler.

In preparation for this training, however, a very young pup should be introduced to collar and lead. Get a small puppy collar and put it on the pup, letting him wear it until he accepts it, maybe only a few minutes a day at first, for hours or permanently a bit later. But keep

69

close tabs on a "permanent" collar. Pups grow very rapidly and you must not let the pup suffer from too tight a collar.

Upon acceptance, attach a long lead or length of rope to it and walk with him on it. He'll tug and tangle and fight when he feels the restraint but give him plenty of leeway and be patient. He'll learn it is futile to fight this gentle restraint. Guide him in the general direction you want him to go. Don't let him get frantic. But show him that if he's reasonable, it's not so bad. This is in preparation for his later formal training in heeling. Accustoming him to the mild restraint of the long lead also will allow you to tie him up when necessary without a great deal of anxiety and frustration on the pup's part.

To start his heeling lessons (four to six months) get a slip-chain collar and short leash. Which side he heels on isn't important, but assuming it's your left side, sit your pup there and attach the leash to the ring in the slip-chain collar so it will draw up like a noose. Then say, "Heel!" and step off. If the pup dashes ahead, jerk him back, saying "Heel!" If he lags, jerk him up, saying "Heel!" If he tries to go wide, jerk him into you, saying "Heel!" If he crowds against you, bump his head sharply with your knee as you walk, saying "Heel!"

If you haven't accustomed him to leather collar and leash you are sure to have a struggle on your hands. It may occur in any event when the pup feels the noose of the slip-chain collar tighten on his neck. (Reasons for using such a collar are detailed in chapter on training devices.) But even if it seems "mean" do not give in when he balks and tugs. Ease up when the dog is in about the place you want him.

Give quick, hard tugs on the leash. A prolonged steady pull will panic a pup, causing either a fight against it or lying down and refusing to budge. The pup must be jerked into the position you want him, head approximately at your knee as you walk. You do not have to be brutal. You do have to be firm. Jerk him over and say "Heel!" When he's positioned right, talk nice to him and tell him how well he's doing. Some pups get it at the first lesson, others in a week or two.

Eventually he'll learn that when the command is given he can walk in comfort on leash as long as he keeps that position. Some dogs will walk along happily. Others never consider it anything but punishment.

Give him plenty of "Alright" release breaks. When he's walked along passably for 20 to 50 yards, unsnap the leash, say Alright and encourage him to cavort and play. Play with him, reassure him and when he's his old confident self put the leash back on and repeat the heeling lesson.

70

When working on heeling off leash, pat your leg and tell the dog to "Heel!" to keep him in close as Dave Duffey does with a Chesapeake.

Once he's walking properly on leash, start off as usual and, when he is moving along properly, unobtrusively unsnap the leash. As long as he holds position talk to him encouragingly. When he breaks or lags, sharply command him to "Heel!" If he does, resume praising and release him from control in a few seconds with an "Alright!" If he persists in bolting or lagging, snap the leash back on and remind him sharply what "Heel!" means. When he's behaving again, try walking him free. Any backsliding means return to leash and collar, which is the only way you can enforce the heel command. Later, when he knows for sure what his response should be, should he get careless, a swat with a leash combined with harsh words will point out his error.

Kennel!

If saying "Get in there" when you want your dog to enter your car, jump into a boat, go into his kennel crate or enter anything you want him to comes easier, use it. But "Kennel" is the customary command

71

and relatively simple to teach. It does impress people when a dog does this with willingness.

Each time you put your pup back into his kennel run, or want him to go into the house if he's quartered there, (you'll have to put him in, he won't go voluntarily), hold him with one hand, point with the other and snap out, "Kennel!" and then by the scruff of his neck and the seat of his pants (skin is loose on the neck and at the top of the hips) hoist him into the kennel. This is informal training since you should be taking him out, and consequently putting him back in, several times a day. But it can cut down on the time it takes or eliminate the more formal method of: opening a travel crate door or car door, leading him up to it, pointing and saying, "Kennel!" while assisting him into it. Praise him. Call him out. Repeat. Repeat. Repeat. Once in a while you may even have to toss him in. But soon, when you point and say "Kennel!" he'll jump or run in. A five or ten minute session will get you well started. Keep at it. He may start anticipating you and entering before you tell him. Then make him sit and wait before ordering him to "Kennel!" so he learns he's to get into things only when told to and avoiding his jumping into, and ramming around, yours or someone else's car.

Hunt 'em Out!

This self explanatory command is used to start a dog working diligently in cover you have reason to believe contains game and to encourage a dog, who's already seeking it, to intensify his efforts to produce it.

Unless you are strictly a duck hunter, you'll want your retriever to work in front of the gun producing game as well as picking up the birds after they are shot. Even if your dog is strictly a retriever, in a hunting situation, you may find it impractical or impossible to handle him in the field trial manner. When your dog hasn't seen a bird drop, you probably will walk him into the area of the fall, tell him to "hunt 'em out" and he will work until he comes up with the bird.

To teach a flushing dog like the retrievers to work a close, quartering pattern, like spaniels do before the gun, please go on to the spaniel section for this information, so I don't have to write it twice. The majority of retrievers will learn this readily, given encouragement and training.

72

Pups learning the command "Kennel!" usually require a shove or boost
to give them the idea of what's wanted.

Fact of the matter is, that a good dog, having been introduced to "Hunt 'em Out!" as a pup, will probably pretty much teach himself how to hunt upland game if you give him the opportunity.

The elder puppy, from about six months of age on up, is ready to learn this command and take that big step toward being a bird producer and fetcher when he's indicated he has a nose, and knows how to use it. A good example of this would be his scenting and working until he finds a dummy you've tossed in deep grass but he doesn't mark it too well.

Most retriever pups have at least acceptable noses. But some seem born with the know-how to use them properly. Others seem to lack this put-it-all-together facility and while catching scent readily, learn very slowly how to *locate* what's giving off the smell.

Hide the pup's bird-wing wrapped retrieving dummy in the grass or other cover. Or you can sprinkle a couple drops of commercially available duck or pheasant scent (such as those manufactured by National Scent Co. and available from Sporting Dog Specialties, P.O. Box 68, Spencerport, N.Y. 14559) on a dummy. Or if your dog has handled birds by this time, use a freshly killed pigeon or recently shot game bird. Whatever, drop it into the cover without the dog seeing you put it there.

Then bring him in at heel, headed into the wind or, if he is running loose, steer him to the downwind side of the object, maybe five or ten yards from where the object is located. Tell him to "Hunt 'em out, Duke!" "Hunt 'em out!" in an excited manner and tone and wave your hand (like you were making an underhand toss when throwing the dummy) indicating the cover ahead. Guide him toward the bird until he winds it and picks it up. Then trot away from him, clapping, calling telling him to fetch. Tell him how good he is when he completes the job.

Almost Ready To Go

That wasn't too bad, was it? You now have a retriever ready to go hunting. Well, almost. You have come this far without even unlimbering your favorite smoothbore. But I haven't forgotten the shotgun.

We are coming to that in a separate chapter. Please see "Introduction to Game And Guns". It is a separate chapter for two reasons.

One, proper introduction to the actual shooting of birds is vitally

74

important and when done properly will do away with the worry about whether or not your dog will turn out gun-shy. A gun-shy dog is the epitome of worthlessness, followed closely by a bird-shy dog. You want neither. So rather than tell you how to *cure* gun-shyness, I propose to tell you how to *prevent* these faults.

My second reason is that I have asked retriever owners, for example, to check the spaniel section for instructions on how to teach a retriever to hunt before the gun, for this is a prime requirement for spaniels, a secondary one for retrievers. I will also be advising readers of the spaniel, pointing and versatile chapters to check the retriever section regarding procedures to use to teach their dogs how to fetch, for that is a retriever's specialty.

I would like readers to peruse the entire book, regardless of their lack of interest in breeds other than the type they own, for it would be to their benefit. But I know there will be pointing dog trainers who will skip the spaniel section and so on.

I don't want any trainer to miss the method of properly introducing a gun dog to the two most important things in his life, game and guns, because it was "buried" in a section of the book various readers might pass up.

Therefore, please, before moving on to whatever is of further interest to you in this book and before you take your young retriever hunting, look up, carefully read and follow the advice given in "Introduction To Game And Guns".

There is much more for you to read. When you've successfully introduced your dog to game and guns and started hunting with him he will be a well started gun dog. But you may want to take him further.

What's more, something may have gone sour in one or more phases of your dog's training. In plain English, you may have a problem. So please see, "Problems, Solutions, And Advanced Training." It will offer answers, suggestions and techniques to aid you in understanding your dog and developing his gun dog potential to the fullest.

5

The Spaniels

IT could *almost* be said that there is one breed of gun dog spaniel used in North America, the English Springer Spaniel. With some justification it might also be argued that the English Springer is the only spaniel needed.

Almost, but not quite. So while most of this chapter will be devoted to the versatile, easy to train and readily available Springer, we needs must include another spaniel breed or two and explain their qualifications as gun dogs for sportsmen in North America.

First, let's summarily dismiss four very limited registered breeds, the Clumber, Field, Sussex and Welsh Springer Spaniels. You will be able to find descriptions of these breeds in books dealing with every breed of dog recognized by official registries. They will also tell you what these breeds are supposed to do, or at least what they supposedly have done in the past. But you will find it extremely difficult to locate a pup of these breeds and experience even more difficulty in finding someone who can actually demonstrate what representatives of these breeds are supposed to do.

If you are looking for an esoteric breed there's no reason you shouldn't try to find one, and your chances are best of locating a Clumber Spaniel and perhaps a Welsh Springer. Those very few sportsmen who have found and use Clumbers have kind things to say about them. But North American hunters will find them slow and ponderous afield.

If you do opt for these very rare breeds of spaniel, the training procedures outlined in the next chapter will apply to them as well as the four Spaniel breeds discussed at some length in this chapter.

Brittany Spaniel

For details on this very popular and useful breed, see the Chapters on Continental Pointing Breeds and on Pointing Breed Training. Brittanies are *not* flushing spaniels, or at least if properly trained and used are not supposed to be. They point their game, hence their inclusion in the appropriate chapters.

Irish Water Spaniel

Thanks to custom, general utilization and the official classification by the American Kennel Club, the Irish Water Spaniel is placed in the Retriever category. Please see the chapters on Retrievers and their training for information about this breed.

It should be noted, however, that in common with the other retriever breeds and in keeping with its name, many, if not most of the Irish spaniels can be developed into capable flushing dogs. So if you get an Irish (or one of the retriever breeds) and intend to use him to produce game in front of the gun it is paramount that you read the following chapter on how to train flushing spaniels.

With that, let's move into our discussion of breed generalities about the flushing spaniel breeds, American Water, Cocker and Springer Spaniels commonly used in North America. Because of its prevalance and to avoid repetition, because the manner of all spaniel work is based generally on what's expected of the English Springer, let's kick off with that breed.

English Springer Spaniel

For the hunter who wants a gun dog that will start at an early age, is comparatively easy to train and useful on a wide variety of game the English Springer Spaniel is a pretty complete package.

Their development in the U.S. has closely parallelled that of the retrievers brought from England and the popularity of the Pheasant, as a game bird north of the Mason-Dixon line, contributed to their acceptance following their introduction to North America in the 1920's and 30's. The big, gaudy bird proved a tough proposition for pointing breeds to handle properly and mid-westerners who combined Pheasant and waterfowl hunting along with Ruffed Grouse and Woodcock gunning in dense cover found flushing dogs advantageous over pointers, and the Springer's popularity spread from there, although eastern sportsmen made the first importations.

In England until about the turn of the 20th century, size and the purpose to which the spaniels were put decided whether they'd be classified as Springers, Cockers, Clumbers etc. As with hounds, up until recently and to some extent to the present in the U.S., spaniel pups out of the same litter might be called either Cockers or Springers. But in North America and abroad today the breeds are now separate and distinct.

It has been argued that there are two breeds, or at least strains, of Springers in North America now, the field Springer and the bench-show Springer. Hunters are advised to select their pups from field trial and hunting stock for ease in training and sporting proficiency.

Depending upon one's frame of reference, Springer Spaniels are small to medium sized dogs about 18 to 20 inches at the shoulder, weighing 40 to 50 pounds, agile and merry in action and most pleasant of disposition.

While they won their spurs on Pheasants, they are equally capable on Ruffed Grouse and Woodcock, can be expected to do at least a passable job on waterfowl under any but the most arduous conditions and to fill in, in a pinch, on virtually any game bird or small animal, like squirrel and rabbit, hunted on this continent.

Springers are truly versatile, multi-purpose gun dogs for sportsmen who want heavy and restricted coverts hunted in a thorough but happily busy manner, flushing the birds within shotgun range and efficiently picking up and delivering game knocked down. The Springer Spaniel can and does do everything except point.

English Springer Spaniels are alert, eager, multipurpose gun dogs.

Spaniels, like this English Springer, are expected to retrieve shot birds that fall into or across water and many can be used for waterfowling.

Many Springers even do that to an extent, and "pointing" by these spaniels is a sore point among their fanciers. Proper form for a Springer is a hard, fast, unhesitant flush of his birds. But some Springers will hesitate just before springing their game, virtually flash-pointing it. There are hunters who find this admirable as a warning that the bird is right there while others claim the pause before flushing allows some game to escape.

You may find either flushing technique preferable, although you may have to accept whatever is dealt you by an individual dog, since training a spaniel that leans either way to do the opposite is very touchy and can make a blinker (a dog that deliberately avoids birds he knows are about) of an otherwise useful gun dog.

The essence of Springer Spaniel work is to busily and thoroughly work his cover close to the hunter so birds flushed are in the air within range of a shotgun, quartering and criss-crossing, back and forth, in front of and to the sides of the hunter rather than making long casts.

Ideally, once the bird is in the air, the Springer should "hup" (sit and stay) until after the bird is shot and the dog is given the signal to retrieve. If game is missed, the dog should be called in and cast off afresh.

Such a dog is a finished dog and methods of developing a gun dog of this caliber will be discussed in the chapter on advanced training. But for most hunters, the Springer's performance will be most satisfactory even if he follows the flight of the flushed bird, just so long as he doesn't run out of the country chasing the misses.

Using those as a criteria, sportsmen will find the Springer a precocious hunter and may expect to get some birds with one at the tender age of five to six months and, with enough experience, enjoy a proficient gun dog at an age (10 to 18 months) when other breeds are just getting underway.

As an additional bonus, the sweet, eager to please disposition of the Springer Spaniel lends itself to wonderful adaptation of the dual role of pet and family dog as well as gun dog. While long-coated, the coat is not difficult to care for. And if the feathers on legs, belly, ears and tail are trimmed during hunting season they do not load up with mud and burrs.

Springers can absorb and should have firm disciplining. Their ingratiating manner can be used to get their own way if their trainers allow themselves to be charmed out of applying rules. But Springers are essentially "soft" in temperament and application of force should not be harsh lest it lead to cowing or sulking.

Springers are tractable, intelligent, practical-sized gun dogs, able to work a day in the uplands at a bustling gallop, cutting and turning like Quarter Horses, retrieving from both land and water whatever falls to their masters' guns.

American Water Spaniels

Perhaps because they are neither "fish nor fowl" and therefore lack a stage upon which to strut their stuff, while not rare the American Water Spaniel is not a common breed in the country of its origin. Along with the Chesapeake Bay Retriever, Coonhound and Foxhound, the American Water Spaniel is one of the few breeds "made in the U.S.A," getting its start and development in the watersheds of the Fox and Wolf river valleys in central Wisconsin.

It is too small a dog to compete against the large retrievers in their field trials, although some classify the breed as a retriever rather than a spaniel. It lacks the style, speed and dash of the Springer Spaniel and no trials are held to display its upland hunting abilities to the public.

Nonetheless, the American Water Spaniel is an eminently practical little gun dog that can give yeoman service to the sportsman who

Saighton's Sizzler, two-time English Springer Spaniel National Champion, demonstrates hard driving style afield.

hunts a little of just about everything with little regard to style and seeks a multi-purpose family dog. A bit sharper in temperament than most spaniels and suspicious of strangers the American is an alert yard dog.

In brief and broad generality, the American can be expected to perform essentially the same tasks in a similar manner to those asked of the Springer Spaniel: find, flush and fetch all manner of upland game and shorebirds and, within the confines of today's waterfowl regulations, handle most duck retrieving chores. The major differences would be lack of speed, style and dash both on land and in water.

They run about 15 to 18 inches high (some leggier strains are bred for heavy marsh work) and weigh 25 to 40 poinds. They are solid liver in color (originally they were called American Brown Water Spaniels) and the coat has a marcelled appearance. The wavy curl in the dense coat is good protection in the water but also mats and loads up with sticktights. In contrast to other spaniels, the tail is *not* docked and is plumed.

Breeding true to type since the 1890s and probably stemming from the extinct English Water Spaniel imported by gunners seeking a dog smaller than the Irish Water Spaniel and Chesapeake, the American was first recognized as a breed by the United Kennel Club in 1920, with the Irish Water Spaniel and the Curly-Coated Retriever probably contributing to its make-up. Between 1920 and recognition by the Field Dog Stud Book in 1938 and the American Kennel Club in 1940, a considerable degree of crossing with the Irish Water Spaniel undoubtedly occurred.

Like the Chesapeake and the Irish Water Spaniel, Americans learned their hunting job by actual doing and they pick up their tasks almost naturally if given sufficient exposure. Training should be mildly coercive as they will buck or buckle under too much pressure.

Cocker Spaniels

Due to being a hair too small to cope with the size of game birds like pheasant and duck and the exigencies of brutal cover, plus breeding programs to fulfill consumer and show exhibitor demands, the Cocker Spaniel has become *almost* a hopeless case when it comes to finding a capable gun dog.

However, that was not always the case and even today if a sportsman can find a pup out of good hunting stock or one in which a few good instincts have carried through despite the puppy mills and selection for certain physical rather than mental and emotional traits, he can have himself a most merry little hunter.

When used, Cocker Spaniels are best suited for Woodcock, from which they were supposed to have derived their name, (i.e. "cocking spaniels") and Ruffed Grouse, chiefly because of their size. Otherwise they can be expected to work in the manner, and on the same game, as the larger English Springer Spaniel.

There are actually two recognized breeds of Cocker Spaniel, the English Cocker Spaniel and the Cocker Spaniel. Casual observers might be hard pressed to tell the difference, but the English Cocker most closely resembles a small English Springer Spaniel. The English are a bit bigger (30–35 pounds) than the diminutive (20–25 pound) Cockers, have well set rather than protruding eyes, longer muzzles and not as much superfluous coat and feather as the so-called American Cocker. They are uncommon dogs in the U.S. but if one can be found it would probably be a better bet as a hunter than its degenerate cousin.

I'm not quite ready to give up on these little spaniels, as most serious gun dog people have done, for two reasons. The first purebred gun dog I had and trained as a teen-ager was an English Cocker named

A rare Boykin Spaniel and the late Charles Morgan, one of the pioneer
retriever trainers in the United States, are shown in a training session.

Tar, about 17 inches at the shoulder and 38 pounds. He was a superlative little hunting dog for a small town boy (and later a young man) working everything from squirrel and rabbit to duck and pheasant.

My second reason is based on the hope that there may be enough importation of working Cockers from the British Isles to restore Cockers to some small niche, at least, in the gun dog world in the U.S., just as serious Springer fanciers gave a shot in the arm to their breed when it needed some straightening out by bringing over some of the best British blood.

As this book is being written, I'm having the privilege of working with some "Working Cocker Spaniels" a strain of English Cocker which were imported from Scotland by Mr. Jack Puelicher, Milwaukee, Wisconsin. Their developers are unconcerned with physical appearance but greatly concerned with breeding for natural hunting ability and a temperament that accepts training well. The pups in my hands have shown that to the nth degree, being tough, tireless little workers on game (despite their small size and crooked legs) and affectionate and biddable around house and yard.

There is one other spaniel extant, which while not recognized by any official registry, does exist particularly in the southeast which readers may encounter or hear of. It has been confused by some authorities with the American Water Spaniel. It is the:

Boykin Spaniel

The ones I've seen looked like a cross between an American Water Spaniel and a Cocker Spaniel (a common cross 30 to 40 years ago resulting in good gun dogs) and were useful on game and worked in the manner one might expect from such a cross. Their liver-colored coats vary from a soft wave to a near curl and are sometimes so richly dark as to appear black.

They are used for hunting turkey in the southeast and also serve well as dove and duck retrievers, probably originated in South Carolina, taking their name from one Whit Boykin, a sportsman who started this "breed", and see limited usage in adjoining states for the most part.

6

Spaniel Training

To some extent it might be contended that all a man has to do to train a spaniel is get a promising pup, turn him out into game cover and let nature take its course.

But it really isn't quite that easy, not if you want a fair shot at the game you see and want what you manage to knock down recovered for the game bag and ultimately the table.

For a spaniel hunting out of control will put out birds too far from the gun to afford a shot and, if not trained to retrieve, will not bring back those difficult birds that you'd never be able to locate and pick up yourself.

Thus, the two basic things a spaniel must learn if he is to be anything approaching a satisfactory gun dog is some degree of response to handling (control) and an eagerness to fetch the game that's put on the ground (retrieving).

For some basic methods of instilling these requirements, I'll ask that you please turn to the retriever training chapter. In essence the same basics that should be given to a retriever in training also apply to spaniels. This also includes the more advanced work which is outlined in the chapter on "Problems, Solutions and Advanced Training" if you want to take the time to turn out a really polished gun dog that will win you exclamations of delight from hunting companions afield and a round of drinks when you get in that evening.

Modifications of this type of training as they apply to spaniels will be noted in the present chapter, along with procedures that are inate to spaniel training.

Because so much is expected of the spaniel, turning out a truly finished performer is a labor of love requiring persistent effort. But on the plus side—for the man in a hurry—the lazy or indifferent trainer—is the fact that even with a slip-shod training effort, thanks to the spaniel's natural proclivities, a sportsman will get some shooting at a wide variety of game at a relatively early period in the dog's life.

So, it's up to you how far you want to go in your "back yard" training and the out-in-the-field workouts and exposure to game. Your spaniel will be just what you make him. So let's get started.

Let Him Be a Puppy

Knowing when to ease up as well as when to put the squeeze on is an important aspect of training and very important with spaniels as well as other gun dog breeds.

If you've read the retriever training chapter, as you were advised to, you have your pup started at the age of two to three months and responding pretty well to "No!" "Kennel!" and "Sit!" (or "Hup" which is the command most pro trainers use).

But all work and no play can make Hobo a dull dog, lacking the exuberance and the merry mien that characterises a good working spaniel. So, from the time your spaniel pup is three or four months old start enjoying some hikes together in the fields, woods, and game cover where he can investigate at his leisure and become accustomed to the many strange things that make up the stage on which he's to perform.

When afield let your pup be a puppy until he is six to eight months old. Let him find, flush and chase whatever is available; anything that leaves scent, whether it flies or runs, including "stink birds", meadowlarks, rabbits or actual game birds, even butterflies. Most pups will instinctively teach themselves many things when allowed to excercise their curiosity in strange surroundings; not the least of which is the rudiments of what his nose can tell him.

Because spaniels start young there is sometimes an inclination to start serious training too soon which may dampen the spirit and dash you want when he's older. The field hikes should instill confidence and independence on the pup's part.

In all your training at this age, treat lapses in obedience tolerantly unless they are anything but out-and-out defiance of authority. The squeeze comes later with the teen-age or young adult dog. So enjoy your pup's antics while you can, being happy with what he does well and tending to overlook his lapses, saving the crackdown for the mature dog.

Purposeful Strolls

During the first few trips afield you needn't follow any pattern in your walking. But, by the time the pup is four to five months old, your walking should no longer be aimless. Set a zig-zag course. Walk as you would when hunting, investigating likely looking cover clumps, marshy spots, fence rows and other places game is probably found.

This type of walking will instill in your dog hunting pattern you will want him to follow when he's old enough to get down to business; quartering uniform cover and poking into likely spots in broken cover.

As your pup gets stronger and more confident, and his investigations start to carry him out beyond gun range, each time reaching the limit you want him to go; change your direction, say his name and blow a couple beeps on your whistle as you walk away from him or angle off his course. Unless he's real interested in something hot he'll turn and come along with you, working to your front once more. It will soon develop as a habit.

This casual type of training may very well be all your dog needs to learn the elements of a quartering pattern across the path you are taking. By now, at six to eight months of age, your spaniel should be sure of himself in the field, have a rough idea of patterning and be ready for an extension, of this play training, to the serious business of learning to hunt within gun range.

Along with this you should have undertaken his introduction to guns, birds, retrieving etc. The methods have been detailed in the chapters on *Introduction to Game and Guns* and *Retriever Training.* You are also ready to teach him to "Heel!" and to "Hunt 'em Out!" as outlined in the *Retriever Training* chapter. The former command plays a big part in learning his manners under the gun and the latter in encouraging his bird finding proclivities.

Hunting for Your Gun

At this stage of the game your pup is going to be increasingly less concerned about keeping in touch with you than in having a time for himself. Now, while afield, keep him brushed up on the commands you've taught him in the yard. Make him sit and heel, and take along a retrieving dummy and toss it for him to fetch occasionally.

87

Allow him to run as hard and as long as he wants, as long as he stays within normal or extreme gun range (20 to 45 yards) as he criss-crosses in front of you as you've taught him to do, by your constant changes of direction. An ideal pattern is an arc, 25 yards or less to your front, and no more than 40 yards to each side.

However, you are now likely to encounter a tendency on the part of your spirited young spaniel to kite out of gun range from time to time. As soon as he lines out straight, and gets beyond effective shooting range, call him back to you and put him at heel.

Keep him at heel for a minute or so, then release him and encourage him to "Hunt 'em Out!" Let him work as long as he stays within range, speaking to him encouragingly and "beep-beeping" on the whistle when you make abrupt changes in direction to keep him on the track—that quartering pattern across your front.

An English Springer Spaniel bitch demonstrates appealing desire and alertness as she sits up to mark the fall of a shot bird.

He's now ready for an introduction to another hand signal. As you beep your dog and make your turns, wave your arm in the new direction. This will be the beginning of his response to hand signals. In time, if he leaves a piece of cover unhunted, you will be able to put him into it with an arm wave or, with no whistling or hollering, cast him off in a new direction when he looks at you.

But any time he kites off on his own hook, call him back and heel him. Then send him out again. Repeat. Repeat. Repeat. . . if necessary. Many spaniels have a strong, natural inclination to quarter before the gun and will fall into this pattern with virtually no effort on your part.

But, regardless of the alacrity in response, by using this method you save a deal of running after your dog, cussing, whistle blowing, rope-jerking and a cowed and fearful dog that's afraid to do anything on his own. The idea is to get it across to him that he can have fun—as long as he moves in a certain pattern, at a certain distance from you. If he doesn't he has to heel. With a field of inviting cover in front of him no dog worth feeding really *likes* to do that.

In these training sessions, always work your dog into the wind if at all possible. It will greatly simplify your training work. Dogs have a natural tendency to work into the wind and they also have an aversion to meeting it head on. Hence they will angle or quarter as you head into it, naturally aiding in the establishing of the proper hunting pattern.

What's been said here about spaniels also applies to retrievers which are being trained to work as flushing dogs before the gun . . . even more so. Being used for so many generations as non-slip retrievers has produced many dogs with little natural inclination to get out and hunt. Use this method to develop his independent seeking and, if he is to be an upland hunter, give him a good season of actual hunting before putting the strict discipline on him that is outlined in the *Problems, Solutions and Advanced Training* chapter, lest you risk stifling what seeking and flushing instincts he possesses.

Dummies and Birds

By this time you should have had your flusher afield frequently, so that he's encountered birds, either by winding them and seeking them out or accidentally running through them, depending upon his individual precocity.

He should be ready for some fake birds: those dummies with the wings taped on, or sprinkled with training scent, which he's been marking and fetching when you throw them in his retrieving sessions.

But now you'll do it differently. He won't see the dummies thrown. Hide the dummies in cover, bring out your dog, start him on his hunting pattern, let him zero in on the scent, "catch the bird" and bring it to you. You can surreptiously flip the dummy into cover as you walk along behind your quartering dog when he isn't watching you. But remember exactly where it landed so you can "steer" the dog so he'll catch the scent or you can find it yourself if he doesn't catch on to this game right off. Remember to use the wind properly. He can't smell it if he crosses on the upwind side of the planted "bird". You can use one dummy at a time or disperse several over the area.

If he's done any fetching at all and enjoys it as he should, Hobo ought to go zinging in on the dummy, pick it up and bring it to you proudly. If he hesitates about picking it up, tell him "Good Boy!" "Fetch!" and encourage him with that reminder. Whenever he "catches a bird" and brings it to you praise him to the skys.

When he's in the vicinity of the dummy, tell him to "Hunt 'em Out!" and if he doesn't seem to be working the scent, keep him there, keep encouraging him with "Hunt 'em Out!" and stick with it until he finds it. If he won't pick up then, it may help to walk in to the dummy, speak to him encouragingly, get your toe underneath it and boost it a few feet into the air saying "Fetch!" so he'll chase it and pounce on it. The dummy in the air and the learned command should get the idea across to him.

Utilizing these bogus birds you can instill the desired response to your "Hunt 'em Out!" command. Since you know the dog's reward for his efforts is there, a dummy to be fetched and the subsequent praise, the dog will come to recognize that you are laying it on the line when you tell him to "Hunt 'em Out!" Once this is instilled, and you are actually hunting, if you *suspect* you may have gone past a bird or he is having trouble locating a shot bird this response will be strongly implanted. Even if his redoubled efforts fail to produce he won't feel that you've tricked him.

This drill is also valuable for retrievers even if they are not used as flushers. Pin point response to hand and whistle signals directing a dog to the area of the fall is advanced retriever work, training methods will be explained in that chapter, and it makes for a spectacular and satisfactory performance.

But, as a practical matter, because of a number of factors, this procedure has very limited usage when afield. Customarily, when a dog does not see the bird fall, the hunter walks to the vicinity of the fall, calls the dog over and says, "Hunt 'em Out!" "Dead Bird, Fetch!" or whatever else comes to mind. The dog then snorts and snuffles around until he hits scent, follows it to the bird and retrieves.

Having established that he can seek out and catch the fake birds proficiently, your dog is ready to hunt some real live feathers. If you want, you can just take him hunting and hope he'll make the transference from the dummy to the real thing. He just might. But to do it properly you should plant some birds for him to work in training sessions before you trust to luck and an ability to put two and two together he may not have.

His proper introduction to feathers should have been done before you undertake this. If you haven't read it, go now to the chapter *"Introduction to Game and Guns."*

"Dizzy" and plant some barn pigeons (if you can afford it use actual game birds purchased from a game farmer) as described in that chapter. From now on you can alternate using the dummies for brush up work, if you don't overdo it, and real birds to keep his interest high.

Kill the birds he flushes. Whether you are a good enough shot to do it consistently, or you have a friend who is a good shot and will help you out in return for some shooting sport, is up to you. You want those birds down for the dog to fetch to reinforce his association with gunfire, something down for him to bring in, and getting him a bird he couldn't catch without it.

Above all, make sure the pup doesn't get sprinkled as he chases a low flying bird. It's an ideal way to make him both bird and gunshy. And he will chase, at least if he's the eager kind you want. When he picks up the downed bird have him fetch and deliver properly — as you've taught him via the methods in the "Retriever Training" and "Problems, Solutions and Advanced Training" chapters. Praise him highly and then throw the bird for him to fetch again. Praise him for that retrieve too and proceed to your next bird.

You probably will be doing a lot of training in barren, birdless areas. But as you work him try to have some "game" out there, even if only dummies, so his efforts to find game are rewarded at least a couple of times; building the optomistic attitude a good gun dog must have when hunting the game-scarce areas which are the lot of most hunters today.

Don't, however, plant so many birds in a small area during one session that your dog will be falling into them. He should learn early that work produces birds; they aren't served up on a silver platter.

Besides, when using actual birds, and he's chasing a flyer, whether it is hit or missed, he may get messed up with the other "plants" which will foul up his training and provide no shooting or fetching. It's sensible and economical to plant one bird at a time.

Let's Go Hunting

Once these introductory procedures have been mastered, your flushing dog is ready to take out hunting. If, and when, the open season is upon you take him. Hunting is something he'll never get too much of.

So he pulls some fool stunts or starts a bad habit or two. So what? These things can be dealt with. Don't leave him home because he isn't fully trained. It takes actual hunting to make him birdwise. You can't do it in the yard or with artificial and set-up training sessions. Besides, giving your dog this experience is a ready made reason for you doing as much hunting as you possibly can squeeze in. If you need the support, tell your wife I said it is vital to your gun dog's development.

It may well be that your dog, as some very wonderful dogs have done for me, will virtually "break themselves" during the hunting season. If you get that lucky, except for some brushing up and conditioning during the off-season you may not need to undertake further training, and at the start of the next season he'll perform as you wish.

But don't count on it. For once your eager rascal starts providing you with shooting, he's also likely to present you with a problem, or two, or three. Since you will be wrapped up in hunting and shooting you are unlikely to do too much about correcting these things in season. You may pass up some shots and do some training if you are unusually devoted. Even then, it might be better to make these corrections a post-season program, after that first season of hunting is firmly imbedded in the youngster's memory.

So look up that pivotal chapter again, *"Problems, Solutions and Advanced Training"*. Let's see if we've encountered the same problems and if what *I've* learned will help *you* out. You can also decide whether you are satisfied, with what you now have in a gun dog, or whether you want to take the time to apply the techniques that will make him a fully trained dog.

7

Pointing Dogs

THERE are on this continent two distinct types of gun dogs, that slam to a halt upon striking hot game scent, or cautiously stalk faint scent until the propitious moment when they stop and freeze, holding this pose until the game is flushed for them by the man or men they are hunting with. This is called pointing.

The two distinct dog types might best be called traditional and modern. The "traditional" types include the Pointer, English Setter, Irish Setter and Gordon Setter. They have been known to U.S. sportsmen in one form or another, pre-dating the War Between the States, and gaining a foothold from the end of that conflict through the opening up of wilderness forests and prairies to farming and grazing in the Midwest and western states and in the plantation country of the South. They have been popular ever since. Their origins were the British Isles but their major development has been in the big country of North America.

The "modern" type of pointing dog's introduction, and zoom to popularity, coincided with the loss by sportsmen of the use of vast areas of open land whether through posting against trespass, reforestation, or crop growing; and replacement of declining bird species like the native Prairie Grouse with imported natives like Pheasant and Hungarian Partridge.

Shooting over a gun dog on point has always been the epitome of sport. While thousands of wing shooters turned to the flushing dogs, (spaniels and retrievers) in order to adjust to more restricted hunting areas, mixed bag shooting and the wiles of the Ring-necked Pheasant

93

there were many other gunners imbued with a preference for shooting over points.

They were less concerned, however, with such qualities as style, speed, stamina, range and gait, and preferred dogs that proceeded at a comfortable pace (hunted only a bit beyond extreme gun range) kept track of their human companions afield, and were reliable retrievers, even out of water if necessary.

They found this package among individuals from a variety of breeds developed on the European continent. Hence the sobriquet "Continental Pointing Dogs". Some promotors of these breeds are seeking a change to "Versatile Gun Dogs," reflecting a multiplicity of duties such gun dogs may be asked to perform.

While some of these "modern" breeds were introduced to North America during the 1930's, it has been since World War II that they've "caught on", adapted to the wants of American hunters, and achieved great popularity.

Modern breeds in this category include German Shorthaired Pointers, German Wirehaired Pointers, Pudelpointers, Weimaraners, Vizslas, Wirehaired Pointing Griffons and Brittany Spaniels. There are a number of other breeds of this type used in Europe but those are the ones known to some degree in this country.

Generalities regarding both the traditional (pointers) and modern (versatile) breeds were discussed in the "Gun Dog Categories" chapter. Specifics about the modern breeds listed above will be discussed in the next chapter. Without further ado let's go into some details about the traditional pointing dogs.

The traditional pointing breeds, as were the retrievers, were developed and accepted originally as specialists. Their forte was, and is finding and pointing upland game birds, just as the prime work of a retriever was on waterfowl. Most of them have remained specialists to this day; although in their use on a wide variety of terrestrial birds some might be accorded the multi-purpose dog tag.

It must also be noted that among the four gun dog categories these traditional pointing breeds have to rank as the least responsive to mechanical, backyard, modified-obedience training methods which today's hunter may be forced to employ in preparing his dog for the field. It takes live birds and game country to both start and develop a traditional pointing dog and a longer time for them to come around to the degree of proficiency satisfactory to either the casual or avid hunter.

In fact, few casual hunters should even consider a traditional

Pointer or Setter. They are dogs for the man who hunts hard and often. But the man who has the country and game available, and takes advantage of it, will settle for nothing less than a bird-wise, stylish Pointer or English Setter that is both proficient and pleasing to the eye, whether in motion or on point.

Pointer

For the man whose passion is upland game bird hunting, particularly Bobwhite Quail, Prairie Grouse or Hungarian Partridge, there is no breed that can equal the Pointer for results and aesthetic pleasure.

With proper introduction, training and experience the Pointer, also commonly called the English Pointer in deference to his origins and to differentiate between the German pointer breeds from the continent, can give a good account of himself on any upland bird.

But if waterfowl gunning takes up any part of a sportsman's hunting season, or if his upland game is frequently dropped into or across water, the Pointer is a least likely candidate for retrieving honors. There are notable exceptions and I have one in my kennel right now.

Cannonade's Salvo, a young Pointer bitch bred and trained by Dave Duffey, shows the high on both ends style so desireable in a class shooting dog.

95

Pointers seldom retrieve from water, but it's nice when one does as Jeb has done for Dave Duffey here.

A white and black male named Stupido (Ch. Cannonade X Seariup Twist) is a strong swimmer and willing water retriever.

He came by it accidentally as the result of seeing, chasing, and eventually swimming after swallows flitting over the training pond and recently-hatched ducklings paddling around on it. He now takes a swim, just about every morning in the summer, seemingly for the sheer joy of it. But three of his littermates, which I also kept, have been strictly non-water dogs although they retrieve well on land. Distaste for water, and sometimes retrieving, is typical of Pointers and even Stupido can not take icy water for long.

Conversely, the thin coated Pointer can put out better than any other breed for longer periods under hot, dry conditions without let up and watering, a situation frequently faced in upland bird hunting.

It can generally be expected that Pointers will range far and hunt independently. Birds are all that occupy their thoughts, once they find out what it is all about, and most have great natural ability. However, as was discussed in "Gun Dog Categories", Pointers do vary in their working style according to natural inclination, training and experience, i.e. hard-driving, wide-ranging "covey dogs", more deliberate working "singles dogs" and somewhat less that inspiring "meat dogs." What type you get will depend on your luck when you pick a pup and the training and experience he gets.

96

The late John Gates, a Field Trial Hall of Famer, in a relaxed moment at the kennel with a champion Pointer and a Pointer puppy.

Pointers have good dispositions, are independent and tough-fibered enough mentally to absorb a few training mistakes without serious repercussions. Most point naturally and can be brought along faster than setters. Pointers are most likely among gun dogs to require force training to retrieve. They adapt well to non-hunting confinement, on chain or in a kennel, and can be satisfactory house dogs. However, Pointers are kept for the most part by serious bird hunters who have a dog, or a number of dogs, just for that. A house-pet Pointer is pretty rare.

Coming into birds unexpectedly, a good gun dog like this Pointer may slam into a low stationed but intense point to avoid flushing game.

Their physical appearance shows their Foxhound ancestry, a lithe, well muscled, easy moving dog of 50 to 60 pounds around 22 to 24 inches tall, with short (and flat) hard coats; commonly of black, liver, lemon or orange-on-white.

For the man who specializes in hunting upland birds, commonly found in coveys, or who may want to take up field trialing to some degree, the Pointer is an odds-on best bet. When buying a pup make sure he is registerable with the Field Dog Stud Book, 222 West Adams St., Chicago, Ill. Pointers registered with the American Kennel Club are seldom of field stock. Serious and devoted breeders, who have developed the Pointer to its present degree of excellence, are affiliated with the FDSB.

English Setter

If the Pointer has a rival in the affections of hunters who gun the uplands and enjoy the grace and style of traditional pointing breeds it has to be the English Setter.

The Setter is second only to the Pointer as an open country dog on covey birds and, on a percentage basis, probably outranks the Pointer for use on game birds, found singly or in pairs, in more restricted coverts. They rate high among northeastern Ruffed Grouse and Woodcock hunters, and share the attention of southern quail hunters with the Pointer. While the second-most commonly seen breed in major field trials, they rank far behind the Pointer as competition dogs.

Their position in that regard and their dispositions are analogous to that of the Labrador Retriever and Golden Retriever in the waterfowl specialist category. Setters are usually "soft" in temperament, responding to gentle coercion rather than out-and-out force. They are very affectionate, make wonderful housepets but require a bit more time and patience in mastering their field work than does a Pointer. Expect that Setter performance at 18 to 24 months of age compares with what's anticipated in a 12 to 18 month Pointer.

The comparatively long, silky coat of the English Setter has advantages and disadvantages. It enhances the appearance, making for a pretty dog. But it will burr up and get water-logged and muddy, requiring more care.

While the Setter may not be the "hot weather dog" that the Pointer is, it has the edge when cold, wet, brambly cover must be worked. If hunting is done during snow time, the hair on the Setter's leg will afford protection for a longer time, from crust that abraids and cuts Pointer's feet and legs in 15–20 minutes.

Given proper introduction and encouragement, most setters, English, Gordon or Irish, take to water quite readily. If a man shoots an occassional duck or drops an upland bird in the water he can fully expect it will be retrieved by a setter, when most Pointers would balk. The last dozen or so setters (of all three breeds I've owned or trained for others) were, for the most part, passable to good water workers.

Perhaps this trait and a general inclination to pick up the knack of retrieving are traceable to the spaniel ancestry of setters, as well as their tendency to investigate and carefully hunt thick cover, rather than skim the edges, as is the Pointer's wont.

There are English Setters available that can "run with the Pointers"

Young English Setters, like this one Dave Duffey is training, require lots of attention and affection to obtain best results.

but on the average they can be expected to be a more moderate in range and more easily broken to hunt close. In physical dimensions and appearance there is a wide range in English Setters.

In fact there almost seems to be three strains, with considerable overlap. Quickly dismissed for the hunter is the "show type": a large, statuesque, full-feathered and plumed, 70-pound dog, with square muzzle, ponderous in movement and lacking in proper bird dog instincts. On the other extreme is a common-looking, little 30 pound dog, snipey of muzzle and with blinding speed that seems on the wane as field trialers, who once harbored them, seem to be turning to a larger dog which might best be termed a hunting Setter.

The hunting Setter is somewhat of a meld of the two extremes, a balanced dog, pretty but not beautiful, about 50 pounds in weight, capable of maintaining a brisk hunting pace all day; biddable and possessed of all the proper instincts. It goes without saying that this type will prove most satisfactory to sportsmen. In regard to registration, as with the Pointer, the field Setter is most frequently signed up with the Field Dog Stud Book.

Talk about precocious style! This English Setter pup is photographed by his owner, David J. Hasinger.

Gordon Setter

The black and tan Gordon Setter is the rarest of the traditional pointing breeds, although serious efforts are now being made to establish it as a gun dog. While never very popular, the breed virtually descended into oblivion until about a decade ago, except for those shown and occasional ones kept by northeastern grouse and woodcock hunters.

They are truly handsome dogs and, I suspect, may have a stronger "shot" of hound blood in them than their cousins judging from the appearance of Gordon pups. They look for all the world like silkycoated Black and Tan Coonhound whelps, and have the temperament of the adults I've known.

Gordons are intelligent dogs that learn by doing, with independent natures bordering on stubbornness and openly resentful when crowded or pushed too strenuously. All the setter breeds become greatly attached to a firm but kind trainer. This inclination in the Gordon is so strong that he becomes strictly a "one-man" dog and will really extend himself only for the person to whom he is devoted.

Find one from good gun-dog stock, give him plenty of attention

A good hunting Gordon Setter delivers a bird to Dave Duffey. When snow blankets the ground, the dark Gordon is easy to spot on point.

and work, and you will be rewarded with extreme loyalty and a close-working hunter, best suited for Pheasant, Ruffed Grouse and Woodcock. Because of their color they are hard to see on point in thick, dark cover but stand out in a snowy setting and, because of their relatively restricted range, are not hard to keep track of.

Their hunting pace is most comfortable and easy to keep up with. They do not "lay out flat" like the racier Pointers and English Setters, nor trot as the Continental Pointers so frequently do, but rock along in a controlled canter.

Gordons seem to run to more bone and height than the other traditional pointing breeds: up to 27 inches and 80 pounds, and the majority are registered with the American Kennel Club, 51 Madison Ave., New York, N.Y. 10010.

Irish Setter

Although one of the more popular breeds of dogs in this country, the stunningly beautiful, flame-colored Irish Setter ranks just a notch above the Gordon regarding the infrequency of being seen afield.

Along with this dubious distinction it shares with the Gordon a general lack of "high style" when on point, usually indicating birds

Red Setter breeders seek this type of style and intensity in their gun dogs.

Even when they are proficient gun dogs, Irish Setters too often display level or low-tailed points.

A Red Setter bred for field work is "stanched up" by pro trainer, Domenick Welsh. (Photo by David J. Hasinger.)

Red Setters, bred for field work, Valli Hi Town and Valli Hi Country point and back as Mrs. David Hasinger moves in to shoot. (Photo by David J. Hasinger.)

with a very merry tail action followed by a low stationed, low tailed point which is less pleasing to the eye of the beholder than the jacked-up rigidity displayed by good Pointers and English Setters.

But there seems to be considerable hope for the man who wants an Irish Setter for the field, if he is willing to turn to a "new breed", termed the *Red Setter* field dog. Under the auspices of the Field Dog Stud Book, field dog fanciers, with judicious outcrossings to English Setters and Pointers, have worked to develop a red dog that runs and hunts hard, and points his game with a high tail. Good looking dogs, they lack the extreme beauty of the show type Irish Setter, whose beauty has been blamed in many quarters for their decline as hunters since the 1930's. People bought them, loved them and bred them for their appearance and personality, with no regard for hunting ability.

With smatterings of success some fanciers of the breed, using promising individuals from AKC-registered show and pet stock displaying some hunting talents, have managed to produce a few dogs that retain their vaunted beauty and hunt well; although customarily displaying soft and unstylish points.

If the buyer of a pup is to play the percentages he must go the Red Setter, Field Dog Stud Book route, if he counts on having a gun dog. If he waits until the younster is started or trained a hard search may locate an unforgettable gun dog from breedings of AKC-registered dogs.

For if an Irish is "right", sometimes even "half-right", he exudes an air of care-free gaiety, when afield, that is infectious. All setters have a reputation for slow-starting and the Irish is no exception. But while their development is not precocious, physically they are long-lived and may be capable of good performance in their advanced years.

A casual, rather than strict schooling approach, is the best training procedure with the Irish, allowing the dog to set his own pace, soft-pedaling force and conning him into believing what his trainer wants done is really his own idea.

Since the developers of the Red Setter are trying to compete on even terms with the Pointers and English Setters in field trials, some dogs from this type of breeding may turn out to be big running. Most Irish Setters encountered, however, rate as no more than medium ranging gun dogs moving at a rollicking canter. Many may prove hard to stanch on point (hold their position, once they've established it, until the hunter flushes the birds) but most take to retrieving training most readily.

8

Continental or
Versatile Pointing Breeds

POINTING breeds from the European continent, for the most part, were "made" during the past 100 to 125 years, and their general acceptance in North America dates back less than 30 years.

The reason for their rapid rise in popularity among North American sportsmen is simple and direct. They are very practical, highly trainable dogs, ideally suited for the hunter who desires his dog to work relatively close to the gun, point the game birds he finds and retrieve them after they are shot. Usually owning only one dog at a time, he wants an animal that can double as a family pet.

With few exceptions the Continental pointing breeds are much happier, and satisfy their owners better, when kept as constant companions in the home and yard as well as co-workers in the uplands and marshes. They'll adapt if necessary but they are not as content with being kenneled as other gun dog breeds.

The Continental or versatile pointing breeds can be grouped according to coat texture. The shorthaired group includes the German Shorthaired Pointer (Deutsche Kurzhaar), the Weimaraner and the Vizsla. The wirehaired group is represented by the German Wirehaired Pointer (Deutsche Drahthaar), the Pudelpointer, Wirehaired Pointing Griffon, German Roughhaired Pointer (Deutsche Stichelhaar) and the (Italian) Spinoni. The longhaired group lists the

Brittany Spaniel (Epagneul Breton), the German Longhaired Pointer and the Small and Large Muensterlander Pointer.

It should be noted here that the very popular Brittany Spaniel, obviously, from its name, of French origin, is the only breed of the longhaired group represented in any numbers in the U.S. The Drahthaar (German Wirehair), Griffon and the Pudelpointer, which is just getting started on this continent, are likely to be encountered by hunters, and all the shortcoats—Shorthairs, Vizslas and Weimaraners are well represented.

The others are too rare to be included in the scope of this book. Throughout the chapter, to avoid possible confusion by less than careful readers, the German Wirehaired Pointer will be referred to by its German name, *Drahthaar* (pronounced Draaht-har), the Wirehaired Pointing Griffon will be called a *Griffon* and the German Shorthaired Pointer a *Shorthair.*

The Brittany and Griffon stem from France, the Vizsla is a Hungarian dog and the others were developed in Germany. I am not about to enter a dispute over what to call these types of gun dogs. In Germany they are called *All Gebrauchshunde* (literal translation, all purpose dogs) and, when introduced to this country, were highly touted for their mastery of a multiplicity of jobs. I have always referred to them as Continental pointing breeds, which is reasonably descriptive. However, as indicated in the chapter "Gun Dog Categories" I am willing to bow to the desire of the North American Versatile Hunting Dog Association (NAVHDA), which is very active in promoting the usage of these dogs in the manner their breeding intended them to be used, which has tagged them with the title Versatile Hunting Dogs.

In my book a dog is versatile if he seeks, finds and points upland game, and retrieves it, and also does a passable job of duck fetching. I feel that any dog, whether flusher, retriever or pointer who manages these tasks can be fairly termed a versatile or multi-purpose gun dog.

However, in Europe and now, to some extent in North America, great effort is expended to teach the versatile hunting dog breeds not only the dual jobs of upland and waterfowl hunter, but also to dispatch vermin, track and retrieve both fur and feather and so on.

There doubtless will be a few readers who may be interested in developing their dogs along the lines of terrier and hound work, in addition to their work on upland birds and waterfowl. This book will aid you in the normal aspects of gun dog training, their work in the uplands and marshes; for I have personally owned and/or trained representatives of the versatile breeds we'll discuss.

But I am not qualified to tell you how to teach a gun dog to destroy a fox or housecat, locate wounded deer, tree raccoon, or fetch rabbits. I do not train bird dogs to do these things. But, for those who wish to, I suggest you contact NAVHDA, through its secretary, Dr. Edward D. Bailey, Rt. 1, Puslinch, Ont., Canada for information about these subjects and the special field trials conducted for Versatile Hunting Dogs.

German Shorthaired Pointer

The German Shorthaired Pointer was the first of the Continental breeds to win acclaim from American hunters and, because of its tenure, has probably undergone more experimentation and change in adapting to what is sought in a gun dog over here.

Although some importations occurred earlier, the Shorthair dates from the late 1930's and was followed in successive waves by other breeds, all essentially cousins, if not brothers, under the skin: the Weimaraner, the Vizsla, the Drahthaar and, in very small numbers at present, the Pudelpointer.

The Weimaraner and Vizsla have more ancient traceable lineage than the others, but the short- and rough-coated pointing breeds from the continent were developed largely through the use of hound, Pointer and Poodle cross-breeding. As you may have guessed *Pudel* means Poodle and is pronounced as such in Germany, where the breed had its origins as a water dog despite the common misnomer "French Poodle," stemming from its later development there.

The early Shorthairs in this country were large, rather ponderous dogs with houndy-heads. They didn't suit many American hunters. They have been refined considerably since, but big-boned, draft horse-like Shorthairs are still to be seen.

Generally, however, the most popular Shorthair type is much trimmer, well muscled, and greatly resembles a dock-tailed Pointer; particularly when their coats are open marked showing a great deal of white, rather than the basic solid liver or heavy ticking.

A third type that may be encountered is a snipey-muzzled, finely boned dog with excessive tuck-up at the loin, with poorly developed hind-quarters, resembling Whippets. Shorthairs should run about 24 inches at the shoulder and weigh 50 to 65 pounds.

Properly the Shorthair is a handsome animal with the endurance to

108

hunt all day at his own pace. More frequently a trot than a gallop. Their pointing style and movement while seeking game seldom is as high, nor displaying the single-minded purposefulness and range, of good Pointers.

Shorthairs are also more often inclined to work with low head and to trail foot scent (probably a result of their inheritance) since they were and are used for tracking game. While this distracts from a dog's hunting style, willingness to put nose to the ground has some compensations in the tracking of wounded game that runs, like Pheasant.

The Shorthair must be rated high as a Pheasant producer. Because their range is short to medium, when they point it is usually possible for the hunter to get to the dog in time to flush the bird rather than have it run out from under a prolonged point. When a Shorthair makes a mistake and flushes a bird, very often it is within range of a reasonable or long shot. It is poor form to shoot a bird flushed by a pointing breed. But hunters who don't give a damn about form are legion. Shorthairs should also provide complete satisfaction on Ruffed Grouse and Woodcock and shorebirds but leave a bit to be desired on covey birds like Bobwhite Quail and Prairie Grouse.

In general they have the proper natural instincts to learn retrieving easily and, with some exceptions, are fond of water work. They cannot be expected to withstand severe conditions under which the retriever breeds are asked to work, nor is their ability to mark and remember falls as ingrained. But they have to be rated superior retrievers over the traditional pointing breeds on land, and their temperament is such that they can be trained to play the role of non-slip retriever on dove shoots, in a blind or boat for waterfowl, and are worthwhile accessories when jump-shooting ducks.

Field trialers have developed "big running" Shorthairs, although, in comparison to "big running" Pointers, that description of range is a most generous one. The field trial type Shorthair is sort of betwixt and between. Not adequate for the hunter that needs a real stem-winder, but too "wild" for most on-foot hunters who prefer a 50 to 150 yard dog, moving at a comfortable pace, easy to keep track of and control.

Most Shorthairs and other Continental pointing breeds with intense hunting desire will be easier for the amateur trainer to confine, within the limits he wants his hunting done, than the majority of pointers. They were designed for, and should be used, as game producers and retrievers for the sportsman who likes mixed bag hunting but wants his upland game pointed. Therefore it is understandable that they

A four-month-old Vizsla pup shows precocity in retrieving a shot bird.

A perfect delivery from a well trained German Shorthaired Pointer.

were first adopted by Mid-westerners and have extended their popularity to the northwest and northeastern regions but are relatively rare in the southern quail belt.

Vizsla

Hungary's contribution to the versatile gun dog breeds is of ancient lineage with a red-gold coat that is very attractive. The Vizsla, when light in conformation, might be described as a racy-looking yellow Labrador or, if heavy-boned and-headed, a dock-tailed Redbone hound. It has also been described as a "yellow Weimaraner". It is none of those things.

Canine historians claim the Vizsla (pronounced Veesh-lah) traces back to the dogs used by 10th Century Magyar huntsmen on European plains. The breed started to catch on in North America in the 1950's.

Considering the relatively short time they've been in this country, Vizslas have made substantial gains numerically. But it can not be claimed they've yet proven the equal of Shorthairs, Drahthaars and Brittanies in standards of performance desired by hunters who want this type of gun dog.

Ideally, the Vizsla should be capable of doing everything any of the other versatiles are expected to do; range close to medium, find and

110

point birds, and retrieve from both land and water. All these the good ones do and owners are high in praise for their handsome animals.

But for the sportsman starting with a pup, good Vizsla hunting and field trial stock will be harder to locate. Expectations of any given pup turning out well are not as high, percentagewise, as among most of the better known traditional and modern pointing breeds. The Vizsla is still in the transitional stage in North America, going through the settling in and modifying which other Continental breeds have behind them; bucking more familiar breeds who have already demonstrated they can accomplish essentially the same things the Vizsla is expected to.

A proper Vizsla is a natural hunter and retriever, 21 to 24 inches high, weighing on either side of 50 pounds. He should have drive and endurance afield, be tractable and affectionate in nature but have strong protective instincts. The breed should be good for, and trainable to, the same duties as the other versatile breeds, as outlined in some detail in the previous description of the German Shorthaired Pointer which, along with the Brittany Spaniel, ranks among the best known of the versatile gun dogs.

Weimaraner

An objective opinion regarding the Weimaraner (pronounced Vymar-honor) is as rare as a meeting of the Orange Order presided over by a captain of the Irish Republican Army. But extreme opinions regarding this once highly touted breed are as common as flies on a barn door.

Recognizing exaggeration and controversy have swirled around this breed since its highly promoted introduction to North American sportsmen following World War II, let's try an objective approach.

Like the Irish Setter, the breed is popular. But percentagewise not too many stack up as premier or even acceptable gun dogs. However, when a good one does crop up, given sufficient experience and proper training, he can be very, very good as a gun dog and home companion, for the sportsman who likes a slow, methodical pointing dog seldom reaching out beyond gun range.

Physically, the Weimaraner should be a large dog of considerable substance (although some very weedy specimens do appear) up to 27 inches high, and weighing around 85 pounds, with a distinctive gray coat that gives him the nickname "The Gray Ghost."

In common with most German breeds, the Weimaraner is highly

111

As with many of the Continental pointing breeds, this Weimaraner is a practical gun dog but hardly stylish on point.

intelligent, respects the firmest of discipline and, unless shown who is boss, will make every effort to reverse the traditional role of dog and master. I have a big, honest Weimaraner in my kennel now, who will go with anyone who has a gun and wins praise from the guests at the hunting club. Most Weimaraners, however, will be one-manish or one-familyish.

Dock-tailed and deriving their name from the German court of Weimar, where they originated as gun and companion dogs, the Weimaraner presently trails most of the other gun dog breeds in popularity among hunters, in both this country and Germany. Fortunately there are serious breeders trying to overcome the unfortunate blizzard of spurious publicity, that accompanied a hard sell of this breed to the U.S. public in the late 1940's and early 1950's, in an endeavor to establish the breed as a serious candidate for sportsman consideration.

Drahthaar or German Wirehaired Pointer

It would be an over-simplification to call the Drahthaar a "House of David" German Shorthair. But, at first glance, his whiskers and rough coat seem to be all that differentiate this breed from his much better-known, smooth-coated cousin, the German Shorthair.

112

Briar, a Drahthaar owned and trained by Dave Duffey, locks up on a bird as a pointing dog ought to.

Jaegerin, a precocious Drahthaar pup owned by Dave Duffey, demonstrates a stanch point at ten weeks of age.

While the physical appearance is similar, and the work to be expected from a Drahthaar is identical to that described in the Short-hair section of this chapter, there are differences.

The Drahthaar is another comparatively "new" breed of gun dog in North America although it was known in Germany well before the last century's turn and is now more popular there than the Shorthair.

While this very promising breed has hardly taken North America by storm in the short period of time, since its official recognition in 1959, by the American Kennel Club (following an earlier nod by the Field Dog Stud Book) the Drahthaar has quietly established itself as a desirable and capable multi-purpose gun dog.

They are very trainable, possessing strong natural instincts to hunt for, point, back, and retrieve game birds; and a clownish sense of humor that is pleasing and generally lacking in other German breeds. They are, however, inclined to be standoffish with strangers and are most appreciated by the people they serve. In common with other German breeds it is relatively easy to make them "sharp" in their attitude toward strangers and they respond best to plenty of attention and intensive training.

They catch on fast, seldom can be pushed too hard and, because their instincts dictate their doing the right thing at an early age, can be expected to turn in profitable days afield at an age (six months and up) when most other breeds are merely tolerated as they gain know-how and experience. Like any breed, they will have their share of

Pups and kids were made for each other. This is Jaegerin, a Drahthaar pup, and Mike Duffey, then seven years old.

spooks and worthless critters. But the percentage of pups from good stock that can be expected to develop easily into satisfactory gun dogs is high.

First established in the Mid-west of America, that area remains the Drahthaar's center of popularity here. The desired dense, harsh to touch, wiry coat is not uniform in the breed; ranging from almost Shorthair slickness to wooliness, with some coats very sparse. They are good sized, from 22 inches up, around 55 to 70 pounds, are agile, alert and generally exhibit a freer gait than the Shorthair.

They have often been mistaken for Airedales and, because of some variance in coat and body confirmation, can easily be confused with Griffons and Pudelpointers. Both of those breeds, along with the *Stichelhaar* and the Shorthair contributed to the Drahthaar in make-up. A good Drahthaar coat is protective, drys very rapidly and helps to give them an edge in water work over some of the other versatiles.

Wirehaired Pointing Griffon

The heaviest coated, and slowest moving, of the versatile gun dog breeds, the Griffon is far from a popular dog, despite the strong

114

natural instincts most display that make them very useful in certain forms of hunting.

This breed is also known as the Korthals' Griffon, named after E. K. Korthals, a Dutch banker's son, who originated the breed in Holland and continued work on it in Germany. But it is generally considered to be a French breed since major development took place there.

The Griffon is a highly intelligent breed, eager to please, points naturally and stanchly at an early age and takes to retrieving easily. It probably ranks at or near the top as a water worker among the versatile breeds, is a good marsh worker and suitable for jump shooting ducks and shore bird hunting.

Hunters who prize style and dash will find the Griffon wanting although their very close range, frequently no wider than a flushing dog's, and deliberate hunting style, may be just what the doctor ordered for the man who wants a dog under tight control, hunting small patches of cover and easy to keep up with.

The Griffon is rugged in appearance but of an amenable and affectionate disposition. While it can be expected to do anything required of a versatile hunting dog the breed has never shown that there was anything it could do better. Unless the specialty involved water work where, as on land, slowness detracts from steadfast endurance.

Pudelpointer

The newest and least know entry among the versatile breeds on the North American gunning scene is the Pudelpointer. Of all the versatile breeds, it may prove to be the most interesting to sportsmen who seek a medium ranging dog, moving like the traditional pointers yet possessing strong natural inclinations to retrieve and take to water.

The Pudelpointer rates as the naturally *widest* ranging of the versatile breeds, except for the field trial bred and trained Shorthairs and Brittanies, just as the Griffon and Weimaraner are the *closest* working.

There is reason for this. As their breed name indicates, Pudelpointers resulted as a deliberate cross between Poodles and Pointers. German sportsmen recognized the abilities of the "English" Pointer and were also cognizant of the intelligence and water retrieving ability of the standard Poodle.

The Poodle (Pudel in German, roughly translated to "puddle" in English) got its start as a waterfowl retriever. Even the later, exaggerated, Poodle coat clips had the original purpose of protecting the

John Kegel accepts delivery of a pheasant by his Pudelpointer during a training session.

organs and joints of the dog from cold water while eliminating excess hair that impeded progress.

Much more recently, since about 1950, North American sportsmen who imported Pudelpointers from their native land have experimented with crossing these dogs with field trial strains of Pointers in an effort to afford the breed some of the "go" and style that is required or prized in many American hunting situations. The Pudelpointer is recognized by the Field Dog Stud Book and Canadian Kennel Club but Pudelpointer breeders maintain their own stud book.

The Pudelpointer greatly resembles the Drahthaar, although considering the early origin of the Pudelpointer (and its use in producing the Drahthaar) it is better said that the Drahthaar owes its appearance and many of its characteristics to the Pudelpointer.

In temperament and ability the two breeds are also comparable, although a sparser coat is acceptable on the Pudelpointer. The whiskers or beard are not as prominent and the Pointer influence is more pronounced, in regard to the more apple-shaped head, expression and gait. Pudelpointers are not pretty, but are practical.

The Pudelpointers I have seen have impressed me enough so that, at this moment of writing, I am awaiting word from the airport telling me of the arrival of a nine-week old pup being shipped to me by a

Canadian breeder and friend, John Kegel of Rt. 1, Goodwood, Ontario.

Brittany Spaniel

In popularity on this continent, the Brittany Spaniel ranks at least the equal of the German Shorthair. This acceptance by North American sportsmen is well deserved, indicating the practicality of the breed, whose origin was the French province of Brittany where sportsmen needed a small pointing dog, suitable for working dense, wet cover.

The breed has changed little in purpose and appearance since importations began in the mid-1930's and its use began to proliferate among hunters in the late 1940's and early 1950's. However, considerable advancement has been made in developing Brittanys that are the answer to many a U.S. sportsman's desires. In this area the Brittany is considerably ahead of many of the other versatiles.

Brittanys seen right after World War II were frequently too timid "shoe-polishers" who seemed to lack the boldness, physical ability and desire to get out from underfoot. It gave them a bad name in some circles, but the good ones were appealing and fanciers of the breed went to work.

One can also obtain a wide-ranging, hard-going Brittany that will run almost as big as some field trial pointers and setters, thanks to the interest Brittany fans have taken in field trials patterned after the traditional pointing dog events.

If a sportsman thinks he may want to dabble in field trials with his gun dog as well as hunt him, the Brittany would be the breed to turn to for the best chance of enjoyment and attainment. While most frequently conducted under the aegis of the American Kennel Club, Brittany trials reflect many of the somewhat different concepts of the trials sanctioned by the Amateur Field Trial Clubs of America, associated with the Field Dog Stud Book.

However, the essence of Brittany work involves that of a close-cover gun dog and most hunters will want a Brittany that falls between the extremes of a "stumble over" dog and a horizon seeker. Because of the upgrading in quality from the original importations, thanks to competitive events, most Britts fall into this mid-range category.

Although they are the only spaniels that point and have a more stand-offish temperament than the other spaniels, the Brittany is strongly spaniel. His spaniel inquisitiveness leads to investigation of scent and cover and makes him ideally suited for the hunter after Ruffed Grouse and Woodcock. A preponderance of white in their silky, setter-like coats make them easier to spot in thick cover than the dark, neutral or dingy colors of the other versatiles. For the same reasons given in the Shorthair section of this chapter, they are also proficient on Pheasant but, while useful, not as satisfactory on covey-type birds like quail.

Persons not intimately acquainted with various dog breeds might take the Brittany for a short-coupled and leggy Springer Spaniel and others might describe them as short-tailed English Setters. There are large and small specimens of the breed but the standard calls for a small to medium-sized 17 to 20 inch animal, 35 to 50 pounds.

As befitting the difference in their origins, the temperament of the Brittany is vastly different from that of the German versatiles. The Britt has strong, natural pointing instinct and lesser, but very evident, desire to retrieve. But a Brittany can not be crowded or "worked over." He responds best to gentle, patient, repetitive treatment. In balancing resentment and sulking when roughly treated, the breed usually catches on naturally and quickly as to what is expected in the hunting field. Their relatively close range and desire to keep contact with their trainers make for a comfortable dog to hunt behind. They are inclined to be one-man and one-family dogs, in and out of the field.

More impatient or "antsy" in attitude than most of the other versatiles, they are seldom suitable as non-slip retrievers (although many take readily to water) most are easily trained to retrieve and if an occasional duck is jumped and knocked down on a bird hunting jaunt a Brittany might be expected to fetch it.

For the most part the Brittany, although classed as a versatile, seems to work out best as an upland bird specialist in the manner of the traditional pointing breeds, at a reduced range and with less style, and should be trained accordingly. Rather than being coerced, and restricted to establish control, most Brittanys need encouragement to excercise independence.

9

Pointing Dog Training

BECAUSE gun dogs that point game must be allowed
more latitude, if they are to go about their work in anything but a
plodding, dutiful manner, it might be assumed that they should be
easier to train than the spaniels and retrievers, who must be taught
more responses to commands and remain under tighter control.

If one has access to a good chunk of country that contains a respectable native bird population, turning out a stylish gun dog that points
birds *will* be a simpler task than the proper training of a gun dog
that flushes birds. Such is not the case considering the situation most
hunters face today. They suffer from a lack of land, game and time.

So, our task is to turn out a good bird finder and stanch pointer,
who will do a reasonable job of recovering what we shoot over his
points and carry it off with an air of enjoyment. To do this we must
set some modest and practical goals.

If the desires of sportsmen, who have brought dogs of the pointing
breeds to me for training, are any indication, they are satisfied or
pleased with a dog that will:

Diligently seek and find game birds. Point birds when he locates
them. Remain stanch (not break his point until the birds are flushed).
Go to and pick up, or "point dead", birds that are knocked down,
assuring their recovery. Refrain from shagging missed birds out
of the country. Respond to hunter shouts or whistles, indicating
direction changes or a new area to hunt. Range at distances between
50 and 250 yards; the scope of this hunting effort and pattern depending upon the game birds sought and the lay of the land.

There's a saying that "there's nothing cuter than a spotted pup" and Dave Duffey obviously agrees as he fusses with a pair of Pointer littermates.

These, obviously, are respectable, perhaps formidable tasks. But a pointing dog who does not perform these basics can not be of much use afield. What about backing? Steady to wing? Steady to shot?

These niceties, all acquired characteristics of top pointing dog work, may also be taught. You will be told how in the chapter "Problems, Solutions and Advanced Training". But first the basics must be put on the dog. After that it will be up to you, and your dog, whether you want to carry on to make a finished performer, or settle for a useful, if rough on the edges, bird producer. So let's get with it.

Come! and Whoa!

Before a pointer, setter or versatile is turned out for his first serious scamper in game cover, he needs to know just two things, aside from responding to his name. He must come to you when called or whistled, and respond to the command "Whoa!" which means just what it says: "Stop, halt, cease all motion and stand there!" This is the equivalent of the "Stay!" "Wait!" or "Hup!" commands used in training flushing dogs.

The difference is that flushing dogs are taught to stay put, while in a sitting position, pointing dogs while standing. The reason for the difference in posture is that pointing dogs should *not* point game from a sitting position. Thus, if your dog should be creeping in on game and threatens to get too close; actually sees a bird sneaking out ahead of him, or is approaching another dog already on point when a back is required; and you want to halt his progress, your command will stop him in at least a semblence of pointing posture.

You may also want to use the command to halt a pointing dog's chase of an inadvertantly flushed or missed bird and he must know this command if you go on to teach backing and steadiness to wing and shot. Then when you discipline him it will be for disobeying a learned command and will not lead him to associate this unpleasant chastisement with game birds.

A back, by the way, is nothing more than an honor of another dog's find, the mark of a well-broke, gentlemanly dog, contrasting to the thieving glory-hog who steals points from the deserving dog by creeping in to the front of the dog already on, or the jealous rascal who ignores his bracemate's point and takes the birds out from in front of him.

Teaching a dog to come when called has been covered in the chapter on "Training Retriever Gun Dogs" in the basics and I refer you to it. While you are there, read about the other basic commands which flushing dogs must be taught. It is desirable that pointing dogs also respond to these commands, eventually, but debatable at this early stage of the game.

You are free to make your choice of starting on the obedience commands now or waiting until you've made sure you are in possession of a gun dog that makes it worth this effort. You may even decide to skip them entirely, depending upon your goals and what satisfies you in a hunting dog. But have a look.

The reason I'm so lenient about free choice is this. A pointing pup should have a lot of freedom in the field, have demonstrated some interest in game scent; and have locked up in some "Flash points" (momentary pauses in pointing posture upon striking scent) before really formal disciplining starts.

The name of this game is finding birds and pointing them when found. If a young dog seems to lack the nose, independence and pointing instincts, he rates as a poor prospect, and it is a waste to put the mechanical responses on a dog lacking in natural qualities. You will be better off with a half-broke dog that will go out and dig up some

When calling a pup to you, crouch down to his level, giving him confidence, and coax him in as Dave Duffey does·with Dillon, a Pudel-pointer.

Once he's come to you, pet him, sweet talk him and tell him what a great pup he is for doing what he's sup-posed to.

birds for you, than with the best trained dog in the neighborhood who can't find a bird unless it slaps him in the face with a wing.

Whoa!

"Whoa!" can be taught in much the same manner as the "Stay!" command. So check the preceding chapter on "Training Retriever Gun Dog". There are also several alternative methods, which can be used to teach the command, or to reinforce it, if you utilize the flushing dog "Stay!" procedure. As far as that goes, the commands are inter-changeable and you can use either. But "Whoa!" is accepted pointing dog parlance.

A practical and effective method of teaching the dog to Whoa! can be used in relation to food. At feeding time, set your dog's food in front of him. Tell him "Whoa!" and restrain him with your hands. When you say "All Right!" pat his head and allow him to eat.

A variation of this method can be used when you have the pup out exercising and playing with him. Put a food morsel in front of him when he's close enough for you to catch and "Whoa!" Through repetition he will learn to stop on that command.

When he stops, before moving in on food, try the "Whoa!" without that stimulus. If he stops, praise him verbally as you go to him, stroke him gently along the back and then tap him on the head and say "All Right!" which is a release command allowing him to move on.

He becomes acquainted with a multiplicity of things during this procedure, learning a command he's expected to obey, becoming accustomed to your hands on him and will associate the pat on the head and the release command, with the privilege of moving on to relocate game, or to start hunting afresh, making discipline applied later afield a mild and painless process.

If he shouldn't stop at the command he's been play-trained into learning, catch him and stand him up on the spot on which you ordered him to halt. If he persists defying the command he should understand, you can introduce him to the checkcord, which is a long rope attached to his collar. Let him reach the end of the rope and say "Whoa!" If he doesn't stop, (you should be set in anticipation of this) jerk the rope sharply and repeat "Whoa!"

It won't take too many of these sharp jerks, or even a tipping-over when he hits the end of the rope hard, to get him to halt when ordered to. It will take longer with a determined "hard-head," but wear gloves and keep working on him. When he'll stop before the rope and collar punish him, let him run without the cord and "Whoa!" him; going to him, praising and stroking; and releasing when he does. If he doesn't. Back to the check cord.

Many, maybe most, pointing dogs are taught "Whoa!" with the rope and collar. Usually when they are between the ages of six to eighteen months when they can absorb this harsh discipline. But there's no reason not to start a pup on this much earlier and avoid the roughness through the other two methods outlined. You probably don't have a string of dogs to turn out in a limited time, necessitating forcebreaking. Most likely you have one pup that you can patiently, and gently bring around with little pain or strain to either of you.

Natural Bent and Bending It

Individual dogs in all the breeds are going to vary in their natural proclivities. Recognize that while getting the type of dog we desire will depend greatly upon our ability as trainers, and the diligent application of training techniques, each dog's inherited inclinations will have a considerable effect.

Generally if we want a wide-ranging dog (one that *hunts* a consider-

123

When a dog does it right, take time to pet and praise the good performance as Dave Duffey does here with Cannonade's Salvo, a Pointer bitch.

able distance from the gun) we can expect it from Pointers and English Setters. If we desire a close worker, the percentages are with the versatile pointing breeds.

Reason will then tell you that you must find some way to curb the run of the traditional pointing breeds, and encourage reaching out by the modern pointing breeds, if you desire a hunting pattern not in keeping with the general expectation of these breeds . . . or should you get an individual who is not typical.

Dogs can be made into horizon-grabbing runners who range a quarter-mile or more from the hunter by working them in open, barren country, where they must reach out if they are to hope to find game at all. Here they can be forced out with whips, shouting or pushing the pace with a fast horse.

By contrast, some recently advocated training methods which impose strict control over a pointing dog, emphasize intensive, artificial training before affording the dog any field experience. This can inhibit a gun dog into becoming an overly-dependent, too-eager-to-obey boot-brusher who never gets out and really hunts.

I am assuming that you will have no more practical use for either of these extremes than I would. What you should want is a happy,

124

independent hunter whose boldness is balanced by biddability, interest in maintaining contact with the hunter, but pleasing to the eye
as he moves out seeking game and locks up pointing it. Essentially,
a dog you can kill birds over and simultaneously thrill to his performance.

An important element in the formula that produces such a dog is
the frequency you go afield with him, long before the actual gunning
season opens.

Walking Your Dog

The simple expedient of taking your pup for walks in areas which
are natural game cover, or at least simulate it, will set the pattern
for his development into a hard hunting producer of game who
keeps track of you afield (hunts for the gun) without a lot of shouting,
whistling or running and cursing on your part.

With a pup from the age of two months, if you will use your legs
and your head, it is unlikely that you will have problems controlling
your dog afield. At least you will minimize your efforts regardless of
his ancestry and natural bent. But, if you wait to take your pup afield
until he's eight to twelve months old, you are most likely to encounter
one of two extremes. One type may be intimidated by the new and
strange "wide open" spaces and want to stay close to the only thing that
resembles familiar surroundings: *you.* Getting him to move out and
investigate can be a tedious and futile proposition.

In contrast, a bold one, turned loose after close confinement, will
be so enthralled by the big wide world that he'll forget you exist;
kiting off and ignoring shouted commands, whistles and you too, during bursts of exploratory enchantment.

By taking your puppy for walks as frequently as possible, from
toddling stage on, you will accustom him to the stage on which he'll be
performing when the hunting season opens. But, of even more importance, he will come to associate your presence with these enjoyable outings and it will become inconceivable to him that to be out
there without you. He'll want to keep track of you, responding to your
voice and whistle and checking on his own regarding your continued
presence.

Such preliminary field experience, coming at an age when he is
still apprehensive and his physical ability will not take a bold pup
out of ken, before he starts wondering about your whereabouts, will

125

also give the more reticent pup time to gain confidence at his own pace. This will be most beneficial as you move into the serious field work.

Making a buddy of your gun dog pup, when at home and around the kennel, will also greatly facilitate the ease in which he is trained to hunt a proper pattern. The closer you can get to him the better. Get him to thinking you are the greatest. Mix this with as many field trips as you can swing and you'll have few, if any, run-away or handling problems.

Handling and Hunting Patterns

Your pup will be ready to start learning what you expect from him in matters of range and pattern and start responding to some orders about the time he starts to hunt boldly and independently. With the precocious pup it may be as early as five to six months, in others delayed as long as a year. But, if you've been taking him afield as outlined above, you can expect to do some serious training starting at about six or seven months. *You* will know it is serious. Your dog should continue to think it's part of the game.

From the ages of six months on, it is doubtful that you can take your dog afield too frequently. How often I leave up to you. If you can, make it daily for workouts of half-an-hour to an hour. 10 or 15 minutes is better than not at all. Much over an hour may prove too tiring until the pup is 10 to 12 months of age.

Don't just stroll around watching the sunset. Act like you would when hunting and put your dog down in the type of country you'll expect him to work in. Running through a cow pasture beats no work out at all. But, where possible, take him to your hunting country or something like it. Again, workouts in the same old place are acceptable, but varying the areas will accustom him to hunting strange places and gain knowledge in going to spots likely to hold birds.

As your dog is swinging along in front of you try to anticipate a voluntary change in direction or breaking his cast. Then hit him with a couple of whistle blasts or shout an appropriate command, like "Get Over!" or "Come around!," angle off your walking course in a different direction and wave your arm in that direction.

(Whistle work begins anytime now.) "Beep, Beep," getting his attention and turning him, a series of coaxing trills, or no-nonsense

126

blasts as the situation calls for, meaning to come in. Do not walk around, tootling on the whistle because you like the sound. Use it only to get attention and transmit an already learned verbal order. When you blow an order, enforce it. (Too much blowing will make a dog either too dependent upon the handler or get him in the habit of ignoring a senseless or unenforced sound.)

Chances are very good, if you've been walking your dog a lot, when notified of the direction change he will swing over to work to your front, preferably in looping fashion.

If he doesn't respond, don't quit in disgust. Keep at it. Few dogs are trained in a day. Do not, however, swing him aimlessly back and forth in some open field just to see if he'll respond. Head him in a direction that will take him to a cover clump, tree stand or some other likely game spot. In time he will start to hunt those objectives on his own. No, not the second time out. But eventually, as he gains experience and finds game he will scent in such places.

In time you will have a dog that hunts in an intelligent and independent pattern, staying out in front of you, and checking back to find you should he be momentarily carried away. He will then require a minimum of handling and be highly prized as a gun dog. When he reaches this stage, allow him a great deal of freedom of choice. For he will then know more about where to find birds than you do. If he's goofing up, or way off course when on automatic pilot, take over the controls and get him back on the beam.

Many a gun dog comes in to check with his master quite frequently. As long as he hunts his way back in over fresh ground this is not objectionable, and may even be desirable if some situation makes proper use of wind direction impossible as you set your course. If you don't like the checking back, when he homes to you, just don't fuss over him. Change your direction and wave him off the right way, advising him to "Get'em!," "Hunt 'em out!," or whatever you deem appropriate.

He'll get the idea to cross in front of you and keep hunting without coming in all the way for a pat and a kind word. When he responds properly, you can tell him he's a "Good Dog!" as he crosses and goes about his business—hunting.

At times, when your dog does come in close, if he should go off in a different direction than you have indicated, hit the whistle and keep at him until he goes where you want him to. This response will be invaluable when you want to send him into some cover he may have missed or put him into the area of a downed bird. Keep at this during your field work prior to the hunting-season opening and you'll have a dog that hunts, and handles, remarkably well for a first-season campaigner.

Long or Short

Perhaps for your type of hunting, you will want a gun dog leaning more toward the "big running" style of the classy field trial dogs. If so, let your pup take the bit in his teeth as much as is practicable and, when he's making a long cast, don't break it with a shout or whistle command. Mostly it is a matter of virtually letting him run to his limits, discouraging him from checking in, and, in effect, letting *him* take *you* hunting. Dogs can be taught to handle when they are hunting up to a-half-mile to your front. But I suggest that this is beyond the capabilities of most gun dog owners, and that ranging that wide is of value only to the field trailer or the hunter who follows dogs on horseback.

You can also encourage big-ranging by working two puppies together, since the "reachy" pup will usually suck the closer ranging pup out with him. I have never seen it work in reverse. Use of a big-ranging adult dog is questionable. Usually the pup can't hold the pace or he may develop the bad habit of trailing a bracemate.

If a close worker is your cup of tea, you can work on shortening your gun dog's range both artificially and naturally. (Subject to argument, my definition of a close working dog is one under 150 yards from the gun. Medium range would be up to 220 yards, or a bit beyond. Anything more than that is wide-ranging to out of sight. A pointing dog that consistently messes around less than 40 to 50 yards from the hunter doesn't deserve to be called a gun dog. If work that close is required, a flushing dog is called for.

For the development of a close worker put him down in very "birdy" cover (commercial hunting areas may provide birds in this number) where there is a lot of scent. His investigation of this scent; instincts causing him to flash point; his correcting when wrong to move on (or even the flush and chase when he has a bird) will cut down on his running.

Or, work him all you can in dense, heavy cover which will impede his progress, or require that he shorten up to keep in touch with you.

Use your whistle and a shouted command to keep him alert and quartering in front of you.

You may be very, very lucky and get a natural that shuts down in thick coverts but steps up the pace in the open when birdy places are scattered about . . . , or if you've been diligent in your puppy walking, it may be the result of your efforts.

An artificial means of shortening a pointing dog's range can be part of his training when you are teaching him his manners or introducing him to birds (See "Problems, Solutions and Advanced Training" and "Introduction to Game and Guns").

When you "plant" your pigeons put them out so that they will be near you when the dog winds them, moves in on them and points. (You know where you have put the bird down. Work your dog in a pattern that will allow you to be waiting near the bird when he winds it, rather than being some distance behind and running to catch the action). Eventually he will associate birds with your proximity and hunt relatively close because he'll figure birds to be somewhere around you.

Wing on a String

While it is of limited value as a training technique there is a stunt you may want to fool with, which may give you a line on your pup's natural pointing instinct. Besides, you'll get a big kick out of it, as will anyone who happens to be watching it done.

Get a flyrod or cane pole, tie on a fishline of equal length. Tie a bird wing (or a squirrel tail or a patch of rabbit fur) on the end of the line. As the wing lies on the ground, let your pup see and smell it; attracting his attention, if necessary, by moving it about.

If he pounces at it, make the "bird" fly away by lifting it into the air and swinging it away from the pup. Land it in front of him again. Pups with strong instincts soon start sight pointing this "bird". If he softens on point (relaxes, or loses intensity) twitch the wing along the ground in front of him. He'll probably react by stiffening up. Praise him! Stroke him if he'll let you get to him.

If he moves in on the bird caution him with a soft, "Whoaauup!," and if he breaks, and tries to catch, try to halt him with a sharp "Whoa!" The very pup who makes the greatest effort to catch should not be allowed to capture the wing. Fly it off before he can grab it. With the more hesitant pup, if he should catch it, it is of little con-

Pheasant feathers and a fish pole, a rig for ascertaining pointing instinct in bird dogs. (Photo by David J. Hasinger.)

Play-training a brace of English Setter pups with a fly-rod and feathers. (Photo by David J. Hasinger.)

sequence and may serve to make him more "birdy." But the rule of thumb is get the wing out of reach when the pup rushes it.

This can be started at a very early age, even before eight weeks in your yard and may continue after you take your pup afield. Some dogs will point wings all their lives. Other intelligent pups quickly lose interest, particularly after they've had a noseful of the real thing. With others it takes quite a bit of teasing with the wing before they start to point it.

In any event, remember it is a puppy or exhibition stunt. It is useful as an indicator of a pup's pointing instinct and suggestive to him that the fascinating object will hold still for him to watch as long as he stays on point. The suggestion may carry over when he scent-points his first birds. But it is sight-pointing and bears no relation to a gun dog's ability to seek and locate birds in the proper manner.

What's Left?

There remain two extremely important things you must do before your youngster is ready for the real thing—his first hunting trip. They consist of his proper introduction to game birds and gunfire, and the association he must make between those. No gun dog can be said to be well started until he has encountered some birds, has been shot over and reacted well to both experiences.

This introduction should take place concurrently with his field work and handling training, (at six to 12 months) and will hopefully occur when you have him afield teaching him his hunting patterns and responses to handling. For, if you are lucky, he will bump into some birds at that time.

So, having read this, please turn to "Introduction To Game and Guns". When your young prospect has stepped up and shaken hands with those major items in his life, he'll be ready to start hunting.

Will he be a trained dog? Will I encounter some problems with him? The answers are he will be a well started dog who may train himself to your satisfaction in a season of hunting. Unless you are very lucky, he may puzzle you, disappoint you or do something wrong you don't know how to correct.

To provide you with methods of developing a fully trained pointing dog, stanch on point, who will back, be steady to wing and shot, re-trieve and other niceties; and to suggest training techniques to solve problems I can anticipate (because I've encountered them) please turn to "Problems, Solutions and Advanced Training". Take particular note of the section labeled "Natural and Easy".

You, as a pointing dog fancier, will share those chapters with the flushing dog fans for they are vital to the starting and development of all gun dogs. At the same time they will help you to choose how far you want to take your dog, or how early you may want to cease train-ing and accept what you have.

This is in recognition of the desire of many men to have a hunting dog of sorts with the least amount of effort expended in training. At the same time, I hope the text and the explanations will encourage persons, interested primarily in hunting and secondarily in dogs, to pursue training as far as those whose day in the field is made by the presence and performance of a well-trained gun dog.

131

10

Introduction to Game and Guns

OUTSIDE of you, there are two really big things in the life of a gun dog. They are game and guns. To really shine, a gun dog must love all three.

Yet, one of the more common inquiries made by hunters of dog trainers is, "How do you cure a dog that's a little bit gun-shy". There are also quite a few dogs who are bird-shy. Some are merely shook up when a bird flushes. Others have become confirmed "blinkers", dogs that will deliberately avoid game they know is there.

There are dogs that wouldn't be gun-shy if they served in the field artillery and others that would spook at the drop of a hat. But, generally, gun-shy and bird-shy dogs are man-made creatures. The "natural-born" gun-shy dog is usually easy to spot because he isn't afflicted with one quirk. He has a total lack of temperament. Just about everything spooks him, and any loud noise or strange thing causes reactions like cringing, urinating, slinking, snapping or wildeyed, tail-down hysteria.

The naturally shy pup isn't worth working with in the first place, although careful and patient application of training methods will bring some of the milder cases around. But never pick a puppy because you feel sorry for a shy, forlorn little feller. He'll give you mostly grief and be virtually untrainable. Pick the bold, happy puppy if you enjoy a challenge that will pay off with real results, or the placid, equable youngster who may not achieve greatness but will train easily and do an honest day's work.

I am not going to advise you how to "cure" gun-shyness in this chapter. For if you properly introduce your pup to gunfire there will be no need to cure him. He will not be gun-shy. This is the easy way. Once a dog develops an aversion for gunfire it takes more than just luck to cure this affliction and the techniques and time are seldom within the province of the amateur trainer.

In fact, the person who has a gun-shy dog is the least likely candidate for effecting a cure, since the fault is generally caused by a man's mistakes. If the man had not the sense to avoid the problem he surely isn't going to have the wherewithal to correct it.

So, if you should be unfortunate enough to be the owner of a gun-shy dog, either get rid of it, keep it as a pet, or turn it over to a professional. But if you start a puppy out right, there's little chance you will encounter the problem.

Step-By-Step or Take Your Chances

Puppies should be accustomed to loud noises early in life. From the time you get your pup; slam doors, bang dishes, clap your hands and be generally noisy around him. Clap your hands when calling a pup in for praise. Do not use noise to intimidate, tease or punish. Use it casually and, if there should be an adverse reaction on the pup's part, just ignore it and go about the business at hand until the pup comes to accept loud noises as part of living.

Particularly with the food pan, it not only doesn't hurt him it provides pleasure. The association of something pleasant, which he likes to do with gunfire, will develop a love of the gun and hopefully, prevent gun-shyness. If you care to, you may shoot an inexpensive blank pistol every time you feed, but you shouldn't have to bother.

If you accustom your pup to noise, from the time you acquire him, when you are ready to introduce him to gunfire, you should have some idea what he's like. Some pups are bold, others cautious. If he's a rough and ready character, you may be able to shortcut introductory procedures. But, if he's of a more hesitant nature, a careful, step by step program is advisable.

Many a dog has been introduced to gunfire on the opening day of hunting season, lived through it, caught on to what was wanted and become his master's pride and joy. But for many others, the first shot, or shots, was a traumatic experience from which he never recovered. Too often the scenario is something like this.

Opening day of duck season, Rover is tossed into an automobile with an assortment of gear and people. It's his first ride in a car and if he doesn't get sick, he's unsure of himself. From there, he's transferred to a new and unstable, strange thing called a boat, which moves over water with a loud roar and upsetting vibration.

But after a time, except for the disconcerting rocking, things quiet down and the quivering dog starts to take some interest in his surroundings. He looks across the marsh grass and cocks his head at the gently lapping water. Just about the time his natural confidence and trust starts to ebb through his being, his master and two strangers swing some long sticks threateningly, and there is a terrific blast of noise as the three-gun salvo startles a high-flying duck.

That does it. Friend dog takes leave of boat and human companions. Who can really blame him? Any animal with any sense at all would get the hell out of there.

Nervous and edgey to begin with, because of the strangeness of all the gear and action; neither seeing, smelling, nor hearing the presence of game, when the dog watches three maniacs rise up to loudly smite some unknown object; not only does discretion seem the better part of valor but sheer terror will propel him out of the boat.

What's worse, that's not the end of it. His ignorant owner starts shouting. Not paeans of praise and encouragement, but dire threats and imprecations, spurred on by shame and disappointment, which are fueled by comments from his companions regarding the worthlessness of gunshy dogs. When the thoroughly frightened dog is either coaxed back or caught, chances are good he winds up being roughly treated or beaten, tied to the boat or blind so he can't get away and undergoes more baptism of gunfire.

Is it any wonder that after such an introduction, friend dog never wants to see a gun again? Thus is made, not born, another gun-shy dog. The wonder of it is that there are actually some dogs who experience something similar to the business outlined above and still survive such fiascos to become useful hunters.

There are also some legitimate shortcuts a trainer can take if he knows his pup and excercises good judgement. I do this frequently with bold pups of sound temperament who have been play-trained to retrieve, show great interest in finding and chasing birds; have been exposed to loud noises and generally comport themselves as characters unlikely to be shook up by the untoward. But I've made some errors in judgement regarding anticipated reactions and the time a pup was ready to be fired over. So I suggest you follow the procedure I'll outline. For you can not count on short-cutting being the easiest, and the step by step is usually the surest.

134

This technique is most applicable to retrievers and spaniels and can be properly utilized with the versatile and even the traditional pointing breeds, although an alternative method for pointers will be described a bit later.

Shoot and Fetch

Formal introduction to gunfire should come at about the age of five to seven months, when your pup is doing a good job of retrieving, thinks fetching is the greatest, and may even have been taken along "hunting", minus the gun but having smelled and chased birds.

You are now ready to give your pup some more retrieving practice and at the same time teach him that this fetching, which he should love to do, is associated with the sharp report of a gun.

Station an assistant armed with a .22 handgun, or rifle, with blank ammo about 30 yards from you. Get your pup in a sitting position at your side, as you would prepare him to retrieve a tossed training dummy, and talk to him in an encouraging, exciting tone to get him keyed up.

When you nod to your "gunner" he should shoot, aiming away from the dog, and toss the dummy high into the air. Make this and other starting-off retrieves easy; not too far from the dog and in plain sight. The shot will get your pup's attention and he'll see what has become a familiar sight to him, a retrieving dummy in the air.

If the pup isn't already on his way to make the retrieve before the dummy hits the ground, say his name and tell him "fetch!" "Hobo! Fetch!" If he's been doing his fetching like he's supposed to, he'll be out and back with the dummy in nothing flat. When he completes the retrieve, make much of him.

Give the pup four or five more such retrieves, each with a gunshot. Usually, your "gunner" can move gradually closer before you wind up your shoot-and-retrieve session. If the dog seems apprehensive about the gunfire, however, move the gun farther from him.

Performing each session over a period of several days, have your gunner edge closer to you as he shoots and throws, until you can do the shooting and throwing yourself. When you fire, aim up in the air. Don't fire even a .22 blank right over a pup's head. You probably know what muzzle blast feels like if a hunting partner touched one off near your ear, and a dog's ears are much more sensitive than a human's.

As a precautionary measure against gun-shyness, early shooting over dogs is best done with a small gauge shotgun as Dave Duffey is doing here with a .410 and a young Labrador, Lady.

Carrol Owens, manager of Gunsmoke Kennels, demonstrates a tried and true method of accustoming pups to gunfire, shooting blanks at feeding time.

Depending upon your interest and your pup's precociousness, you can run these drills off in a few days or spread them out over weeks. But most dogs quickly associate the sound of gunfire with a falling object to retrieve, and this is a big step in assuring that yours will be a gun dog you can depend upon.

Isn't there a difference between a .22 blank and a 12 gauge shotgun blast? Of course there is. But it's mostly a matter of degree and I sometimes think if a dog is going to be sensitive about gunfire, the sharper crack of the .22 may be more likely to cause it than the shotgun's roar.

But by all means, move up to the shotgun after you've accustomed your pup to the .22 blank shot and tossed dummy. You can usually start with a 12 gauge, making sure your assistant is about 50 yards off and aims away from you and the dog. Follow the same procedure as with the .22 until the shotgun is moved in close and eventually is in your hands. If you want to be ultra-cautious you may use a .410, 28 or 20 gauge shotgun here for most gradual introduction, but that is seldom necessary.

Perhaps this word of caution is unnecessary. But it's better to be safe than sorry. You can use live rounds when doing your shotgun training, utilizing old, left-over shells you might not trust to do the job when hunting. But be careful. Also on the market are blank shotgun shells called "poppers" which are specially loaded just for dog training and well worth consideration. They make the proper noise but contain no shot. But with these and with the .22 blanks—in fact anything involving guns— caution and good sense are the order of the day, because even a blank at close range can inflict damage to man or dog.

You can introduce your dog to birds almost simultaneously with his introduction to gun procedure. But before telling you how to do that, let me offer some other procedures I've found useful to get a dog accustomed to shooting, associate gunfire with game birds and fetching, which can be used as introductory methods or in conjunction with the method outlined above.

Blank Pistol

It is possible to introduce a dog to gunfire without the aid of an assistant and in a most casual manner. It involves carrying a blank pistol and a training dummy with you when you go afield.

I've found an inexpensive cap pistol about the handiest thing to have in your pocket when you take a pup afield. When the pup is busily bustling around 15 or 20 yards from you, shoot a cap. The noise will attract his attention. When he looks up at you, throw the dummy for him to fetch. Repeat this in your walks as often as he remains interested in fetching.

If the pup flushes and chases after any kind of bird, pop another cap, or two or three, while he's chasing. He may not even hear it, except sub-consciously, because he's interested in the chase. But it will accustom him to shooting and form the desired association between birds and gunfire. You can then step up to a .22, .32 or .38 caliber blank or the shotgun. In the spring of the year, after a spaniel or retriever pup is well accustomed to gunfire and shows no adverse reaction, I frequently shoot blackbirds which are unprotected and plentiful. They are easy to miss with a .410 but the occassional retrieve spices things up for the pup, and gives him needed experience seeking and handling feathers, which outweighs the remote possibility you may develop a hunter of non-game birds.

Pointing Breeds Introduction to Gun

A variant of the above procedure can be utilized to get pointing dogs to connect gunfire with the result—birds in the mouth that he couldn't

Using a dummy and a blank pistol, a trainer can give his retriever practice at steadiness, marking and retrieving when his time and facilities are limited.

Frequent breaks in the training routine are beneficial to both trainer and dog. Dave Duffey and Stupido enjoy each other's company here.

otherwise catch. If you've taught your modern or traditional pointer to fetch at an early age, as with the retrievers or spaniels you can also use the same introduction to gunfire method that led off this chapter.

However, there is good reason, which will be explained in the chapter on Problems, Solutions and Advanced Training, why it may be desirable to delay retrieving training for the pointing breeds, precluding the early doubling up of shooting and fetching that can be done in the yard with a spaniel or retriever.

So you may want to start by firing blanks at feeding time, having someone shoot some distance away just as you put the feed pan down

138

in front of a hungry pup; eventually working the gun closer until the pup pays no attention to the noise even five yards away. Do not discharge blanks inside a building.

When you are afield with your pointing breed pup and the dog is running, particularly if he sees and shags any kind of bird, shoot your blank. If the shot stops him, ignore him as though nothing happened and keep on walking. He'll go back to what he was doing if you don't fuss over him. Ten minutes or so later try another shot. Repeat this a couple of times during each field trip and he'll learn the noise isn't harmful. Then move up to a small gauge shotgun and follow the same procedure.

If he continues to chase a bird without paying any attention to the shot, you can dish out some verbal praise which will lead him to figuring that the enchanting bird and the bang are allied, and his performance on them is praiseworthy.

Should your pup tuck his tail, run to you or run away, ignore this action and keep walking. But don't shoot again that day. You will then have to turn to discharging blanks around his kennel at feeding time. When he accepts this, try a shot again the next time out and keep at it until it no longer bothers him. This pup will probably require care and caution in everything you do with him. Some breeders and trainers test for "sensitivity" to gunfire in a manner similar to this and discard pups that over-react. But, properly handled, this can usually be overcome.

I also prefer to make sure that a pup has had at least half a dozen or so actual contacts, with either planted or wild game birds that he's smelled, seen and chased, before actually shooting a bird over him.

Once he is accustomed to and has accepted gunfire, your dog is ready to go hunting. You may very well introduce him to real birds during the hunting season and put the show on the road successfully.

But just as I'm cautious about introduction to gunfire (even though I know it can be done at times without the routines I've suggested), I also suggest some pre-season work with birds to assure performance when the gunning seasons are open. I repeat, avoiding gunshyness is relatively easy. Curing it, regardless of the degree (there *is* such a thing as being a "little bit gun-shy"), is difficult or nearly impossible. So until you acquire the experience, know-how and insight it pays to be conservative.

Before moving on to the introduction to the game section of this chapter, let me suggest a couple of "don'ts" in regard to dogs and guns.

Don'ts

Should anyone, friend, enemy or casual acquaintance suggest to you that "we ought to take that pup of yours out and shoot around him a few times to see if he's gunshy," don't. If you do you'll be taking a foolish and unnecessary risk you'll come to regret.

During your pup's first season of hunting, do your hunting by yourself, and with a trusted companion who understands and appreciates dogs. A battery of guns going off can unsettle a youngster, particularly if your introductory procedures have been sketchy. Don't hunt your first-year gun dog with large parties.

Finally, don't take your gun dog out to the trap or skeet range to "get him used to shooting". The calm, easy going dog will come to ignore gunfire while the senseless (to the dog) banging away will drive a high-strung youngster out of his skull.

You want a dog that knows gunfire for what it is—the sound that provides the reward for the work he's done. He should try to spot a flying or falling bird when the gun goes off and, if he doesn't look quickly enough to see it fall, will hunt dead in the area you send him because he knows there's got to be something there for him.

Early Birds

How and when you start your youngster on real birds may depend upon a lot of factors, including your personal circumstances and the type of dog you have. Generally, the retrievers and spaniels, and, to some extent, the versatiles, may be started earlier and more artificially on the real thing than the traditional pointers.

Once you've got the preliminary training already outlined on the dog, and have properly introduced him to gunfire as described earlier in this chapter, your pup is ready to hunt. So you may opt for letting him learn a lot of things as part and parcel of his first gunning season.

But you'll be able to expect more from your gun dog, and will have a much better season, if you take the time to introduce him to birds and bird work in the months that precede the season's opener.

You may be starting from scratch. Or your pup may have an inkling of what birds are all about because he has fetched dummies with bird wings taped on them, had a dead game bird brought home from the hunt thrown for him, or enjoyed chance encounters with birds when taken afield. But let's begin from a dead start and let you decide which steps you may be able to skip as your pup develops.

140

Flushing Dog Introduction to Game

Because spaniels and retrievers possess strong, natural retrieving instincts and their proper hunting procedure is actually an effort on their part to catch live game, introduction to game can come at a very early age and chiefly involves proper "handling" with the mouth.

After your pup is retrieving wing-wrapped dummies, get yourself a few barn pigeons or pen raised game birds, if you can afford them. Pigeons rate tops because they are not too big, readily available and comparatively cheap.

Kill one by wringing its neck. Then there is no blood. Take the youngster out in the yard or afield, discharge your training gun and toss the pigeon for him. You may have to encourage him to pick up this new "dummy" but it's unlikely. When he brings it to you, really make a fuss over him and toss it for him to fetch again. Give him half a dozen or so retrieves a session. By that time, the pigeon will be about worn out.

Just because the bird gets bedraggled does not mean your dog is hardmouthed. But, if the pup actually does some feather-pulling, chewing or munching, you should immediately turn to using "cold birds." Kill a pigeon and store it in your refrigerator. Use the same procedure with this chilled bird. Dogs are less likely to hard mouth such a bird and some trainers advocate a cold bird to start, then progressing to a "hot" one. Some pups may be less likely to snatch up a cold bird.

Using cold birds has another advantage in that the wings are tight to their sides and they will last longer; while a soft, floppy bird may spook a shy pup and wear out faster when roughly handled by an aggressive one. I often have had 10-12 week old puppies handling cold birds which I alternate with the glove or sock they've learned to fetch.

The next step is to hide a dead pigeon in the grass and run your pup through his "Hunt 'em out!" drill, so he learns to seek and pick up a bird he hasn't seen fall. You may well be able to do this after you've thrown the bird for him a couple of times on your first outing.

If you've come to the conclusion that we are simply substituting a pigeon (or duck or pheasant or what not) for the dummy you are right. Once we've made this transition, the next step is to live birds. He could be ready to learn while hunting now. But let's make sure he knows what the score is.

If you have friends who like to shoot, and are good shots, you should be able to enlist some help. Take half a dozen barn pigeons afield in a

141

Poncho, a black Labrador owned and trained by Dave Duffey, emerges from the water with a pigeon shot during a training session.

Barn pigeons are inexpensive and available birds for use in accustoming retrievers like this Labrador, Poncho, to handling feathers.

bag or crate. Sit your spaniel or retriever as you would when working him on dummies.

Have one friend toss a bird into flight and have the other shoot it. Send your pup to fetch. A half dozen retrieves will be plenty for the first time and one bird is better than none. Later on shoot as many pigeons as you can. Any work the dog can get will be to the good. Take the dead birds home, refrigerate them, and use them for yard training until they wear out.

A major reason, besides the training it affords, for doing some gunning over your dog before the season opens, is to give him experience. Then he won't get goofed up if you miss the first bird when you are actually hunting or it falls when or where he doesn't see it. Success is what counts and the first birds killed over him are important.

When the pup is retrieving flighted birds satisfactorily, get to some cover, take a live pigeon and dizzy it. Hold its wings close to its body and swing the bird in a counter-clockwise circle until, when you put him on the ground, his head lolls to the side. If he's alert and wants to run, don't release him, spin him some more. Make a kind of form with your feet to set the bird and he'll hold for some time.

Now bring your spaniel or retriever up, working into the air currents and if he isn't hunting encourage him to "Hunt 'em Out!" When he homes in and the bird flushes, shoot it or have your companion do the gunning. Make sure that the pup chasing the bird won't be sprinkled with shot.

When he brings the bird to you, take it from him and praise him sky-high. Then toss it for him to fetch again. A few of these flushes and retrieves and you are sure he'll acquit himself well afield when season opens. For the first part of his first season continue to throw each bird he brings in for a second retrieve. The retrieving is fun for him, keep it that way. Don't just snatch the delivered bird from him after you've shot and he's fetched. Reward him with another toss and fetch and give him lots of praise.

If you can get them and it's legal in your state by all means utilize game farm pheasant, chukar, duck, etc. as an alternative to pigeons, if you can afford it. Or, if possible arrange to hunt at a commercial hunting club where birds are released. The more birds that are shot and handled over your dog before season the better he will be that opening week.

You *can* wait to show him what birds are all about during the open season. But don't. Get him at least a shot bird or two that he's hunted up himself and it will pay you many times over.

Pointing Dog Introduction to Game

Because you want to give every encouragement to your pointing dog to hold the point his instincts freeze him into when he hits hot bird scent (rather than rush in to catch, resulting in a flush) his introduction to birds is a bit different than in the case of the breeds used to flush game.

Therefore, as pointed out earlier, mechanical methods of familiarizing a pointer of any type with birds are not as readily applicable and may even be undesirable. Because I lean toward encouraging natural traits to the fullest, I suggest that the actual hunting season is the time and place to start shooting birds over the pointing breeds.

Now, I'm not suggesting a total unfamiliarity with birds. If you've been doing the basics suggested in the chapter on "Pointing Dog Training," you've been lucky and your pup will have found and chased, hopefully after a flash point, some game birds and been praised for it and a blank discharged when he was chasing.

But the hunting season is here. With the training and experience you've given your pointer he should be ready for it. You too should be prepared . . . . prepared to treat this first season more as a training period than a hunting season. Bag as many birds as you can. But do it the proper way with the intent of instilling in your young pointer habits that will pay off in the future by avoiding many of the obedience sessions needed to assure a dog's stanchness. This may mean passing up some shots and spending some time when you might be seeking more birds in an effort to get the proper response from your dog.

It's opening day and you pick a spot where there won't be a lot of other hunters. Obviously a public hunting ground would be a poor place. Save those lands for later in the season. Try for a sort of semi-private spot for that first hunt, which may mean buttering up a friendly farmer or other landowner before season.

You cast your dog off and almost before you've walked the squeak out of your boots, there he is. On point! If you're lucky and the point is established within gun range, take your time, walk up, keep your mouth shut. If the stationary dog is a long way off, you better stir your stumps. But be as quiet and calm as possible. Your dog will not only sense excitement but if you speak it probably will break the concentration that is holding him in the spot where his instincts stopped him. (There's an explanation for this and a training procedure to follow in the "Problems, Solutions and Advanced Training" chapter).

If your approach scares up the bird or birds or if you get out in front

144

of the pup and flush them, wonderful! But, more than likely, he will dive in and do his own flushing. That's why you should hustle up to his point. For whether you or the dog puts the game in the air, shoot and *kill a bird.* Dropping a bird to reward that first point is of great importance.

If a covey is flushed, the pup is likely to go rattling off after the flying birds not paying attention to the one that falls. If a lone bird gets up he'll probably be on the shot bird before it can bounce.

Should he pick up the bird, even if you think he's chewing it, don't get excited and run at him yelling. He'll then probably run off, bird in mouth. Break your gun or return it to safe, squat down and coax him to you. Now is the time to talk. Tell him what a *goooood* dog he is and call him, "Here, Hobo! Fetch!" repeating this like a litany interspersed with the praise. Hopefully he'll come all the way. But if he gets a start back in your direction, lays the bird down and you can't get him to bring it all the way, pick up the bird, pet and praise him profusely. Take your time.

Then tease him with the bird and excite him with your voice and when he's fired up toss it out about five yards and tell him to "Fetch!" He probably will, at least partially, even though you may not have taught him to fetch. There are reasons, explained in the next chapter, "Problems, Solutions and Advanced Training" for delaying retrieving work with gun dogs that point until they have attained some degree of stanchness. Should you decide, however, to give your pointing gun dog some introduction to retrieving before that time, the most acceptable means of doing it is also detailed in that chapter.

In any event, it is a training shortcut worth trying. No harm can be done and you may be able to make an acceptable retriever of him right in the field.

Should young Hobo just sniff the bird, or if he actually picks it up but spits it out and moves on, still no sweat. Pick up your bird, pocket it and go on hunting when you are through telling him what a good dog he is. You can start the retrieving drills at home, when you are not hunting.

But how about that wild-eyed guy that chased off, ignoring the shot bird or doesn't have one on the ground because *you* missed? Whatever you do, don't climb his frame. Don't yell angrily at him. If he doesn't immediately respond to your calls and whistles wait for him to come back. In all probability he'll stop chasing when he loses sight of the bird and will be looking for you. That's the time to call, not when he's in full stride intent on catching.

145 .

When you get him back, if there is a bird down, work him into the area of the fall so he's downwind from it telling him "Dead!" "Birds!" "Hunt Dead!" "Hunt Close!" "Hunt 'em Out!" or whatever you deem appropriate. Upon winding it he may point the dead bird.

A dog that will "point dead!" is not to be sneezed at, even though retrieving is preferred. Recovery of about everything except a lightly crippled bird is pretty well-assured, there's no danger from a rough-mouthed dog and it'll do your waistline good to bend over and pick up your own birds. You may want to encourage this trait.

If you insist on retrieving it can be taught later or it may come naturally. Gun dogs in their infinite wisdom often learn to differentiate between dead and live birds, very likely because they eventually come to associate a shot with a bird to fetch and most reasonably because of the "blood scent" that comes to them off a bird that has been hit.

If there is no bird down, when you get your dog back after his futile chase, call him to you and lead him over to the place where he locked on point. "Whoa!" him there. Stand him up and stroke him, lifting his tail and running your hand from his shoulders to his rump, sweet-talk him with soft "Whoaauups!" and tell him what a good dog he is. Bird scent may still linger. And he's been taught to Whoa! on command. When he's stood for half a minute to a minute under your stroking and praising, tap him on the head, tell him "All right!" and move him out. He may snuffle around a bit on the old scent, but walk on and encourage him to get out of there without being harsh about it.

A few of these episodes and you are likely to have yourself a gun dog, depending upon fortunate or unfortunate circumstances and each dog's natural proclivities. Some may catch on after two or three encounters and on the spot training. Others may need a couple dozen experiences, but stay with it.

You can crack down later, if necessary. The use of the check cord and mechanical methods of assuring stanchness will be detailed in the next chapter. My personal recommendation would be to wait until the hunting season is over and if the severe mechanical discipline is necessary do it in the off-season after the dog is a hunting fool. If the season indicates that the dog lacks desire, stamina, nose and bird sense you will be better off to expend the training effort on a more promising prospect. And it may be you won't have to force-break to stanchness. Quite a few dogs learn by experience and from their mistakes. They literally "break themselves." Let me tell you about a couple of ways that can contribute to bringing this happy happenstance about.

Hold Your Fire

When you start a pointing dog's gunning career, either hunt by yourself or in the company of a good buddy who will give the dog consideration and appreciate what a good gun dog can accomplish — but keeping his mouth shut about what you should or shouldn't be doing for and with the dog. If he wants to praise or criticise or suggest at the end of the day, fine. But you'll have your hands full concentrating on the dog without having to keep an ear cocked to a stream of suggestions and gripes.

However, pay off for this consideration by letting your shooting buddy have the lion's share of the flushing and shooting while you spend most of the season field-training your gun dog. You can start applying the advanced training methods detailed in the next chapter "Problems, Solutions and Advanced Training" right now and may wind up with a near finished or at least "country broke" bird dog to start the following season.

If you follow but one principle when hunting alone and have your trusted hunting buddy agree to do the same you may never have to use a check cord to assure that your dog will point birds and hold that point until the hunter does the flushing.

When the bird or birds get out, *shoot only if the dog has been stanch on point,* or if he stopped to a wild flush which he *did not* cause. Pursue that principle, making exceptions only for very good cause and you are likely to find with a dog of intelligence and good breeding that the idea will percolate through his skull that the only way to get him a bird is to do things the right way.

When he does bust his birds, do not shoot. Let 'em fly off and get your dog back. Scold him, stand him up, "Whoa!" him. Make him hold the semblence of a pointing posture (don't expect intensity through all this disciplining), then tap his head, "All Right!" him and let him go on with the hunt.

Then each time he points, should he see a moving bird or be otherwise tempted to break you can "Whoa!" him, softly in encouragement for his doing right or loudly in an effort to stop him if he starts to go. If he goes, it is disobedience of a command he's learned and he'll recognize that the scolding is for that, not for being bird crazy.

Once this is established you'll have a gun dog you can enjoy and take pride in. You will also have taken a large step toward putting the finish on a dog that will mark him as a gentleman and a gentleman's gun dog.

147

11

Problems, Solutions and Advanced Training

MUCH has been made throughout this book of naturalness and proper introduction. The reason being, in my opinion at least, that a pup's inherited qualities (natural ability) and the manner in which he is started are the most important factors in determining what kind of gun dog he will be.

Up to now, what I've tried to do is to help you recognize the natural qualities your pup may or may not possess, and show you how to start him up the right path by channeling these instincts and proclivities into the particular stream of behavior you want navigated. This has been accomplished largely by natural or "play-training methods", a form of soft coercion that will encourage the capable pup to learn by doing.

Along the same lines, natural retrievers start picking up and carrying on their own and natural pointers, with no training will freeze in pointing posture when encountering bird scent. With dogs possessing a high degree of such instincts, training is merely a matter of channeling and common sense obedience which will reinforce what the dog knows to do naturally and provide the means of enforcing what we desire without seriously altering or destroying the spirit and natural qualities of the dog being trained.

For good dogs can virtually make themselves. And the very poor dogs can not be trained into usefulness in the field by *anyone*. If you have drawn a good dog, by the time you finished him out on the introductory procedures outlined in the previous chapters and give him a season afield, he will probably rate the accolade "fine gun dog". You may not want to go further. But you should. For there is virtually no end of things such a dog can learn. He can with a comparative minimum of effort on your part acquire the polish that is the mark of a thoroughly broke gun dog.

At the other extreme, if you have been half-diligent in applying introductory techniques to your pup and the response and success is nil, you haven't been blessed in your selection of a candidate for good gun dog honors. If that is the case, there is only one thing to do. Bite the bullet. Give away or shoot the worthless one and start all over.

If you've goofed off and haven't given the dog a chance, turn him over to a good professional, who should be able to evaluate his potential in two to four weeks, tell you whether he is worth training and in two to six months turn over a useful gun dog to you.

Between these extremes of virtually self-trained and actually impossible to train dogs lie the bulk of the pups produced by breeding hunting dogs today. So, percentagewise, that is most likely the type of pup you will acquire. Some will lean strongly toward the self-made category and probably will be most satisfactory for the amateur trainer. Pups of really great potential may turn out to be just too much dog for the "average hunter".

Others will be a shade or two above the useless class, but still possess enough of the proper instincts and temperament to be molded into reasonably useful gun dogs. Such a dog is virtually man-made and his trainer can take real pride in having accomplished what he has with his dog.

Obviously along the way you will have encountered problems.

The first portion of this lengthy chapter will try to anticipate the problems you are most likely to encounter and offer a method of dealing with them.

It will not cover *every* problem a trainer of dogs encounters. The solutions offered will not work on *every* dog. But they have worked on more than one. If you can come up with a better answer, my congratulations. The mark of a really good dog trainer is his ability to come up with ingenious improvisations that will apply to an individual dog.

The second section of this chapter will go into what I've classified as advanced training techniques, even though some may consider them rather elemental. They have been so classified because there is no natural way, as a rule, of getting a dog to perform these tasks. It takes repetitive, mechanical training to put manners on a dog.

Four Retrieving Problems

While you are play-training your pup to retrieve it is very likely he may do one or more of four things: refuse to pick up the dummy, play with or chew on the dummy, run away with the dummy instead of bringing it to you, or drop it before he gets it to you.

These might well have been included in the preliminary sections for they are basic but not too serious problems when caught early. But they are problems, hence the inclusion in this chapter.

No Pick-up

When a pup is reluctant or refuses to pick up a tossed glove, sock or dummy, tease him with the object, encouraging him to grab at it. Slither it around on the ground so he'll chase and catch it, get him to reach and jump for it. When you've got him interested, anxious and keyed up skid it out on the floor for a couple of yards. He'll chase, pounce on it, grab it, maybe even bring it to you as the source of all this fun. You have aroused his latent urge to hunt just as a wild predator will encourage her whelps to catch crippled prey.

You run some slight risk of developing hard mouth. But first things first in dog training and it is often necessary to gamble about the development of future problems to solve the one confronting you.

If he doesn't bring the object to you, move away from him and call him. A great deal of teasing and fooling around is warranted to get him to pick up and carry. Once you've accomplished that, in a few paragraphs you'll find out how to cope with the "run-off" problems.

Runs Away With Dummy

When a pup picks up the object you want him to retrieve but insists on gamboling around with it, DO NOT chase him. That's the game he wants to play, as it is played among litter mates.

Instead, move away from the pup, calling and clapping hands to attract his attention. Hide from him by ducking out of sight. He isn't as cocky as he acts. You're his best buddy and he doesn't want to lose you. He'll come looking and hopefully will bring the dummy along. Don't hide if you don't have to. Just your moving away from him probably will be enough to bring him in pursuit. Fuss over him any time he brings the dummy to where you can reach it without moving toward him.

If he doesn't pick the dummy up from where he's left it, start over, teasing and skidding it out for him. (As pups progress in age and ability dummies should be tossed, but at the very early age you'll be starting, he will follow it better on the ground than in the air).

He'll bring the dummy near you sometimes, even if by accident. Praise him when this occurs. You may solve this in a session or two. It may take a number. But continue to move away and/or hide on him if he continues to run off (he can't go far because he is small and you are inside). As long as he picks up and carries, this is not a serious problem. A refusal to pick up may be. If it's worth it, force-training to retrieve may be called for if a pup can't be play-trained into it by the age of six or eight months. Taking the time to force train a pointing breed to retrieve may make sense. With retrievers and spaniels I question whether an individual who must be taught by punishment, pain and dull routine to do what his heritage should provide "naturally" is worth the bother.

Mauls or Plays With Dummy

If a puppy lies down with the object to be retrieved and chews on it, tosses it around playing with it and is generally having a ball "killing his prey", call him a couple of times and move away clapping.

If he doesn't respond, go to him and chew him out verbally. Don't struggle with him over possession of the dummy. Just snatch it away and swat him lightly on the rear with your hand. You've made your disapproval evident, so move away from the pup, squat down and call him to you. Make up with him and when you've sweetened him up, tease him with the dummy and skid or low toss it again. Repeat. Repeat. Repeat.

If your patience wears thin if the pup continues this antic, or in the case where he insists on running away with the dummy, you may want to try an acceptable short-cut by forcing the pup. Once he's become accustomed to a collar, attach a light cord to it, long enough so the pup can reach the tossed dummy without restraint. When he picks up the dummy, reel him in as you tell him to "Fetch!" Don't be rough or jerk. Play him like you would a big fish. Praise him highly once you've "boated" him. Repeat this until he starts back with the dummy of his own accord.

Short-circuited Delivery

Failure of a pup (or older dog) to bring the object he's sent to retrieve to hand, or at least within arm's reach of the trainer, is most often caused by anxious trainers moving toward the puppy or dog to

151

Even Pointer pups which seldom have the natural instinct to pick up and carry that retrievers and spaniels demonstrate, can be encouraged to retrieve naturally at an early age. Pictured is Bug, a nine-week-old sired by Bullock X Cannonade's Salvo. The pup is first allowed to see and smell a glove he is then teased with. When the glove is skidded or tossed out a short distance, the pup runs to it and pounces on it.

Picking up and carrying, he starts back towards Duffey. The wise trainer does not chase a pup, but grabbing the glove when the pup comes within reach is permissible. The pup is then gently steered into the trainer via the glove and he is praised and petted as the glove is gently extricated from the pup's teeth. Now, with repetition of this training exercise, clean happy retrieves are assured.

make sure the delivery is completed. To a puppy this can represent a threat and defeats the intention of the trainer. This anxiousness can also cause a pup to run away with the dummy. Dropping the dummy before the retrieve is completed may be caused if the object is too large. Hence the glove or sock recommendation for small pups.

Always move away from your pup as he comes in, even to the extent of taking the dummy on the run as he catches up to you and goes by. Squatting and coaxing the pup to you is most practical and probably will suffice between the ages of eight to twelve, even sixteen weeks. But with the older pup, the strategic retreat, or "advance to the rear", is the method to use.

152

Hardmouth

You are free to determine to what degree your retriever is munching on birds before you charge him with being guilty of "hardmouth", which rates as a serious sin. But the term is difficult to define. In this matter, I am rather liberal and permissive in contrast to the accusative conservative opinion that will fault a dog for a missing feather.

A bird made unfit for the table because of the severity with which a dog "mouthed" it during a retrieve is commonly offered as proof of hardmouth. But even this guideline is debated. A toothmark in a bird's carcass will turn off some gourmets. A less-sophisticated chowhound will happily consume a well-crunched offering.

Before I'll cuss dogs out for hardmouth, bird-mangling must be *deliberate* and *consistent.* When you hear a man claiming his wonderdog has never ruffled a feather during a retrieve, write him off as an inexperienced gunner or a natural-born, double-barreled, revolving, prismatic prevaricator. Any way you look at him he's a liar.

Dry feathers can adhere to a dog's wet mouth. Wet feathers come out easily. A struggling cripple may force a dog to squeeze too tight in order to maintain control. Dragging a bird through thick cover, a streak of orneriness or over-excitement on the dog's part can cause inadvertent and occasional "hardmouth."

A dog is *deliberately* hardmouthed when he mashes a bird, rips it up or runs off and eats it. And there are unusual and puzzling cases. I owned a real good Labrador who had been field trial trained, won placement in licensed stakes and was a terrific pheasant hunter and duck retriever. But if he wasn't fed an hour or so before he was taken hunting he would absolutely savage the first bird knocked down. After that no problems. But it was either feed before or throw the first bird away.

Some trainers reward their pointing dogs by twisting off a quail's head after it is delivered to them and giving it to the dog to eat. I have seen pointers refuse to retrieve if they didn't get this tidbit regularly, but deliver tenderly as long as they did.

A prominent trainer friend of mine, when confronted with a retriever disinterested in birds, fed them freshly killed pigeons on the theory that it would arouse a dormant interest in hunting. Then he'd force-break them to retrieve tenderly, since he advocated forcebreaking every dog regardless of its natural ability anyway, and believed in taking each step at a time and drilling a dog until he was letter perfect before moving on to the next procedure.

Once instilled hardmouth can be impossible to cure. It won't get better as the dog gets older. Many excellent retrievers as they get older become rough on birds. I wouldn't fault them too severely for hardmouth. After hundreds, maybe thousands, of retrieves, they've learned that a quick squeeze means the end of their difficulties with a struggling cripple.

Hardmouth is most likely to occur in either the tough, hard driving type or in a shy, flighty dog. It is easier to correct the tough dog because some harshness won't agitate him as it will the spookier animal.

If you fear your dog is getting too rough on birds you may be able to halt the onset of hardmouth by adapting a portion of the force training procedure which will be outlined in the section on advanced training. Make your dog sit and hold a dead bird. If he works it around in his mouth, tap him under the chin until he holds it still, saying "Ah-AhAh!" until you get this compliance, then praise. If he clamps down hard, grab him across the muzzle, pinching his upper lip against his teeth, shake him and say "No! No! No! until he holds gently.

To prevent and, in some instances, correct hardmouth, the most effective means I've found is a large dose of fetching and *carrying*. Unfortunately most dogs are allowed little chance to savor their triumph and carry the "caught" bird around. When they deliver to the hunters, birds are jerked out of their mouths and stuffed in a game bag. A dog's enjoyment is over almost before it starts.

After your dog delivers in the hunting field, praise him and toss the bird for another retrieve. Or take it from him, praise him, put it back in his mouth, order him to "Hold it!" and "Heel!" and let him walk along carrying it for a few yards. Sweet talk him all this while which he'll appreciate. He'll be eager to turn it over to you when the prize becomes a burden and he'll like to be released to get out hunting once more.

Keep something in his mouth constantly around home when he is under control, gloves, socks, newspapers, dead birds, anything he can carry. Have him carry at heel. Have him sit and hold. If he starts rolling the object, biting, chewing or doing anything but holding it firmly, you are close to him, he is under control and you can make him hold properly by "AhAhAh-ing" him. You can see it and do something about it.

But when the offense is committed afield, the damage will be done when and where you are powerless to do anything about it, while the dog is picking up and returning the bird. At delivery time, it's too late. You can't punish or correct for bringing the bird to you, which is the likely canine interpretation of any disciplining at that time. Nor can you race the dog to the fallen bird shouting threats and expect him to be much of a retriever.

If your dog isn't incorrigible, he should get the idea that whatever he picks up and carries is to be held "just so." If a youngster shows good potential otherwise, don't give up. He's worth some work or even a fight to salvage. Should your dog go bad when he gets older, try correcting. But you may just have to live with it.

Turning Down Woodcock

Some dogs seem to develop an aversion for a certain type of bird as far as retrieving them goes. Most commonly it seems to be the Woodcock. But some dogs detest pigeons and give vent to their feelings by crunching them or balking at picking them up.

This is simply to warn you that such a thing can happen, although I can not recall a personal gun dog of mine over the past 30 years who refused to fetch Woodcock. Maybe it was because dead Woodcock were used to start them retrieving as tiny puppies. When they were started afield, they were usually in the company of an experienced dog who did fetch those birds and the youngster sought the same praise the older dog received.

Outside of recognizing this aversion can occur, if my dog fetched everything else to my satisfaction, I wouldn't make an issue of it. If he's just a poor retriever, however, don't make excuses for him by blaming the distaste some dogs exhibit for certain bird species.

Blinking

A dog who deliberately avoids a bird or birds he knows are there, pretending he doesn't know; or starts to work scent and then leaves it; or upon establishing a point on game, leaves it to come to his handler, or makes a pretense of hunting by moving on, is a "blinker".

Blinking is a man-made fault and a serious one usually caused by too early disciplining and severe check cording or whipping in an effort to make a dog "mannerly".

Because the dog comes to associate birds with the racking up he gets, not understanding the punishment is for his "misbehavior," he will decide to shy away from game rather than undergo all the unpleasantness. Because of what's required and training methods commonly used, the fault is more commonly associated with the pointing breeds

156

than the flushers and retrievers. But too early or over-zealous appli-cation of routines to instill steadiness in spaniels and retrievers can also make blinkers of them.

The solution is to make your blinking dog birdy once again. It won't be easy. It will cost you a hunting season to correct this unless you spend a great deal of time in the off-season using planted game farm birds or pigeons. You must encourage the dog to find birds and let him flush and chase. It helps to kill as many as you can over him. You want all this unrestricted fun to wipe out the unpleasantness he's come to associate with birds.

Once you get him birdy once more you'll have to start stanching him all over—slowly and gently. A dog of soft temperament usually suffers this affliction. If he is *really* sensitive, you not only will have to delay steadying him to wing and shot but forego it entirely. When you return to your stanching and steadying program, go easy. If he shows signs of being "bird bit" again, lay off until boldness returns.

Some confirmed blinkers are very crafty. You may think your dog is pointing and then correcting a mistake he made when he moves off point, or slinks along as though trying to trail and pin a running bird, until you walk up some birds he has run away from. But don't be too quick to label a dog a blinker. Confirm your suspicions by producing birds the dog has left before badmouthing a dog, re-training or getting rid of him.

Disinterest

Some people call a dog "birdy" if he shows a great deal of interest in everything that flies from early puppyhood on, including butterflies. For myself I think "birdiness" involves more of the dog's interest in bird scent than in the sight of a bird in flight. When you use that defi-nition, no dog can be "too birdy". But the one that chases after every-thing that flies can damn well be.

If your dog shows little interest in birds, all you can do is offer plenty of opportunity and a lot of praise for any interest shown on game. Sometimes a dog can have what birdiness he possesses knocked out of him by too early or too much disciplining or punishment at the wrong time. This may be restored by letting a dog have his head, hunt and chase. If a pointing dog goes sour, shooting birds for him to re-trieve may help. But some dogs just don't have much "hunt" in them. Lack of birdiness is cause for discarding a dog.

Incomplete Water Retrieve

Upon emerging from water, too many dogs lay down the bird they are retrieving and shake off. It is all too common, but not too serious in a gun dog as long as he picks the bird up again and finishes the job by delivering to hand without a lot of coaxing, whistling and shouting.

But if it becomes an established habit, it can develop into the dog figuring the delivery job is done when he hits land and it breaks up the continuity of a signal accomplishment, a good retrieve from water. Accept this broken retrieving pattern if you will. But you don't have to. If you correct it, you'll save flaring incoming ducks because you had to direct your dog to do the whole job, or else were forced to get out of your blind or hide and pick up your own bird.

As soon as the dog approaches shore, trill your whistle and start moving back so he'll follow or chase you, if it's necessary to run to stir his interest. If you can walk slowly backwards, encourage the dog to keep coming and pat your chest with your hand rather than slapping your leg. This will keep the dog's head and eyes up and on you, and he will be less likely to drop the bird and will make a better delivery.

If he does lay it down, get to him at once, telling him "No!" put the bird in his mouth, make him hold it and bring it to you as you back off patting your chest. It is a repetitive process, as are most corrective actions. You must, in training sessions, instill this habit of completing the delivery before shaking off. When working on multiple retrieves, permit the dog to shake before sending him again. No big problem. He'll most likely do it anyway. You can impress the tourists though if, after you take the bird, you tell your dog to "Shake!" They'll think he's marvelously trained.

Gun-shyness

This fault has been discussed in the chapter on introducing a gun dog to gunfire. If your dog is even "a little bit gun–shy" and, certainly, if he's badly frightened you have the two sensible solutions already suggested, get rid of the dog or turn him over to a pro. He won't be gun–shy if you properly introduce him to guns and shooting.

Sometimes an unfortunate happenstance, like being shot by an irate neighbor while running loose, firecrackers, lightening bolts or a queer combination of circumstances, ruins an otherwise fine dog. Believe me, a gun–shy dog *is* a ruined dog.

If you decide to effect a cure yourself, there are all kinds of methods

A live pigeon may be used to introduce a bold pup to birds or in an effort to instill interest in birds in a pup that lacks enthusiasm. The pup approaches the scent of the tossed bird which was thrown in light cover so it could be easily spotted. Wing feathers were pulled so the bird could flutter and run but not fly off. This is a 4-month-old Pudelpointer.

Curiosity overcomes apprehension and the pup, after chasing and playing with the fluttering bird, grabs it. Mission accomplished! The pup picks up the struggling bird and runs off with it, and although it took much coaxing to obtain the semblance of a retrieve, an avid interest in birds was instilled, which was the purpose of this lesson.

that expose a dog to unpleasantness so great he'll brave gunfire to avoid it. Probably the "starvation method" is as effective as any.

Put food in front of the dog and shoot off a blank. He'll slither off and hide. Remove the food. Allow no food (but be sure he has water) until you make the same offer the next day. Put down the food, discharge a blank. Keep this up until he's starved into gobbling his food despite the shot. Then you are over the hill and once you get your skinny dog in shape you can entertain the hope he won't run away the first time you shoot afield. If he does, back to the starvation ploy.

If you have a dog already trained who turns gun–shy, if he loves to retrieve and the fault is not too ingrained, you may overcome it by using this interest in retrieving to straighten him out by following the procedure outlined for introduction to gunfire in the chapter "Introduction to Game and Guns".

Advanced Retriever Training

Some of the things a Retriever must do to be accorded the "well-trained dog" tag are elemental and come almost naturally, while others require a great amount of mechanical repetition.

A good gun dog from the retriever breeds should know about water and how to fetch out of it, be accustomed to boats and motors, decoys, know how to track and capture crippled game, mark and remember the fall of more than one bird at a time, remain steady until sent to make the retrieve and obey hand signals directing him to a fall he hasn't had the opportunity to observe.

Spaniels and the versatile gun dog breeds who are going to be expected to serve in much the same capacity as the retriever specialists should learn the same things by the same methods. Much of this type of training has very little to do with a dog's natural bent. It is more a test of the trainer's ability.

Retrieving From Water

The earlier pups are introduced to water the better. Probably the most important duty of the Retriever breeds is recovering shot waterfowl and it is of considerable secondary importance for spaniels and versatiles.

Pups from the age of eight weeks on can be induced to splash around in shallow water. If a pup is whelped in winter or spring wait until the water is warm, which will vary depending upon your locale, even if you have to wait until the pup is a bit older. Use some common sense

160

and don't pick a raw spring day right after the ice is gone to take a pup to water for the first time. This is essentially play training. When the pup finds it's fun, a later occasional unpleasantness won't instill water fright.

Should you obtain a late summer or fall whelped pup, wait until some hot spring day when the marshes are wet and the fields puddled and take your four to eight months old youngster afield while you do some sloshing around in hip boots. He'll follow you through the shallows, get used to water and at that age on a sunny day a pup wading, running and swimming won't get chilled. He'll enjoy the temporary relief from heat.

Play in the water with your pup at every opportunity during the summer months and it will be unusual if you can't entice him to follow you when you don waders or swim trunks. But pick a calm shallow pond or lake until he's well started, confident and swimming, not a surf or a strong flowing stream. As you coax and talk sweet to the pup, move slowly, don't frighten him. Make an enjoyable game of it. He'll be in over his depth and swimming before he knows it. He'll swim naturally, although he may splash some with his forepaws. In a few sessions he should be entering and swimming boldly and with obvious enjoyment. If not keep playing with him.

Why all this folderol? Aren't good Labradors, Chesapeakes and Water Spaniels born with a love for water? Well, some is, some ain't. You'll be most likely to encounter pups who are bold around and in water and just take to it with no coaxing among the retriever breeds and to a lesser extent among spaniels and versatiles. The thing is you can't count on it. I'd just hate to see prospective waterfowl retrievers who could serve very well with a gradual and proper introduction to this element washed out because they were expected to leap in and fetch a duck the first time they ever saw water.

Don't expect and don't even encourage your pup to jump off a bank, a deck or out of a boat. If you've one that does it on his own hook, great! Such dogs do come along. Others have to wade in or even fall in a few times. Frolicking with an older dog or another pup who is bold in the water is a useful means of introduction.

Never, never throw a pup into the water, particularly if his extreme reluctance to enter and puddle around tries your patience. For all but the foolhardy, such an unwilling immersion will not only set you and the pup back but could be permanently damaging. But if you insist that all this is a lot of Micky Mousing around and you want to get on with things, maybe this will work.

First Fetch

Should you have your pup wild about this retrieving game and fetching right well on land before you undertake to acquaint him with water, you may be able to eliminate the introductory stuff and double-up on your training. If your pup is precocious and bold he may do this at a surprisingly early age, like even eight to ten weeks.

Find a shallow, warm-water place, take your pup and his dummy to it. Toss the dummy on land a time or two for him to retrieve and then flip it just a foot or two out into the water. The pup will step out into the water and reach to pick up the dummy, cautious but following a procedure he has learned is fun. Some will even pounce on it. Gradually increase the distance until the pup must wade to get the dummy. Then as his confidence builds up, gradually extend the tosses until the dummy lands just beyond his depth. When he makes a lunge to grab the dummy, his front feet won't find bottom.

The next obvious step is to toss the dummy far enough so the pup must swim a few feet to the dummy, pick it up while swimming, turn and come back with it.

The rapidity with which you progress and the shortcuts you take may be greatly determined by an individual pup's precocity, or lack thereof. But the rule of thumb is take it easy. This is not a test to see how far he'll swim or how well he'll mark a fall. And you don't want him to quit because you throw too far or too often. Four or five fetches a day for the first few days will be enough. Don't try to do it all in one day.

While you are doubling-up your training procedure, this is a part of water introduction and that's the phase in which you want success. To achieve success the pup must wade before he can swim.

Even though he shows more than average aptitude, don't push too fast or too far. That temptation is difficult to resist. But eventually you'll have him going out as far as you can throw the dummy and swimming strongly. When you've achieved this, should he return without the dummy you can wade out to him and make him pick it up. Just be sure that whenever a dummy splats on the water your pup completes a retrieve.

Once he's entering the water with a rush and swimming well you can get him to enter from a low bank or jump off a dock by teasing him with a dummy. When he's excited, drop it into the water just out of reach. He'll probably leap on it. This will help get him to "hit the water hard" rather than slipping in. Get the pup jumping from some-

When introducing a pup to water retrieving, toss the dummy barely into the shallow water, as the author's son, Mike, does for this yellow Labrador.

thing stationary before you expect him to jump out of a boat into the water. You don't want him spooked by the boat's rock or striking his legs on the gunwales as he goes over the side.

Boats and Motors

Speaking of boats, sometime during his hunting life any dog used for waterfowl retrieving is going to be transported in some kind of boat. If you can arrange it, by all means have a boat around where you do your water training. Let him play around and jump in and out of that boat or else do it in your yard with the boat on dry land. In the absence of a boat you may be able to accomplish much the same thing by having your youngster jump in and out of a bath tub, a box trailer, a large box, etc. The idea is to develop his confidence.

You may have to climb into the boat to coax the pup in with you.

If he's learned to "Kennel!" as he should, you should give that command and he should jump over the gunwale and into the boat. Don't make him sit and stay before giving the command or in an effort to keep him in the boat. Let him jump right out if he wants to, order him back in, let him jump out a few times until he's confident around this new thing. This can all be done on land. You can then stand in the boat, or sit on the seat and have the youngster (5 mos. or more old) sit quietly for a time while you talk to him in preference to rapping him one if he doesn't settle down right away.

When you get into a boat that is actually in water, repeat this procedure. Or, you can start right from a floating boat taking the risk that it's rocking will spook the pup a bit. Pet him, tell him what a good boy he is as he sits by you.

When the pup is not dejected, shivering or apprehensive, tell him to "Stay!" step out of the boat and walk around it, cautioning him to wait there. If the boat is in water, it should be shallow so you can wade. When you release him with an "All Right!" the chances are good he'll leap out. If he doesn't, call him to you. If that doesn't work, coax him out. If that fails, walk off and leave him there. He won't stay. He'll come after you. He's now learning to enter and leave a boat.

When you start with the boat in the water you'll want his feet to hit bottom when he jumps out of it, avoiding the possibility of total immersion, which could frighten him until he's become accustomed to water. Once he's jumping out and coming to you in water, no more than belly-deep, have him sit and stay in the boat until you toss a dummy, near enough the first few times to tempt him to leap right onto it. Gradually toss it farther. Repeat. Repeat. Repeat.

Then get the boat out into swimming water and have the pup start jumping out of it to retrieve a tossed dummy. When he starts his return, dummy in mouth, row into the shallows, step out and have him deliver while you are standing in the water. Praise him. For his first ride, use a stable boat which will allow some movement without danger of tipping. When he's quiet and obedient afloat you can trust him in a skiff or canoe. For you must let him get accustomed to the motion and the boat before enforcing regulations about sitting quietly, lest he think the boat is the cause of his punishment. When he's secure and happy in the boat is the time to make him sit and stay. Row or paddle your boat at first. Introduce the motor later.

The next step is to get Hobo to jump from the shallow water into the boat and hand over the dummy there. You may even have to beach the boat to coax him into it. But you want delivery to hand, regardless of

164

where you may be. Teaching deep water delivery is a step following this one.

Once he's learned the boat is a safe resting place, loves swimming and enjoys riding and working from the boat, sit him on shore, paddle or row out and call him. He wants to come and he's accustomed to the boat. When he swims up alongside, help him in. He'll try to hook his forelegs over the gunwale. Then put your hand at the juncture of his head and neck, pull toward you as he braces against it, coming up out of the swimming water into the boat.

When delivering a dummy or duck in deep water, because he may clamp hard if it's in his mouth when he struggles to come aboard, it is worthwhile to teach him to release the duck or dummy in your hand as he swims alongside, and then pull him in. He should "Drop!" on command and you should be able to take what he retrieves from him before assisting him into the boat.

When introducing the new noise and vibration an outboard motor represents, row out into deep water where he won't be tempted to leap back onto the dock or shore if the starting of the motor prompts desertion. Then start your motor and take him for a ride. Accept a bit of restlessness at first but talk him calm, reassure him and he'll find everything in order. Then enforce the sit quietly regulation. Take him boat riding as often as possible before season opens. Hobo will probably love it as much as the car or at least accept it with equanimity so he offers no pre-dawn complications when you head out on those mornings the ducks are flying.

Decoys

Sometime or another your "duck dog" is going to encounter decoys. Getting him to ignore them in favor of the real thing is so simple it's worth doing if only to save you embarrassment should they spook him when he has to swim through them or should he become confused and fetch a fake.

If you pass or jump shoot, or waterfowling is secondary to your upland hunting, you may want to skip this procedure. But every serious waterfowl gunner should make sure his retriever knows about decoys.

You can use discarded blocks or buy half-a-dozen cheap paper mache-type decoys and scatter them out on your lawn. Walk Hobo through them at heel. If he shows the slightest interest in them after your first pass through tell him "No!" and give him a swat on the flank. Once you've convinced him of the worthlessness of all fakes, throw a dummy beyond them and send him through them to fetch. Then

165

throw it to each side of your stool layout. Finally drop it right down among them. He'll pick out what he's been praised for and avoid what's earned him a cuff.

When you go to water tote the decoys along. Set out a few. Work him among them and through them with dummies. To make real sure, shoot or throw dead pigeons among the blocks, or use shackled ducks. But it probably won't be necessary. Several lessons will have convinced him retrieving decoys just ain't proper.

Steadying

You will want to be at least reasonably sure your dog won't leave a boat, blind, shore or muskrat house where he's stationed until he is sent. This is known as steadiness. It saves energy and avoids unnecessary moisture and discomfort if your dog refrains from taking off every time a gun goes off.

So keep working on your "Stay!" command until you can depend upon Hobo's staying put until sent, or at least until he sees the bird or dummy hit the water. Unsteadiness may be accepted in a dog's first season, encouraging eager retrieving. But by the end of the season, some pressure should be exerted to start the youngster settling down and you can get serious with him after the season closes in your training sessions to assure that you can demand his steadiness the second year.

This is instilled by having the dog wait at your side during the retrieving lessons until you send him, a procedure outlined in the early chapter on training basics. You can keep him in practice obeying this command (Stay!) by stationing him a spot and walking off or going about something else. If he "breaks" or tries to follow you, take him back and harshly put him in his place, repeating until he stays put until you call him to you or give the "All right!" release. Tempt him to go, by making quick and unusual motions while he's watching you or having someone or something else interest or distract him. If he succumbs, put him back to stay for a while.

The major purpose for this type of control over a gun dog is to make sure that he is in position to mark the fall of more than one bird, as commonly happens when a barrage of shots have been fired at a flock of ducks. If you seldom shoot more than a duck at a time, you may decide to accept unsteadiness if it seems too difficult for you to instill.

If you get a particularly recalcitrant dog who can not be steadied by words of caution and the sharp restraint of leash and slip chain collar as outlined previously, you may have to resort to tipping him over with a check cord when he breaks, thrashings, or lassooing his middle with the check cord which will cinch him up tight and make him yowl when it tightens around his middle when he breaks.

Seldom is this necessary and since you want a dog who sizzles out to retrieve you are more likely to find encouragement and less drastic restraints preferable to harshness. But if the dog is real tough and over-eager, getting rough is the only way to get things done. He'll probably have the temperament to accept this treatment without it affecting his desire to retrieve.

I wouldn't require even the semblence of steadiness before the age of six months and then only with a precocious pup. From then on, once you have your pup waiting until he is sent to fetch a single thrown bird or dummy, you may progress to multiple retrieves— throwing two or three dummies or birds in succession and teaching the dog to remember the falls of each one, simulating work he may be asked to do when several ducks are dropped out of one flock.

Obviously, if Hobo isn't steady he'll have trouble seeing or remembering the second or third falls of dummies or birds as he dashes out after the first one, or will be distracted from the first bird he zeroed in on by the subsequent falls. So Hobo should either be steady off the leash or be restrained so he will see what's occurring when you move him up to "doubles" and "triples".

Doubles and Triples

Starting a dog remembering more than one fall means you go gradually, very gradually and make your first falls very short. By this time Hobo should have mastered long (50 to 75 yard or further) single falls.

Sit him at your side, make him stay steady. Throw one dummy 10 to 20 yards to either left or right of you and the dog, the second to the opposite side. As the second tossed dummy hits the ground and the pup has his eye on it send him by saying, "Hobo, Fetch!"

Send Hobo quickly. Don't hold him steady beyond the time that second tossed dummy thumps the ground or splats the water in those early sessions. You want to keep *both* falls as fresh in his mind as possible and make sure he takes the second fall first. Holding him too long will have him looking back and forth between the two dummies, unable to make up his mind which to start for or switching "birds" after he does start. Holding steady for a longer period should be delayed until he is thoroughly drilled.

These first multiple retrieves should be on dummies that are on

167

open ground or in open water where they can be seen by both you and Hobo. At the start it will often require visual stimulus to help him remember that there is a second bird out there. Early work is best done on land, for you can then walk Hobo out to the second bird if he forgets it and doesn't respond to your urging to "line out" to it.

When you send Hobo for the dummy, as you should have been doing when sending him for singles, coinciding with your verbal command, swing your arm in the direction of the dummy in a bowler's motion. This hand signal will be used later as you teach him to "take a line" to a bird he hasn't seen fall. It's use now will instill responses that will facilitate that training procedure.

He doubtlessly will sizzle out for the dummy he's just seen drop if he's done well on single retrieves. The first thrown dummy, which will be his second retrieve is the problem one. It may not be. Some youngsters have phenomenal memories, will look toward or start toward the remaining dummy as they return with the first one in their mouth. Do not allow switching dummies. Insist on delivery before sending for the other.

Be delighted with this display of memory. Just don't let him do it. It will lead to his dropping birds he's already picked up to race after another flush or fall when hunting, with no birds being recovered.

If he won't respond to your whistle beeps and continues to the second dummy, run out and intercept him if you have to. But if he comes to you as he should and delivers the dummy he is carrying, give him a quick "Good Dog", have him sit at your side once more in retrieving position, aimed generally at the remaining dummy lying out there in plain sight.

Now, it is in plain sight for you. But at the dog's level and because stationary objects don't quickly attract the attention of animals, you can only hope that a fragment of memory directs your pup's gaze on that dummy. Don't waste time. Canine memories are short. When he's looking that way, send him with the verbal "Hobo Fetch!" and that bowler's arm swing in the dummy's direction.

The dummies were widely spread when thrown to cut down the chances of the dog's crossing or switching when going out or coming in. The spread will also accustom him to heading in a different direction, the one you signal with the arm sweep, when cast a second time whether or not he remembers that second fall.

When you cast him the second time, he may start out in the direction of his first retrieve. Stop him, start over. He's forgotten all about the second bird but remembers where he got the one just delivered and is willing to try out there again. Or he may start in the right direction, spin around and look at you. He's confused too. If you are lucky, as you continue to urge the pup out he may spot the dummy in the open, pick it up and bring it to you. Praise him.

Very often, if the dummy is in the open and close enough your pup will either remember or see it, go right to it and get it. Wonderful! Remember this is no long marking test. It is a drill to accustom your dog to starting out for a second bird in the direction you send him. To do this, he must succeed. So stack the deck every way you can to assure this with short easily visible tosses.

Remembering long falls and taking lines to those he forgets will come later, with experience and training. You are concerned here with instilling the idea that there's more than one bird out there for him to fetch, whether he remembers or you tell him there is.

So repeat and repeat and repeat, gradually lengthening the distance of the throws and altering the angles dummies are thrown. As the dog indicates he remembers the areas of those falls gradually hold him longer before sending him for the first bird. Never cast him unless he is looking in the direction you are "bowling".

If necessary keep walking out to that second dummy with him, making the underarm sweep and encouraging him to fetch. When he does locate and pick up, trot back to your original position with him coming with you, take the dummy and praise him.

Before long (unless if his brains were dynamite he couldn't blow his nose) even if he doesn't remember the second bird he'll start out on faith alone in the direction indicated and upon spotting it will fetch it. Even the slow pup, upon completing his first delivery will sit and look off in the direction of his second bird, remembering and waiting to be sent if drilled enough.

Once the short ones are mastered, the longer retrieves well-remembered, you can start tossing your dummies into some cover so he will have to remember the area of the fall and then use his nose instead of his eyes to come up with the dummy.

You can also have an assistant shoot and throw a "long bird", while you throw a "short bird" to test his memory and drill him on any kind of fall, including two birds dropping virtually in line with each other, one fairly close to the dog and handler, the other much farther out which is called an "over and under" or "in line" double retrieve, in contrast to the "spread doubles!" you started with.

For three birds, triples, the procedure is the same, except you are adding one more dummy for the dog to remember. Expecting a dog to remember more than three falls could lead to confusion and grief with any but the most unusual dog and there is little point in training for it.

Taking a Line

In contrast to hound terminology where "taking a line" means following the scent line left by the quarry, in retriever patois it means making an undeviating cast in any direction the dog is signaled to go until he scents or encounters the downed bird or is stopped by a signal and re-directed.

The "bowler's sweep" of your arm, which you've been using to send your dog off on a retrieve he has marked and remembered, is the same motion to use in "giving a line" to Hobo when he either did not see the bird fall or has forgotten it. Recovery is made possible in those circumstances (a "blind retrieve") by the dog's obedience to hand and whistle signals. The most important such signal is giving the line. With diligent training retrievers learn to make spectacular casts of up to 200 yards.

However, on command a good hunting dog should be taught to make a straight-line cast of about 50 yards which may be necessary to put him in the area of a fall. So teach it this way.

Put down a dummy in plain sight about 20-25 yards away from you and your dog. Keep increasing this distance as you progress. Let the dog see the dummy placed. From a retrieving position, send him with the usual command and underarm sweep. He'll retrieve it. When he's gone out as far as you want him to on signal for the dummy in the open, let him see you drop it in some cover.

(If you are working alone, station your dog, order him to stay, go out, drop the dummy, return to the dog and send him. It's good steadying practice too. But if the dog starts foot-tracking to the dropped bird rather than zinging out there, get someone else to toss the bird).

When he takes a 50 yard line into the cover and finds the dummy, station him where he can't see, in back of a building or your car etc., (good steadying practice) while you leave him and plant the dummy. Then call him, position him and give him a line to it. Don't hide the dummy too far away at first. But keep increasing the distance until he goes out on that line until he scents or stumbles onto the bird.

If you want him to take lines of over 50 yards, or if your dog isn't grasping the short stuff as you are giving it to him, you can help him stay on course by sending him down a trail, a mowed strip in a hayfield, a narrow snowplowed road or some other "path of the least re-sistance." Always put the hidden bird and dummy on the side of the path that will give the dog the benefit of the wind so he'll run down the path and hook into the scent when he hits it.

No Switches Allowed

Repetitious line work will be less tedious if you mix it up with a variety of marked retrieves and other training lessons. When he's coming in with a dummy he's been lined out to, shoot and throw another dummy, tempting him to switch. But don't let him. Then send him back for it after he's completed his original retrieve. Do this in water too, but in the shallows so you can run out there just as you would on land, and tell him "No!" and prevent his switching.

This drill is to prevent his swimming around like a dervish should you happen to score on some ducks that came in while your dog is out after birds that were knocked down earlier. It's also a good memory jogger for him when you send him back for the dummy he "ignored." You want him to be aware of it and remember. But you also want it fetched at the proper time and sequence.

Marking or Lining

There is some real danger that if you overdo the giving a line bit you will never develop to its fullest a dog's natural marking ability — the facility of following the flight line of a bird and correctly es-timating and remembering the area in which it fell. This has been done to a great extent in field trials.

Too seldom do trial dogs get the opportunity to display their mark-ing ability which is, to a high degree, a natural ability, as opposed to the mechanical response to hand signals learned by rote. So do not use the "giving a line" signal to any great degree except when the dog has not seen a fall or has obviously forgotten it, lest Hobo comes to rely on this handling rather than on his own judgement. Controlled independence is highly desirable in a gun dog. Overly-dependent, mechanical response is not.

Keep that in mind in regard to the application and use of any train-ing procedure. At this stage of the game your dog should be reliable in stopping to sit at whistle blast, upraised arm and verbal command to halt, particularly if being worked as a gun dog producing game as well as picking up what's shot.

171

Don't undertake the trial training procedures until your dog has had a good season or two of actual hunting under his collar and has demonstrated the natural ability and independence that will make putting the mechanics on him worth the time and effort it will take. Of course, if you are planning to trial your dog, you must push him much harder and faster. But it takes an unusual dog to soak up this discipline and many a dog who can be brought along most satisfactorily with a more natural and casual approach will turn sour.

Cripple Catching

In no way does a gun dog contribute more to the conservation effort than in recovering downed birds that a hunter would never find without a good dog, particularly cripples. If you wait until a dog gains enough experience in the field to cope with downed birds that still have enough life to attempt an escape you will lose some birds that could be recovered if you'd spent a little time on pre-season training.

If you want your dog to recover "runners" a long way from where they dropped, or come out of the marsh with a duck another hunter lost, start out with a wing-clipped barn pigeon. Toss it out on the lawn or a mowed field where the dog can see it and send him for it. It's no challenge. But he'll get used to running down and catching live game and returning it to you intact. If your dog is a proper retriever you can use the same pigeon many, many times.

Don't get shook up if a few die during these drills. It could be from shock, fright or a grab in the wrong place. Unless your dog is actually mushing them he isn't hardmouthed.

When your dog has caught a few pigeons (or the same pigeon a few times) turn it loose in some heavier cover where the dog must hunt and use his nose. Then turn to a wing-clipped or shackled domestic mallard. (Wing-clipped pheasant are a bit too elusive at this stage of the game, when success is important. Ducks can lead a dog on a merry chase but are easier to recover).

Don't release your duck just willy-nilly. Toss it into a small field or marshy plot and send your dog after it. If the area is too big, it can escape. These first few times, make sure his chances of success are good. Make it tough later when previous successes prevent discouragement. Being virtually indestructable, unless your dog is hopelessly hardmouthed, a pair of mallards will last as long as you want to train.

After he's caught ducks on land, work your retriever in the water, utilizing a pothole, ditch or small creek where the duck will head for marsh and shore cover rather than staying in open water. A dog can collect a "cripple" in a marsh, but in open water even a shackled duck can elude a pup for so long he may get discouraged and quit. You don't want that to happen, even if you have to catch the duck yourself and hold it for the pup.

Later on you can test your dog's perseverence and give him plenty of conditioning if you wing-clip your duck, tape its feet together and toss it out in an open pond and let the dog try to catch it.

Live Birds

Game farm birds, when available for legal use, will go a long way toward giving your dog a "jump on the season" when used in place of or alternating with training dummies. Ducks can be used in all aspects of a retriever's training and should be used every now and then to pep up and sharpen a dog.

Ducks will last longer if their wings are taped to their bodies when used in water work or they can be encased in a "sweater" with draw strings on both ends which can be made from an old sweat sock or purchased commercially. Since ducks can get sassy when they find out dogs don't hurt them, a rubber band wrapped around a duck's bill is a good idea. It will prevent a duck's grabbing a pup's lip or ear, often resulting in two understandable reactions. The tough pup will bite back, the soft puppy will be frightened. Don't let it happen.

There's no reason you shouldn't use game farm birds like pheasant and chukar in your retriever training. In fact you should if you can. The only difficulty is their availability and cost for one-dog, amateur trainers. You will find the common barn pigeon most satisfactory for teaching your gun dog about upland work and by alternating pigeons and ducks with dummies you can train for just about anything in a limited time and area.

Directional Signals

Just as steadiness to wing and shot marks the finished pointing dog, so does complete control and a response to "handling" indicate the finished retriever. This involves your dog going to the left or right or straight back when he's some distance from you and you signal with an arm wave what you want him to do.

It all started back when you taught your dog to plunk his fanny down when you blasted on the whistle and raised your arm, pointing a finger skyward. It is completed when, with a wave of your arm, you can put him onto an unmarked bird if he deviates from his original line, passes it upwind or doesn't get out far enough.

A young dog should be able to clearly see the first birds shot over him in training so he associates the birds and retrieving with the gunfire.

In that context, it is largely a field trial "stunt" demonstrating the ability of a diligent trainer and his complete mastery of the dog. The hunter, dressed in drab clothing, is too often obscured from his dog when a bird is downed some distance off. To respond to these arm or hand signals the dog must be able to see who is giving them. It is more practical for most hunters to send their dogs to the area of the fall, as described in the "Taking A Line" section of this chapter, and order them to "Hunt 'em Out!"

But for the man who thinks he may have use for precise handling response to put a gun dog right on a bird the retriever didn't see go down, the formal method follows. Whether your dog responds precisely, casually or "sometimes" depends entirely on how much you drill on this phase of "blind retrieving."

Use one dummy at a time. Sit your dog about 10 yards to your front and visualize a baseball diamond with you at home plate, the dog on the pitcher's mound. Let the dog see a dummy placed some 25 yards to his left, right, or directly behind him, corresponding to first base, third base and second base. Place the dummy, position the dog, step back about 10 yards and you are ready to go.

Start with the second base dummy. To encourage your sitting dog to spin around and go straight back to the dummy behind him, as he sits tight under the signal of your upraised arm, jump toward him decisively, sweep your arm down toward him, snap out "Hobo, Get Back!" If you are real lucky and his mind is on the planted dummy he will whirl, see it and fetch it.

If he hesitates on this new command, keep moving toward him repeating the "Get Back!" and the arm wave in that direction and crowding him toward the dummy.

To send him in either direction, leap to the side and sweep down hard with the left arm if moving to the left, the right arm if moving to the right. As you sweep down, point dramatically in that direction and shout "Get Over!" If he starts in the wrong direction, blast the sit command on the whistle (he must obey this with alacrity before you start this handling) and redirect him.

If he hesitates about getting over, keep hopping sideways waving, pointing in the direction you want him to go and repeating "Get Over!" If the dummy is in plain sight and not too far, this urging won't be as strenuous as when you advance to hiding the dummy. Passing motorists and neighbors upon witnessing that performance may question your sanity. But ignore that and persevere.

It is preferable that a dog pretty well master the "Get Back!" before you start working on the "Get Overs!" which are usually easier to teach because the dog doesn't have to turn completely around and the waving and body English resembles how he's asked to change direction afield. But the "Get Back" will probably find more use in the hunting field than "Get Over" since it is common for a retriever to "mark short" or halt at some obstacle when he should go farther.

Keep working your dog until he begins to anticipate your signals by looking in the direction of the dummy, edging that way or bounding over there at your first gesture. Have him properly deliver each pick-up and praise him when he does right. When he does it wrong, stop him, keep urging until he goes where you want. Don't be severe in shaking him up or whipping him until he has learned the proper response and defies you. Insist however, that he sit and sit tight on the one blast of your whistle.

When he masters the in-sight dummies, hide the dummies. Start all over with the signals. If you've worked the routine hard enough, it's been implanted in Hobo's mind that he's to go in the direction you wave. He should start off properly. He shouldn't be expected to go too far at first until he's onto the dummy. Gradually lengthen the distance he must go in the direction you signal and also the distance between the pitcher's mound, where he is seated, and home plate where you station yourself. In time you can hope to obtain good response when the dog is 50 to 75 yards from you.

Then have him sit next to you. Start giving him a line from this retrieving position at your side, sending him from the plate to the mound and stopping him with a whistle blast when he's out there. When he swivels and sits facing you at your whistle signal send him in whatever direction you've hidden a dummy. Give him the wind's benefit to start. Then when he starts in the proper direction he'll have a chance to smell and home into it. Later, when he trusts you to put him on a bird or dummy, make him work downwind.

If you seek precise response, allowing you to put your dog right on a bird via signals, you must not allow the dog any leeway to hunt aimlessly just because he might stumble across his bird. This is precision work and put on a dog mechanically. It is not something he will learn by doing, through experience or on his own hook. It is strictly a learned response and this sort of training should be done only after a dog has some actual hunting behind him and enjoys it, lest he lose some of the initiative so desirable in a gun dog.

Advanced Spaniel Training

Since hunters use their spaniels and retrievers for much the same purposes, and expect them to hunt in a similar manner, some of the training procedures which may concern primarily either a spaniel or a retriever can also be beneficial to both.

It is for that reason that the retriever and spaniel advanced training sections are placed cheek by jowl in this chapter. It is hoped the retriever fanciers will continue on reading into the spaniel section and spaniel adherents will page back and pick up some helpful information from the retriever section.

176

Retrieving

This most important aspect of spaniel work can easily be taught by following the procedures detailed in the chapters on basic and advanced retriever training, whether the spaniel will be expected to work non-slip on dove or duck or as a combination flusher and fetcher on upland game.

The other major requirement of a gun dog spaniel is that he hunt, find and flush game within shotgun range and this has been detailed in the chapter on "Spaniel Training." However, while they may be satisfactory bird producers and recoverers of shot game, well started spaniels may be pretty rough on the edges and there are refinements a man serious about his dog's performance may want to add.

Controlled and Steady

My assumption is that when you've reached the point where you want to put some added touches on your spaniel under normal conditions, your spaniel (or retriever if you are using him as a flushing dog) will respond pretty well to any one of three signals indicating he should nail his butt to the ground—one blast of the whistle, an upraised arm or a verbal command.

But during the hunting season or in training sessions afield, there are birds getting up, guns going off, all kinds of stresses and distractions. Your young dog just doesn't seem to hear and you don't want this "deafness" to become permanent.

Take your Hobo, the training dummies and a blank pistol to a field of light cover. Cast him off and when he is working busily shoot a blank in the air. He'll look. Hit the whistle and throw your arm upright. He should sit down if you've yard trained right. If he doesn't, get out there and *make* him sit.

Keep him sat for a few moments. Then give him the go ahead, "All Right! Hunt 'em Out!" and wave your arm, right or left as you move out in that direction. Should he go the opposite way, stop him with the whistle or a shout, repeat the command and signal. Do so until he follows your direction.

We're two-birding it with one stone again. In addition to this start at steadiness, Hobo is getting some work on directional signals. Continue this and you will be able to get birds out of places that Hobo may have bypassed. For a wave, backed by a "Hunt 'em Out!", will put Hobo into a spot of cover you want worked out that would otherwise have remained undisturbed. This is most pleasing and productive and is sure to impress your hunting buddies since they are unaware it's no big deal to teach.

When your young dog starts stopping and begins to sit at gunshot, anticipating the whistle blast, which means do just that, start tossing dummies for him to fetch. Shoot, throw, whistle and gesture in that sequence. He's been sitting for the shot, but he may break when he sees the dummy in the air.

Anticipate this and throw the dummy in such a manner or direction that you can intercept him before he gets to it—if he should break. If he doesn't, test his steadiness a few times and then throw the dummy any place you want. But you want to be able to discipline him for breaking. This can't be done after he reaches the dummy or it will confuse him. So toss the dummy so, if necessary, you can get between it and him to short-circuit his disobedience. Stop him. Take him back. Set him down, ungently. Make him stay for a few moments. Then order and wave him in to fetch.

When you give the command to retrieve, the dog should be at the spot he should have stopped at had he obeyed properly and you should be at your original post. If during the returning-to-position interim the dog has forgotten about the dummy, direct him to the area with hand signals (the wave in the direction you want him to go). You then are taking advantage of a foul-up to get in some additional training. This sort of practice is good for Hobo. Praise him when he completes his retrieve.

But Hobo surprised you and did it right! He kissed the ground with his fanny and didn't break. Just keep him steady for a few moments, then send him to fetch in the normal manner. Spread out over an hour or two afield you may be able to instill this response in a single session, and you'll reinforce it if, on occasion, you make him hold his steady position for quite some time, leaving no doubt in his mind that he must stay put until sent on.

When They Run

During this same training stroll, begin stopping him without gunfire or dummies. When he's busily working, hit him with the whistle. He should stop and sit, same as at home. (If he doesn't, get out there and make him.) Hold him in position as you walk toward him. Then cast him off with a wave of your arm in conjunction with the release command and insist that he move off in the direction indicated.

Even though your spaniel hunted within gun range during the open

178

season, he probably encountered more than one running pheasant and hot-footed it after the bird, flushing it out of gun range at the end of a corn-row.

You are now taking the first step toward being able to stop your flushing dog when he's on the line of a sprinting cock Pheasant so you can close the gap between the dog and yourself and have a chance to shoot when the bird flushes. This training session and the subsequent ones to be outlined will also help solve the problem of having Hobo shagging after a bird you've missed or one you've passed up, costing time and energy, and perhaps wild-flushing other game during this unauthorized chase.

Once Hobo has learned that a shot and a bird in the air mean "sit and stay" and retrieves are started only from a sitting position—it may take two, it may take twenty sessions—you are ready to move from dummies to live birds.

Ready for Birds

If you can afford it pheasants or other game farm birds are fine. But you are going to need more than one or two birds so I suggest pigeons, which fly strong and far and are cheap. You also need an assistant who is a good shot.

Put your birds out as you did for your pup's basic training. Have him flush two or three, allowing them to fly off without being shot at. But when he puts his bird up, hit him with the whistle. If he skids to a halt, wonderful! Get to him, heap on the praise, then cast him off.

But since you've allowed him to chase flushed birds during the hunting season (or you should have if he was between six and eighteen months and in his first season) this remembrance is likely to set him off in pursuit of the flushed pigeon despite your whistle blast and shouts. Figure on it. When he goes with the bird, *get on him*.

He knows what the whistle blast means and he's responded to it when being worked under gunshot with dummies. He's defying you. Transmit your dismay to him. If he'll stop after a short chase go to him, grasp him by the loose skin on each side of the throat just under the ears and shake him up. (This shake is a very effective way to discipline a dog, perhaps because it simulates the way a bitch punishes a pup, avoids a lot of flailing around with a leash or whip and allows control over the dog should he get resentful and try to bite.) Then plunk him back where he should have sat and make him stay put for a time. If you can't catch him 'cause he chased out of the country, wait for him to come back, then take him to the place he flushed, do your

179

scolding and make him stay for a time. Then have your next bird planted and move on to it.

Once he is steady to wing (the flying bird with no shot), ring in the shotgun. You'll have your hands full with the dog. That's the reason for having your good-shot buddy along. Have your partner do the gunning.

Also, during the "no shoot" portion of these sessions, you may find some pigeons you allowed to fly free will eventually wing back over you. If you have your dog under control at that time, no sense wasting them. Sit and stay your dog and have your gunner drop the bird. Watching a bird in flight, the shooting and the marking of falls at different angles are all excellent experience for a gun dog. Just make sure he remains steady until sent. That's what you are training for in these sessions.

It may seem tragic to let some planted birds get away without shooting at them. But there is a reason for starting to steady a flusher on game without shooting it. If you shoot the bird and your dog breaks, he'll be on the bird before you can get to him or it. For you can not control the bird's flight as you did the dummy in your introductory lessons. That then knocks out the chance to intercept the dog, punish him and put him in his place. You have to let him make his retrieve and praise him for it, just as you did when he was hunting when he got the notion that's the way it's supposed to be done.

Now you must teach him that he fetches only when told to. But in putting such manners on a dog, you do not want to reduce his desire or confuse him regarding his retrieving duties. So you must steady to wing before moving up to the ultimate, steady to shot.

What's more, once a dog has been trained not to chase a free flying bird, probably a majority of hunters will be willing to halt training right there. You can if you want to. This assumes that if a hen Pheasant, for example, gets up, and there is no shooting you want your dog to stay put—no shot, no chase. But it may be that in the instances when you shoot you want your spaniel to break shot, figuring he will get onto the dead or crippled bird faster when it is hit and you will, therefore, accept a short chase should the bird be missed.

Start Shooting

Making a dog steady to shot is largely an extension of steadying to wing. You prepared Hobo by having him stop for random shots afield and he's steady to wing. Now have your partner start shooting the birds. When you do this, if the dog breaks to make a retrieve, use every means possible to halt him—whistle, yells, grabbing—*before*

180

he reaches the bird. If you don't stop him, shrug it off, accept delivery without comment and start over. You can't punish or scold. But don't let him think you are happy about his disobedience.

If you do stop him before he gets to the bird, drag him back and make him stay steady until you send him. If he has a memory lapse, direct him to the bird with hand signals.

He may put it all together. After all, he's been taught to stop when a shot is fired. He's also been steadied to flush. If "naturally" or at your command Hobo stays steady to shot, don't hold him too long at first. Send him as soon as the bird hits the ground. Then gradually make him sit steady for longer periods until you can trust him completely — well, almost completely. No matter how well-trained, there has never been a dog whelped who won't break under any circumstances.

The gunner you select is very important. He should be the collected type who will pass up shots that might endanger you or the dog, but score at every opportunity because it is important to get these birds down for the dog. It helps if he knows something about dogs and understands what you are trying to do. What he *must* know is that he shoots only when the dog remains steady. To do otherwise will defeat the purpose by allowing the dog to think he'll have a bird to fetch regardless of his behavior.

Hand Signals

Chances are the response you get to the hand signals casually taught as part of your dog's repertoire when afield, outlined in this and other chapters on spaniel training, will fulfill your desires regarding hand signals, which for spaniels are largely a matter of reminders to stay put and guides to change direction.

But spaniels can be taught the same precise responses to arm waves as the retrievers can and if you want your spaniel to do more than stop or proceed in the general direction of an arm wave, as you've already trained him to do, please turn back to the section in this chapter devoted to "Advanced Retriever Training."

Wet Work

Whether it is an American Water Spaniel (which was developed as a "skiff dog" for the duck hunter), Springer or even a Cocker Spaniel, every good gun dog spaniel should be expected to do some water retrieving. Except under extreme conditions, spaniels can be expected to retrieve all the ducks the present law allows a sportsman to shoot and to work very well when upland hunts require retrieving from or across water and in bogs and marshes.

181

You want a water-loving spaniel. To get one and train one, again, please page back to the instructions in the section on "Advanced Retriever Training" in this chapter.

Runners

If enough game is shot over a gun dog, he will eventually learn how to cope with running birds and collect lightly hit game that makes its escape by legging it or skulking. But before a dog's first season, or in the absence of game abundance, a gun dog can be taught to work cripples and runners.

Spaniels should be good at this task. Most take to it naturally because they hunt by utilizing both foot and body scent, in contrast to the hound that trails primarily by foot scent and the pointing breeds that work mostly from body scent. To do some training on tracking and producing running birds please refer to this subject in the section on "Advanced Retriever Training" in this chapter.

Early Breaking

Some very competent dog people will assert that a spaniel should be completely yard-broke and steady before he is ever hunted. I respect that opinion but disagree with it, very strongly. What you and I are after is a hunting dog. I do not want any portion of the "hunt" knocked out of him before he ever discovers what the game is all about. Too early discipline can do this and you can't instill desire or restore spirit.

To instill complete control over a dog when afield can require some pretty stringent corrective measures. If applied too early or without considered judgement, they can retard a dog's natural development. Furthermore, many dogs can not take the pressure necessary to the development of a really finished gun dog, much less the requirements of a field trial performer.

So don't fret about having a completely broke spaniel until you've put a couple seasons of hard hunting on him. You got him to hunt with and if you wait until you develop perfection you'll miss out on a lot of shooting and you may never get your dog afield.

True, some training is necessary. But it takes hunting, hunting and more of the same to develop a really great gun dog. Yours will never get too much of it. Finally, you may very well be satisfied with a "half-broke" or not overly obedient dog as long as he gets you shooting and picks up what you've knocked down.

But if you've been lucky enough to acquire a pup of good natural ability it behooves you to carry him as far as he'll go so he'll be a truly great gun dog. But take your time and put the training on him after he's shown you he has the stuff to take advantage of your tutelage.

If that still doesn't convince you and you want to be serious and formal from the start, exercising rigid control early, bear in mind that you may get away with cracking down quickly on a tough, aggressive rascal, but it is mandatory that you go easy and encourage, rather than discourage, the softer, more conscientious individual.

Speaking Frankly

Hunting behind a good flushing dog, whether spaniel or retriever, is *not* a leisurely pastime. Particularly when hunting pheasant, which often flush some distance from the dog, there will be times when you have to hustle to move up within gun range when your dog's animation indicates he is working a bird.

So be on your toes and prepared to get your rear in gear when hunting with a flushing dog. To put birds into the air, a gun dog must push them *hard*. The slow cautious dog may never close with a bird or at best wastes a lot of time and may lack the necessary desire and drive to really bust tough cover. So if you have a hot dog, accept in good grace occasional wild flushes, particularly in light cover.

You should get to see at least one Springer Spaniel field trial in order to see just what a top spaniel can be trained to do. But recognize that you may not be able to, and perhaps should not try to, emulate some of the things professional trainers elicit from their charges.

Never call your spaniel off a hot line, as is sometimes done in trials where the birds are planted and a dog must stay on a prescribed beat. But when hunting, that running bird (or the one that doubles back behind you) may be the only one you'll see all day. You can't afford to have him escape or lose a crippled bird by calling a gun dog off and confusing him. Stop him if you can. Catch up and send him on. Or, in desperation, leg it to stay up with the dog.

The gun dog who doesn't know the meaning of "quit" and hunts hard and long will seldom be rock-steady. I for one have never had a really good spaniel or retriever I trusted implicitly to stay steady in every *hunting* situation. Training sessions, yes. But when actually gunning, no.

So, let's provide an explanation—or excuse—for our gun dog's bad manners, as compared to what can be accomplished in flushing dog control as exemplified in field trial performance.

In a field trial for spaniels, the handler's responsibility is the dog. He can concentrate on seeing that what he's trained the dog to do is carried out. Dogs sense when you are "on them." Even if they decide to have a fling at disobedience, alert handlers can anticipate such a move and avert it with a quick command.

The hunter can not concentrate on his dog. He's got to shoot the bird or birds produced. This takes concentration in itself. Dogs sense when you've "lost touch." Take your eyes off a dog for the seconds it takes to swing on a flushing bird and shoot and friend dog is on his way. He can hardly be disciplined when he returns, bird in mouth.

All of which is to say that if, despite your best efforts, your dog comes unglued when hunting even if he has had manners put on him during the training sessions, the world hasn't come to an end. No one will cuss a dog much if he breaks shot as long as you can stop him from chasing more than 40 or 50 yards should the bird be missed. While we should set a polished, mannerly performance as our goal, we must also accept with equanimity the very real possibility that we won't quite attain it.

Advanced Pointing Dog Training

A mannerly pointing dog is a joy to behold, a true canine gentleman and a great credit to his trainer. In a preceding chapter, "Pointing Dog Training," you've already learned how to train your dog in the two most important Emily Post requirements, handling response and stanch pointing.

But you may well want to go a bit further, putting on the gloss that is represented by such necessities or niceties as being steady to wing and shot, backing, stopping to flush and some variants of tried and true training procedures. So let's kick off with that logical extension of stanchness, steadiness to wing and shot, explaining once again that stanch and steady deal with two different degrees of manners.

A stanch-on-point dog is one who will hold the point he has established on game until it is properly flushed by the hunter. In other words, he does it right by not jumping in and flushing game he has found, but may chase as soon as the birds get into the air.

A dog that is steady to wing will retain his pointing posture throughout the flush but will break and chase when the gun is fired. This is called "breaking shot". A dog steady to wing *and* shot will not leave his position until after the shooting is over, moving out on command to either retrieve downed birds, hunt singles off a covey flush or seek a new covey.

Steadiness to wing and shot is generally accepted as the mark of a "broke" dog, a requirement in field trials but seldom seen in gun dogs that regularly and as part of their normal hunting procedure retrieve shot birds.

Steadying

When working on making your dog steady you can do with an assistant. It is difficult to do alone. A helper to flush and shoot the birds while you work on your dog will greatly facilitate things.

There's a good chance you've already introduced your dog to a "check cord," a long length of rope attached to his collar, if you've had difficulties making him stanch on point. If not, do so now.

Plant a dizzied game bird or pigeon. If you are sure of your dog's stanchness, you can confine it in a release trap (See chapter on "Training Devices and Accessories"). But if you are doubtful about his stanchness or immediate response to "Whoa!" do not use the trap. If your dog fouls up, you want the bird to escape. Finding out he can catch them can make a confirmed flusher of him. But by the time you are ready to work on this gamut, your dog should be reliably stanch. If he isn't, train him to be as has been outlined.

Fasten the check cord to his collar and turn him loose, if you want to do this as naturally as possible. If you want this to be a mechanical lesson, hang onto the end of the check cord and more or less steer him into the bird where he can wind and point it.

When the dog points, caution and praise him, work up the check cord toward him, pet and reassure him. Have your assistant flush and shoot. Use blanks here if you wish. During the first few flushes, you are not going to kill the birds. Let them fly off. Your dog should have had some hunting experience by this time and probably has been breaking and retrieving. The falling bird will only tempt him to go.

Hopefully, he will hold steady as you remind him to "Whoa!" when the bird goes out and during the shooting. Likely he won't. All too seldom is the easy way your lot. If he starts but stops at your shout of "Whoa!" that's great, too. Move up to him, praise him stroke him, then tap him on the head and send him on. You may be able to work this bird again if your companion has marked it down, or put out another.

If he doesn't obey, brace yourself. When he hits the end of the cord, rare back and tip him over. A few such experiences should hold your wing and shot breaker or bring him to a screeching halt when you holler "Whoa!"

When he regains his feet, *do not* whip him, bawl hell out of him or otherwise add to the punishment he's already been dealt by the collar and cord. Matter-of-factly haul him back to the place he pointed, set him up in pointing pose, stroke and praise him. He tangled with the cord because he disobeyed a command. He should learn that standing properly is praiseworthy.

If you have a soft dog, it might even be wiser to have a reliable assistant do the check cording while you do the flushing and shooting if this meting out of punishment seems to adversely affect your relationship with the dog. But seldom is this necessary, unless your dog is that provoking combination of sensitive and stubborn.

Keep at your dog until he is reliably steady and you can move out in front without an assistant, flush and shoot, stopping him with a "Whoa!" if he does forget his manners. Steadying to wing and shot is mostly a mechanical process and actually is a single training step. Requiring *complete* steadiness to shot, as well as to wing, is stretching the step into a stride.

You must use some judgement, since too harsh discipline, too frequently without just cause may turn a dog to blinking birds, a subject discussed in the problems section of this chapter.

Alternative or Reinforcement

Another steadying procedure I use, which varies from the more or less traditional technique outlined above, may be used as an alternative method or to reinforce what your dog has already learned when you are fooling with him in the yard.

He must know how to retrieve and be responsive to the "Whoa!" command. Let him frisk around in the yard or afield when you've taken him out. Holler "Whoa!" and when he stops, raise your left arm (if you are right-handed) cautioning him to stay put and throw a dummy. When it lands, send him to fetch it. If he breaks, stop him (Whoa!), set him back where he should have stayed. When he's doing this well, use a blank pistol in left hand high above head (same cautioning gesture) shoot and throw. When he holds steady awaiting your command, send him to fetch.

You can also frequently drill your dog on "Whoa!" when you have him out so that regardless of where he is or what he is doing he will stop and await praise and further instructions upon command. You'll find this invaluable in matters of stop to flush and backing.

As an added precaution, when cracking down on your dog to teach and enforce steadiness, it is politic to use pigeons rather than work him on birds he will be expected to hunt. Then if you should get too harsh and he develops an aversion to birds it is better that it be the scent of a pigeon than a game bird you prize.

When using dizzied birds or one confined to release traps during training sessions, take time to fool with your dog, lifting tail, stroking, pushing
into birds. This will increase stanchness and assure you your dog will hold
his point until you get to him.

Two other forms of mannerliness which are closely allied to steadiness are "stopping to flush" and "backing". I believe these to be more
important to most hunters than complete steadiness and they can be
readily taught if your dog knows what "Whoa!" means and knows you
mean what you say when you say it.

Stopping to Flush

Sometimes it is difficult to decide which is which, but there is a difference between a "stop to flush" (a credit to the dog) and a "flush and
stop" (a black mark on his performance). While a dog should be given
the benefit of the doubt, if the doubt exists in your mind "hold your
fire".

A stop to flush is no fault of a dog's. When a spooky bird or one
accidently bumped when the wind is the wrong way takes off, a
mannerly dog halts, watches it fly and refrains from chasing. That is a
stop to flush.

But when a dog deliberately knocks his bird or birds, either by
crowding too close, creeping in, or banging in and taking them out,
even if he "Whoas!" on your angry and startled command, that is a
flush and stop. It should never be honored with a shot. If he flushes

During a Missouri quail hunt, Stupido, a young Pointer, locks up on a single bird. Dave Duffey cautions his hunting partner to wait before moving in to flush so he can reinforce what the Pointer does naturally with a simple praise training procedure.

Duffey starts stroking and reassuring the intent young Pointer while the partner stands on the ready to shoot in case the bird flushes during this activity.

Duffey strokes, pushes on and praises the young dog which serves to make him hold tighter and lets him know he's done and is doing the right thing. Satisfied that the dog has the idea and is holding properly and stylishly, the hunting partner moves in to kick out the bird which flushes and swings to the right. Still not having been steadied to wing and shot, the young dog goes with the bird and the hunters go into action.

The bird makes a crazy loop around the cover's edge and Duffey turns to take him going away, since the hunting partner cannot safely shoot at the bird. It is important to kill the bird, both for the dog's reward for good work and to give him practice retrieving.

The shot connected and the hunting partner who knows his way around dogs stands quiet while Duffey concentrates on trying to get Stupido, who retrieved the quail, to deliver to hand.

When a young dog makes a mistake and goes with his bird, he should be brought back to the scene of his crime, whoaed, styled-up and talked to before being sent on to hunt.

and stops on command, a severe tongue lashing may suffice. If he chases, lay on the real thing when you get your hands on him and stand him up near where he misbehaved.

You may shoot and kill birds over a legitimate stop to flush, should you be in range or if the bird comes toward you when you are out of range. With Ruffed Grouse or any species in a spooky mood, these shots may be all you get. This is in keeping with the axiom that you honor only proper work. In any event, always Whoa! your dog when the bird is in the air and insist he stay put until you send him on, or until you shoot if you allow him to break shot.

Backing

If you never work your dog with another, "backing," the honoring by one dog of another dog's find and point, may be something you'll skip in the realm of manners.

But if you go afield with other men who also own gun dogs or you like working a brace of dogs yourself, it is a must. For backing is not only the mark of a gentleman, but is vital if friendships are to continue and a well-broke dog should not be subjected to this breach of manners by a jealous, glory grabbing thief.

Any dog that moves in front of another dog on point to stake a claim on that find, or even worse, charges in to knock another dog's birds, is a thief, pure and simple, or worse.

If you are lucky, the teaching of a dog to back, will be relatively simple. It can also take considerable drill and work. It is essential that your dog know "Whoa!" the most basic thing in a pointing dog's lexicon. If he knows this you may teach him to back when afield, actually hunting. But if your hunting opportunities shared with an honest, well broke dog are limited you may have to train artificially, in much the same manner as steadying to wing and shot.

When he is instantly obeying a "Whoa!," a dog should learn backing on command relatively quickly. When he is in the vicinity of another dog who is pointing stanchly, "Whoa!" him, even though he may not yet have seen the dog, chiefly to avoid his messing up the other dog's work. Make him hold where he stands. He'll spot the other dog when you or the other hunter move in to flush. When the birds go and the shooting starts, and this is repeated a number of times, your dog will associate a stand by another dog with the production of birds. This in turn will lead to his "backing on sight", a voluntary honor of another dog's find that will warm your belly like a belt of good booze on a damp day.

But it will take plenty of opportunity and repetition to assure an automatic back by your dog whenever he spots a stationary dog. In the instances where the pointing dog is obscured and your dog doesn't see him, he must learn to back on command to avoid interfering with his bracemate. But once a dog learns to back on sight, he probably will lock up whenever he spots anything stationary, a weather-whitened stump or anything else resembling a dog on point.

If this opportunity does not exist or if you have been working your dog with a dog that false-points and he is sceptical of birds being produced, you may have to resort to more mechanical training.

Get a reliable, well broke dog, who won't be distracted or spoiled by your commands to your dog, set up on point on either a wild or planted bird. Bring your dog in on a check cord. When he catches sight of the other dog "Whoa!" him immediately, stroke and praise as you do when he's on a point of his own. If you bring him in so he can also get a whiff of bird scent this will facilitate matters.

When the bird has been flushed and shot for the other dog (you should have an assistant to do this, but if your dog is steady you can try it) cast him off. If he doesn't seem to be catching on or doesn't seem to see the other dog, take him in close for a noseful of scent. When he points (and this will be a point on scent rather than an honor) pick him up and drop him a few feet *behind* the pointing dog and make him hold there until the flushing and shooting are over.

Retrieving

The difference between "natural" and "forced" retrieving has already been discussed, pointing out that my reference to a natural retriever does not mean a dog that fetches only when *he* feels like it. But the natural inclination of many, if not most dogs, to pick up and carry should be utilized to the utmost in making a reliable fetcher of birds out of any gun dog.

In fact, I use the willingness or unwillingness of any pup (regardless of breed) to pick up, carry and come back in your direction with an object as an indicator of how easy or hard he may be to train. In my experience, pups that will "retrieve naturally" are the ones that "break easily" and often learn what's expected of them with a minimum of formal training, regardless of what you are trying to get across to them.

With retrievers and spaniels, play training at retrieving should start at a very early age and they can be well versed in the art before they've ever encountered birds. There has been and is a valid reason for delaying retrieving training in pointing dogs until after they've had some experience with birds and are pointing stanchly. The basis for this delay rests on the possibility that, having "caught birds" by retrieving them, a young pointing dog will try to catch everything rather than pointing it.

Some pointing dogs are not allowed to retrieve at all for fear it will affect their stanchness or later steadiness to wing and shot. Others have their training delayed until they are a year or two old and then usually must be force-broken to fetch. If you have field trial aspirations for your pointing dog, that will be the best program to follow.

But for most hunters, recovery, at least, of what is shot is of prime importance to them, even if they do not require a complete snappy retrieve and clean delivery. So I am suggesting that it is worth the risk of requiring more work to stanch and steady a dog to do at least a little elemental work on retrieving at an early age, following much the same timing and procedure as previously outlined for the flushing breeds.

This is particularly true of the Versatile pointing breeds of which a high proportion have strong natural retrieving instincts, as do a lesser but significant number of the traditional Pointers and setters.

Since you may expect some water work from the Versatile breeds or

193

Hunters who pause to admire the picture of a mother and son point and back on game birds before moving in to shoot, get greater enjoyment out of a day in the field.

the setters, you can double-up this facet of training with play-training to retrieve, taking every advantage of the pup's natural inclinations with little risk of affecting his instincts to point and hold.

Simply have your pupil do all his fetching out of water. Then you will have instilled the elements of picking up, carrying and returning to you; but when he encounters his first birds afield, it will be in another element and his strong instinct to lock up won't be watered down by the fun he's had fetching. After you've stanched him, you can progress to having him fetch both on land and in water quite easily.

As pointed out in the chapter, "Pointing Dog Training," you may find your youngster picking up the first birds shot over him, thereby recovering the birds or making at least halfbutted retrieves for you. By all means encourage this.

But you may make virtually sure that this will happen. Your dog will become a reliable fetcher of game if you give him some play and more serious practice with retrieving dummies, or throw dead birds from puppyhood on and link up the simple transition from artificial to actual.

But you may find some of the pointing breeds reluctant to pick up or, if they pick up readily, inclined more than the flushing breeds to clamp down too hard, play or chew rather than carry and deliver properly. They may require force-training to retrieve.

Mechanical Fetching

I'd just as soon not write this section. Telling someone how to force-train a dog to retrieve is just as tedious as the actual doing. There are force-broke dogs who do their work happily. Others treat it for what it is to them—a rather distasteful chore they have to do. For in essence mechanical fetching is instilled by a procedure that makes a dog do what he is not inclined to do in order to avoid a painful alternative.

I am inclined to look on it as a last resort measure. As such it must be carried out all the way, once started. If you want to turn out a satisfactory retriever don't start unless you are prepared to take it all the way.

Have your dog sit or stand steady and with the retrieving dummy in your right hand say, "Take It!" or "Dead!" As you say it open the dog's mouth by grasping his lower jaw, sliding your thumb into his mouth and pressing his lip against his teeth. Immediately slip the dummy into his mouth. The dummy can be anything from a piece of broomstick to a regular dummy but success will come faster the smaller the object.

You may have to hold his jaws closed to keep it there, but keep it in his mouth as you repeat, "Hold it! Hold it!" or something similar. You must persevere, even if it means a tussle. If he holds it by himself, tap him lightly under the chin to encourage keeping his head up and his mouth closed on the dummy. Lowering his head usually means a dropped dummy so keep him looking up at you as you stand bent over in front of him.

When you tell him to "Drop!" squeeze his lip against his teeth if he won't release as you draw the dummy from his mouth. He may be eager to spit it out, but tell him "Drop!" none the less.

After he will accept and release the dummy, back off a step or two cautioning him to "Hold!" He should sit or stand and hold while you walk around him, a procedure similar to the "Stay!" training routine except that he is holding something.

Then step back and call him to you. Praise him highly if he does and brings the dummy along, just as you praised when he held correctly. If he drops the dummy as he comes to you, cram it back into his mouth and tell him harshly to "Hold!" He must learn to hang on until you tell him to "Drop!"

195

Pointers are not as inclined towards natural retrieving as spaniels and retrievers, but they can be dummy-trained in order to insure recovery of shot birds. Here Twist, as a nine-month old, picks up a wing-wrapped dummy.

Once he is coming to you carrying the dummy, have him walk at heel carrying. If he's assured he's doing right he'll come to be proud of this and you can have some fun having him carry packages or newspapers for you.

You have forced the dummy on him. Now he must "voluntarily" open his mouth to take and release it. To get him to open up without your prying fingers, you pinch an ear, squeeze a paw, or apply pressure with a spiked training collar. See the "Training Devices and Accessories" chapter. When the dog opens his mouth in protest, or to take hold of your hand, insert the dummy. Say "Take It!", pinch, insert. Immediately let up on the pinch (pressure between thumbnail and forefinger) and order "Hold!" If he's been completely drilled on his previous lessons he should do it.

There is no short-cutting in this procedure. It's one step at a time. It takes more than one or two lessons. Keep at it once or twice a day but never for more than about ten minutes.

Twist starts in a bit reluctantly but carries firmly and gently.
Confident now that she'll be praised for her efforts, she comes in happily
with her "bird."

It shouldn't be difficult for a pleased sportsman to take time to admire
the game his dog has produced and let the dog know he is happy with him.

When he's learned to take the dummy on command, opening his
mouth when you say "Take It!" so you can put it there, start to lower
the dummy toward the floor or ground when you tell him to "Take It!"
so he must reach for it a bit.

You may have to push his head down toward the lowered dummy
until he gets the idea. The next task is to get him to pick it off the floor
on command.

When he will pick up the dummy placed on the floor, drop it in
front of him and order the pick-up. When he does that readily, toss
it a couple of feet and tell him to "Take It!" If he's reluctant, try teasing him with the dummy before you toss so he'll want to grab or chase.
Gradually increase the distance you toss the dummy. Never forget to
praise when the dog does right, comes close to it, or makes any com-
mendable effort. Keep working to get it completely right.

Once he will go and pick-up, if he doesn't want to return to you
when you say "Here! Fetch!" attach a long lead or rope to his collar
and toss just a few feet so he can reach it without the lead tightening.

Then draw him back to you when he picks up, repeating the "Here! Fetch!" until he will turn and come without being pulled. Then work him off the lead.

Once this is accomplished you're almost home. Turn now to giving retrieving practice as outlined in the instructions for working a dog who has learned this trade in a more natural manner. If he balks, go back over the steps you've used to force train him. Since you want him to retrieve shot birds, you should use dead pigeons or at least a wing-taped dummy as a substitute for the stick or whatever you started with once he's willing to hold the dummy on command. He learns that he must pick-up and hold *anything* you tell him to and he'll be ready for the first real bird you throw or shoot.

'Specially for Versatiles

While the Versatile or Continental pointing breeds *are* distinctly different and this difference should be recognized, there is no real reason to write a book dealing exclusively with this category of dogs.

However, there are a few things that will aid the would-be trainer of German Shorthairs, Brittanies and the other utility gun dogs previously mentioned by breed and lumped into this classification.

You must understand that these dogs, with the possible exception of the Brittany were not bred and developed as specialists like the traditional pointing breeds or the retrievers. They were intended as multi-purpose workers who pointed and retrieved on land, fetched from water if necessary and capable of working both feather and fur. Traditionally the American hunter has looked askance at a bird dog that pointed rabbits. But if you should choose to utilize your Versatile gun dog for this purpose there's no real reason why you shouldn't and you will find him willing and able.

Your Versatile gun dog can be trained to hunt and point in the manner outlined in this book for training *any* pointing dog. Your favorite breed can learn his fetching duties via the routine recommended for the flushing breeds, spaniels and retrievers.

In a sense, that is the key to understanding your Versatile gun dog. He was intended and is a combination pointer-retriever. The breeds selected to "make-up" these new breeds were of those two specialist persuasions, the Britt again rating as an exception. In temperament and ability they are a meld of the qualities one looks for in a retriever on one hand and the traditional Pointer on the other.

But I would not, and you should not, expect the confirmed "Pointer man" or the admirer of Labradors to be readily sold on the virtues of the Versatiles as specialists or even as combination dogs.

199

But don't let that bother you. The criteria of a good dog is how well he satisfies his owner. The Versatiles are practical and will satisfy most hunters. If you care to specialize or are disappointed in your individual dog, try a traditional pointing breed or a retriever. It could be your personality just doesn't mesh with that of an individual dog or what is generally expected of an entire breed.

You are virtually sure to find the Versatile breeds, largely German in origin, highly intelligent and begging for training and discipline. They respond to firm, no-nonsense treatment and become bored only when neglected. If they do not receive attention and training they will devote their energies to destructiveness and make noise. Make companions as well as gun dogs of these breeds wherever possible.

The Brittany is a special case, responding best to "kid-gloved" treatment and patient coaxing in contrast to the militaristic drill and stress that other Versatiles seem to thrive on. While often aloof, as compared to the other spaniels which *do not* point, the Brittany is essentially a "soft" dog, just as the Golden is among the retrievers.

Natural and Easy

There are some dogs that will never be stanched on point without a lot of hollering, whipping and jerking around with a check cord. But there are lots of others that can be stanched on point without all that fuss.

Therefore, it behooves a trainer to try the natural and easy way first. Chances are good it will work out. If it doesn't no damage has been done the dog, no bad habits instilled and the mechanical procedures can be instigated to force the dog to do what he won't do naturally.

Essentially this system, which I use myself and stumbled onto because it seemed to work with most of the pointing dogs I was training, consists of keeping your mouth shut, interfering as little as possible with a young dog's natural reactions and rewarding rather than punishing.

With most well-bred individual pups of the pointing breeds, whether traditional or modern, the instinct to point is very strong. You have discovered this, or will, when taking your gun dog afield. Virtually every pup will "flash point" instinctively when the scent hits him just right, some will even stop when they see a bird in the air —so ingrained is the pointing instinct.

Some dogs hesitate so briefly before jumping in to flush and chase that it hardly seems fair to describe that pause as even a "flash point." But in time these youngsters will come to holding point longer. Other

200

youngsters lock up and remain mesmerized by the scent, and will hold stanch until distracted.

If you are alone in the field with your young gun dog, as you should be, there are only two things that will readily distract. The birds themselves and *you*. As long as the birds hold tight, it is a good bet that the dog will hold tight. Most youngsters will dive in and flush only when the bird moves and they can see it as well as smell it.

However, I'm convinced that over-anxious, over-eager trainers cause youngsters to become unglued when they charge up to a pup on point, verbally cautioning or ordering him to stay put. If the birds cooperate and you walk up quietly, chances are very good your dog will hold and you'll be well on your way to stanching him, regardless of whether the birds flush as you get close or hold until you have time to stroke and pet your locked up pup and then go out to flush.

Let's take the typical trainer reaction when he sees his pride and joy, still really a puppy, slam into a point. The sight will stop a man in his tracks and stultify his physical and mental processes. He's pointing almost as surely as the dog.

But rational, thinking man recovers much faster. He becomes apprehensive and wishful. "God! I hope he holds". With that he starts running toward his dog.

As he rushes up he converses with his dog, crooning praise or encouragement or shouting commands. "Good boy! Good dog! Easy boy, Easy! Hold it! Hold It! Easy! Whoooaaup! Whoa! Whoa! Dammittohell anyway!"

What happened? It happened that the youngster didn't wait for the trainer to get close enough to be responsible for the flush or to get his hands on the pup to stroke, praise and steady him.

Instead he jumped in, pushed the bird out and disappeared in hot pursuit, the frustrated shouts of his trainer ringing in his ears. Had the trainer kept his lip buttoned all might well have gone properly.

The pup did not break because he couldn't stand the tension. That was what locked him up in the first place and he'd stay mesmerized until distracted. But the trainer's voice broke that concentration and brought the pup down to earth. When the wheels started to turn in his skull once more he couldn't resist finding out what smelled so good and where it was.

Furthermore, the human voice alerts and spooks game. It may cause game to either move or prepare for flight. Most young pointing dogs will hold as long as their quarry is still. But the slightest motion will key them up, particularly if they can see what it is they are pointing, and an overt move by the bird will trigger a chase-and-catch reaction.

The trainer's "commands" were further pointless in that at the age most young pointers start locking up, too few have yet developed reliable response to the "Whoa!" command and no dog should be expected to obey something he hasn't been taught.

So, what should *you* do. First, zip your lip. Then put your legs in gear and get to the pup. Bite your tongue as you hasten to him to prevent it's flapping. Even if the bird flushes wild, or your approach puts him up, you will be in the vicinity and it is important that the pup associate your activity or presence with the flush of the bird. He will come to understand that you, not he, are responsible for producing what he has found.

If the season is open or you are using planted birds and are toting a shotgun, if the bird gets out at your approach shoot. Kill it if you can. If such circumstances don't exist, discharge a blank or, if you have no gun, shout encouragement to the pup as the bird leaves.

If you are very lucky, both bird and dog will hold. The pup probably will for as long as the bird sits tight. Then you will be able to get your hands on the dog. This is the time to dish out verbal praise or caution him, while you are stroking and even restraining by the collar if the bird decides to leave then. If the bird still holds, push against the pup's hindquarters, as though shoving him into the bird. He'll resist and his stanchness will increase.

Should the bird hold through all this activity, leave the stanched up pup, move out into the area he is indicating and then with uplifted hand, verbally caution him to "Whoa!" while you try to get the bird into the air.

It's likely your pup will try to help you produce the bird. If verbal threats and gestures don't halt him when he moves in, grab his collar, take him back to his original stand, pose him again and go through the stroking-praising routine.

If your pup does elude you and finds and flushes the bird, or is rooting around when it gets out, while undesirable it can be accepted. The seriousness being reduced by the fact that you are in the immediate area and have played a part in flushing the bird. It is much better than having the pup bust the bird while you are some distance from him.

Unless the pup is an extremely unusual individual he will chase the flushed bird, regardless of when it elects to leave. If it flushes while you have your hands on the dog, restrain him for a couple seconds if you can. Then let him go. If the cover is thick and the bird quickly disappears the chase may be short or the pup may go to the spot the bird flew from and ran around sniffing up the scent. If it's in the open the pup will probably chase it out of sight.

Don't waste your breath yelling at the chasing dog. Take a deep breath, relax, congratulate yourself and your dog and wait for him to come back. When he does, call him to you, stand him up on point, stroke him and tell him what a good dog he is. Then tap his head, tell him "All right!" and take him on, preferably in a direction not in line with the bird's flight.

If you have killed the bird, encourage his retrieving it. If he brings you the bird, praise profusely and toss it for him to fetch a second time.

The general idea is to have the pup associate *you* or another hunter with the bird's flush, to connect the gunfire with the excitement of it all and may even demonstrate the futility of his flushing and chasing. Never shoot if he does the flushing.

Eventually the pup becomes convinced he needs you to get the bird and high praise, his rewards for doing things right. Like any training procedure it will not work with all dogs and it requires repetition. But in my estimation this "gentle-breaking", if it doesn't do the whole job, will at least help in the training for four out of five young dogs who are worth taking afield.

Starting with this closed mouth approach will never harm a dog and may even salvage sensitive individuals who would be cowed by the tried and true mechanical means, which can always be resorted to and have been fully explained in this book, should individual pups not respond to this technique.

12

Traveling With Your Dog

THE good old days of walking out to the edge of town to go rabbit or quail hunting are really a thing of the past for most of us.

Lucky is the man who needs to drive his car only 10 or 20 miles to get in some hunting. No one thinks much of making a 50 to 100 mile drive to get to even mediocre hunting and sportsmen drive to the far reaches of their home states or halfway across the nation to get really good hunting. When time is the essence, the avid sportsman goes by air.

For the hunting dog this has meant considerable change. No longer does he trot along with his master, to go stiff-legged and bristle-backed when a town dog challenges the passage of his master's horse and buggy. Even the baggage car of the passenger train is denied him.

Instead, he travels by motor vehicle or jet plane. Such travel is stressful and the considerate dog owner recognizes this and does the best he can to make such trips as comfortable as possible.

Virtually every hunting dog must spend some time in a motor vehicle going to or coming from the place of hunting or sleeping in it on long trips. Yet thousands of dog owners introduce their dogs to automobiles on the morning they pull out and are dismayed by the dire results. Messes to clean up or damaged car interiors may be their lot and a frightened or upset dog will prove a disappointment when afield.

So what's the magic formula for successfully transporting a hunting dog—or any dog for that matter? Like just about everything else involving dogs it depends upon proper introduction, adequate experience, equipment and the common sense of the dog's handler.

If a hunting dog is acquired as a small puppy this introduction is simple. Just take the pup along in the car, holding him in your lap. Ideally, the trips should be short. Perhaps just around the block to start. If his first trip in an auto is a long one, like bringing him home from the kennel from which you purchased him, the lap treatment is still good. Given a chance to dump out and piddle before being taken in the car, it is surprising the high percentage of pups that will ride contentedly, snuggling next to a person.

Car sickness, on a dog's part may very well have to do with motion. But the stimulus for sickness is usually fright, tension and nervousness or a restless discomfort brought on by the call of nature or excess energy. So play with the puppy to tire him and get him to relieve himself, withhold water for at least an hour before starting on the trip and above all quietly reassure him so he will relax and accept the strange smell, noise and motion which is the interior of a motor car.

If you are afraid of an "accident" soiling your clothing, then fix a box with soft bedding and put it on the car seat next to a passenger who will pay attention to the pup.

Vomiting is usually preceded by drooling and if this occurs or the pup starts retching, if you can pull over to the side of the road without hazard to your vehicle, other traffic and the pup, bail out with him and he may settle down. Actually, with a very small pup (under 10 weeks of age) it is no great concern if he should suffer an upset stomach his first trip. For seldom, as in the case of an older dog, will this be the start of habitual almost conditioned reflex. Just have some old newspapers or other absorbent material on hand to soak up and clean up.

An older dog may require more careful introduction, depending upon the temperament of the individual dog. If your dog is kept as a companion as well as a hunting dog seldom is there any problem. The dog comes to love the car because it means going with you.

If your dog seldom is in the car except when you go hunting, you should expend some effort to see that he accepts the car and travel so as not to be a nuisance. You may want to coax him into the car with you. Or if he is trained to do so, order him to "kennel" or "get in." Then sit with him and talk and pet him before you start the car and drive off.

If possible take a drive of 20 miles or less to a place where the dog can get out and run, hunt or be trained. Do this a few times and the dog will come to associate the car with being with you and doing something he likes to do. In a short while he'll be dancing around at the car door wanting in. I had an English Cocker who used to go everyplace with me. He'd get in and curl up on the back seat and never move until we'd go off the hard surfaced road. Then he'd be up standing with front feet on the front seat looking around. He knew back roads meant going hunting.

There are near-ideal or at least superior vehicles in which to haul dogs. The family car is not one of them. But if it's all a man has, it has to do. The easiest thing is to let the dog sit on the seat. Many owners do this because it doesn't involve much training. If you don't mind dog hair, moisture and mud on the seat and the dog sits or lies quietly so he's no hazard to the driver or passengers, this is okay.

But if there's room (there isn't in the sportier models) everyone is better off and the dog is safer in case of panic stops or accidents if he's taught that his place is on the floor.

Field Trial Hall of Famer Herb Holmes, owner of Gunsmoke Kennels, uses a specially built truck to carry his field trial dogs. Holmes is shown with Stupido, a Pointer (Cannonade X Seairup Twist) belonging to Dave Duffey.

Most modern cars have trunks large enough to accomodate one or two dogs comfortably. Be sure there's nothing loose to fly around or be chewed up and lay an old rug or blanket on the floor. But if you utilize a car trunk be very conscious of proper ventilation. There are small ventilators that can be installed on the trunk top or fender well commercially available. Or you may find that it is easy to put a vent hole or two through the ledge between the back seat and the back window. In any event, do not drive with the trunk lid "cracked" open. Dust and exhaust fumes will be sucked up into the trunk, at best fouling up your dog's scenting powers, at worst asphixiating him. And don't park in the sun for long periods.

Speaking of ventilation, whenever you leave a dog in the car for a time, be sure to crack your windows as wide as possible but not wide enough to let the dog squeeze out and run off. In warm weather a dog can suffocate in a closed automobile. This is a horrible death and no dog should be subjected to heat prostration or even extreme discomfort in warm weather. Even in bitter cold weather a slightly opened car window will cut down on the steaming up and dog odor inside a car.

One of the greatest boons to a man who does any traveling at all with his dog or dogs is the travel crate, either commercial or homemade. They may be of wire mesh, fiberglass, plywood or aluminum construction. For many reasons, my personal preference is the collapsible wire crate. My crates are in use year around so the fold up for easy storage feature is of no importance to me. But it may be for the sportsman who uses the crates for only a few days, weeks or months of the year.

There's no question about adequate ventilation through the open wire mesh, dogs can be observed at all times, the crates are comparatively light in weight and do not block out vision through a rear-view mirror. In cold weather an old rug or blanket can be draped around or over them if the dog is to sleep crated in the car over night or manufactured canvas covers are available, keeping in body heat. However, if the crates are to be carried in an open box of a pick-up truck, the wind and rain breaking solidity of fiberglass, aluminum or plywood is preferable.

The use of travel crates presupposes the ownership of a van-type vehicle, a pick-up truck or a station wagon in which the crates can be placed. For a "dog car" that can double as a family or recreation vehicle, I don't think the van-type, cab over engine wagons can be beat. They handle and ride well, the enclosed cargo room is near-unbelievable even with the back seat installed and there is access from the front, side and rear to dogs and hunting gear.

A pick-up truck with cover or cap over the box probably rates next best with the conventional station wagon third choice. Much depends upon how many dogs and companions you want to haul and how much seat folding and removing you want to do to obtain space. Some may even opt for the short-wheel based 4-wheel drive models, (Scout, Jeep, Bronco etc.) particularly for short trips and when room for dogs, gear and passengers is not of an essence.

Travel crates can aid in car-breaking a dog, if a week or two before you plan a trip you confine the dog from time to time in the crate either in the car or in your home. He will look upon it as a familiar bed and be at home in it when the trip starts.

The large crates give the biggest gun dogs plenty of room and if two smaller dogs get along well there is room for the pair. If you are doubtful about the compatability of two dogs strange to each other,

A light trailer and van-type vehicle full of wire crates can transport a lot of dogs. Here Mike Duffey and Dale Fellman unload a Pointer on the Montana prairie.

208

two crates will keep them separated. You can leave your dog in the vehicle for extended periods or overnight without worry of damage to the interior (a bored dog, bent on destruction can really wreck the inside of a car) and in hot weather can leave windows open for plenty of ventilation with no worry about the dog's escape. Crates can be padlocked to prevent theft.

If you are burdened with one of the rare dogs who is frequently car sick, the messes will be confined to the crate. You will also find with a nervous or apprehensive dog having a tendency toward car sickness that if you position the crate crosswise in the cargo compartment rather than facing front and back it will reduce or prevent this incidence. Put to use, you will find travel crates advantageous in many more ways.

A professional in the dog game, or rarely a very serious amateur may give consideration to built in dog boxes that fit on each side of pick-up truck boxes but for most sportsmen they'd be inconvenient or impractical.

However, a dog trailer will be a practical, if somewhat costly, conveyance for the hunter who wants to transport more than one dog or doesn't want the dog inside the vehicle with him. It also allows him to buy the kind of car he wants without giving consideration to how suitable it is for canine transportation.

Like all dog transportation items, trailers have advantages and disadvantages which every owner should be aware of and consider. When two of my Pointers got tangled up with a skunk I was most happy they were in a trailer and not inside the vehicle with me.

When the day's hunt is over, on a trip, the trailer can be unhitched, left in a friend's driveway or motel parking lot with the compartments padlocked, and the dogs can sleep without being jostled around when your car is being driven to a store or restaurant. Because the glass floor is slippery I put a swatch of indoor-outdoor carpeting in each compartment. The dogs can also be fed and watered inside the compartment or they can be staked out on chains. If your dog power is limited, extra compartments can be used to stow and haul gear.

Four circular ventilators on the top and air holes in the upper part of the compartment doors provide adequate air circulation on even the hottest days when the trailer is moving. On most days during hunting seasons the dogs won't overheat when the trailer is stationary. But on hot days it should be parked in the shade to avoid extreme discomfort to dogs from heat buildup. In bitter cold there are no direct drafts on the dogs when moving and overnight with a deep bedding of hay or straw the compartments are snug and warm to the hand when opened in the morning.

When transporting your dog or dogs on hunting trips a lot of little considerations can mean the difference between full and good performance and a disappointing, half-hearted effort. So give your dog every break you can.

Before loading my dogs to take off hunting, I let them have a brief run and try to make sure they lift their legs and squat. If it's going to be a long drive, within a hour or two I start looking for a place to pull off to let them out or exercise them on a long lead. Even though they've done their duty before we left, it's my experience that after an hour or two of riding they will be ready to dump out again. Once this is done, if necessary they can stay confined for 12 to 14 hours without answering nature's call.

This is another advantage of crate or trailer compartment travel. Dogs so confined lie down and stay quiet. Moving around stimulates kidney and bowel activity. When let out and moved around they usually will eliminate quickly. Dogs that travel a lot seem to pick up the idea that's the reason they are taken out. They should also be offered a drink at exercise time.

Of course, if the drive to the hunting spot is only a matter of a couple hours, all this will be taken care of when you let them out to start hunting. But if it's a long trip be sure to plan it so you can get your dogs out before you hit a long stretch of freeway where it is dangerous to the dog, time consuming or inconvenient to stop.

Whether on long or short trips drive considerately and carefully, avoiding jack rabbit starts and panic stops and lurching around curves which can jostle or slam the dogs around. They should ride as relaxed as possible without having to tense up and brace themselves.

After a long trip, bear with your dog when you start hunting. The country and maybe even the game is going to be strange to him. The climate may be drastically different. Long travel is tiresome. Allow your dog to get acclimated. It's been my experience that it usually takes a dog at least half a day, maybe a day to get his "hunting legs" under him and his bearings straight and unless you hunt with a local man and his dog, the start of a hunt of several days may be less than you expect. On short runs this should be no problem unless you haven't accustomed your dog to the car.

But do have patience with your dog if you hunt a long way from home. If your dog is accustomed to relatively cool and damp atmosphere and you put him down the next day on the arid Nebraska or Montana rangelands, make excuses for him without apology.

Individual dogs will vary in how quickly they adjust and in how relaxed they ride. I had one Labrador that I finally hunted only "around home" because he hated travel so. After a long trip he would be physically ill, with fever and partial paralysis. A Drahthaar I had never put his head down and slept while traveling but would bounce out of the car and hunt all day with no obvious delayed effects. A Springer Spaniel of mine would curl up and sleep for the entire trip and seemed to need no adjustment period in strange country or on strange game. You may encounter dogs of all inclinations.

If you return home after a day's hunt, your dog will be well treated and happy when you let him into the house or turn him into his familiar kennel where food and water is available.

But if you are on an extended trip and the dog is literally living out of the car, at the end of the day, see to your dog before you do anything else. That hot shower, the welcome drink and the big meal can all wait until you've checked your dog for burrs and other irritations, put food and water down for him and know he's set for the night. Then you can relax and enjoy the amenities.

A tired dog may not eat right away, but he'll probably do justice to it during the night. He'll need food to work properly. Even if you feed him dry or mixed meal dog food as his basic ration, you may consider splurging on a trip and providing him with some hamburger, canned dog food or the packaged moist-dry foods which are convenient to feed and which he'll usually eat even when bone tired.

A dog who's hunted hard will sleep well during the night and probably will not have to eliminate until he is let out to start the hunt the next morning. But he should have water available to him through the night, both as a necessity to replenish the moisture he's lost and a comfort for his thirst. He'll lap it from time to time during the night.

If you eat lunch in the field share it with your dog whether it's a peanut butter sandwich or a steak scrap. A little to eat at mid-day won't make him logy and some protein, sugar or even starch may be the fuel that keeps him going.

Proper introduction to travel, the use of good equipment and some consideration on your part can mean a happy dog and sterling performance at the beginning, during and end of a hunting trip.

13

Random Tips

IN any trainer's repertoire there are assorted odd-ball things he does and ideas he has regarding dog "psychology" which do not fit neatly into the mold that makes up a manual of instruction.

Most are things picked up along the training way and may be generally or specifically applicable but are seldom scientifically provable. But they work well or have born,fruit enough so they are worth passing on for what they are—random tips and observations.

All Bets Off

The assumption throughout this book is that the reader will be starting with a pup or young dog in an effort to develop his own personal gun dog. Recommendations regarding which breed is best for what and so on have been based upon that assumption.

But if you are going out to purchase a trained or well-started gun dog, all bets are off. Breed, color, appearance or expected temperament and the expected percentage of pups that will develop properly carry no weight in this instance.

You can expect to pay a pretty stiff price for a trained gun dog, so ask the seller to demonstrate the dog's worth. If that particular dog does it like you want it done, forget the fact that he's not the breed you favor or that Dave Duffey or Herman Schlagelheimer said other breeds could do it all better. Buy the dog that does it right.

Praise and Punishment

Through the book you have frequently encountered the admonition to praise or pet your dog when he does something right. There are times when he should be punished too.

It is important to strike a balance, so that when you do raise your voice or threaten, the dog will pay attention. But when he is doing right he will perform in a confident and happy manner secure in the knowledge that he will get the welcome pat or sweet-talk that is the only reward a good dog needs.

As far as meting out punishment is concerned, I can't give you exact measures or methods. The severity of the punishment depends upon the offense and the degree of defiance of a known command.

So while your conscience must be your guide, I suggest that you will find a couple of swats across the flanks with a strap or leash, or a shaking up by grasping the dog on each side of the throat right under the ears, as the most generally effective means of making your point. Don't beat on your dog with any hard, inflexible object. You can cause serious damage you'll regret when your temper cools.

Consistency and Other Virtues

Be consistent. Do not punish for something one day and the next day let the dog get away with the same act. Don't ever give a command unless you are prepared to see it through and enforce obedience. Like children, dogs will push you to the limit of your patience if they can get away with it. That's why I don't put patience high on the list of requirements for a successful dog trainer. Some, yes. But a more useful asset is persistence. Together, persistency and consistency will assure a well trained dog.

No dog should be asked to do anything. He should be told. How firmly you tell him depends on the circumstances. But when you give a command, your dog should know you aren't just talking to him. And virtually every dog will give you just cause at one time or another to holler at him. When such a circumstance arises, go ahead and yell. Both you and the dog will be better for it.

Always encourage your dog if his *reaction* to something new or strange is good, but ignore him if it is bad. If he's leery or unresponsive to a given situation, you don't want to enforce this apprehension or failure by administering punishment. Punish only when the dog has disobeyed a command he knows and understands and has responded to consistently.

Finally, your dog must trust you. A normal dog's trusting nature is built in. It's up to you not to change this natural attitude but to reinforce it. So never fool your dog, even in play.

Believe in Your Dog

Just as your dog must rely on your probity, so must you honor your dog's ability and honesty.

When your flushing dog indicates he's making game, show your

213

interest by getting up close to him, fast. If you are out of position to kill birds for him, he might conclude the game bird species are to be ignored like all the non-game scents. The reason the dog hunts certain species and ignores "stink" birds is because you've indicated to him what you want produced.

If your pointing dog vanishes, better head for the direction you last saw him. He might not be on point. He might even be chasing some farmer's chickens. But if he is on point, get there so you can reward his find by shooting over him.

Show Him the Bird

It is all too common for a pointing dog to be doing a decent job of holding his birds, but then to start creeping in on them or diving in to bust them, particularly pheasants. You may be able to prevent or correct this by always producing a bird for an honest point.

Get down on all fours to understand this. The dog wants birds. He points. A pheasant sneaks out on him, but true to his training he holds. You come up, thrash around, produce nothing. You go back and send him on. If he relocates accurately and you get the bird up and shoot, fine. But it doesn't always happen this way. Sometimes the bird escapes and there is no shot, no mouthful of feathers.

To keep track of the bird, your dog may start creeping. Or in the hope of getting a mouthful of feathers, he dives in to catch himself. In either event, he gets to see the bird and is not frustrated. If you fail to produce for him too frequently he may conclude that his chances of getting his reward are better if he takes the initiative.

To prevent this from becoming ingrained, make every effort to get a bird up to honor his stanch point. If you fail, send him on to relocate. If he fails to lock up again, call him back to the place he originally stood, stand him up, make him hold, pull a previously shot bird out of your game pocket, walk out in front of the dog, shoot and toss the dead bird for him to fetch. You want to make sure he gets a bird by holding his point but gets nothing for breaking it.

There is a very slight risk that you will encourage "false" or "non-productive" pointing by following this procedure. But as you gain experience, you will come to know whether your dog is really on game or not and as your dog gains experience he will usually correct on his own long before you reach him. If you are positive there can be no bird where he's indicating, ignore his point and walk on. But do so at the peril that there *might* be one there. Dog training isn't cut and dried. You deal with situations as they arise and take the necessary risks.

214

Flushing Techniques

Once a dog is broke, the classic way to come up on a point is to walk in from behind, get out ahead of the dog, cautioning or praising him if necessary as you go by, and put the birds out in front of him. But in training and until your dog is reliable, approach your dog from the side or from an angle where he can see you coming in. Don't be in a dither, but don't waste time.

In the case of pheasants, particularly, you may be able to produce a bird that would otherwise sneak off if you make a loop in front of your dog and come in toward him, making the bird freeze and finally flush between you and the dog.

Reading Your Dog

Individual dogs have different pointing styles. But usually if a dog stands in cover and feathers or flags (tentatively wags his tail) he is puzzled because he has birds but he's not sure just where, or they may be moving on him.

Other than cautioning him if necessary, let him alone until he pinpoints his game and his tail goes rigid. Then produce for him. Some dogs never stop flagging, even when they have their birds dead to rights. You must learn to read your dog.

Accelerated tail whip usually means a dog is working game scent. Some dogs "road into" their birds, breaking their pace and homing in on the scent. Others break off in mid-stride and come down pointing. You can't teach a dog style. He's born with his particular set of responses. It's up to you to interpret correctly.

Some pointing dogs "soften" on point, losing their intense attitude, even cowering upon the handler's approach, or if he's a long time getting there. This may be caused by fear of punishment and you may have been overzealous in your breaking efforts. Some dogs just don't give a hoot. They relax to watch you do the rest of the job.

A crouching or low stationed point, however, is not necessarily softening. A dog may have found himself in the middle of birds because of the vagaries of scenting conditions and instinctively dropped down to avoid flushing. Some dogs just naturally crouch or set every time they point.

Even a drop or crouch as you approach, could indicate his awareness that birds are about to flush, which he wants to avoid. In years gone by, but to a very limited extent today, dogs were taught to "drop at shot" to avoid any chance of interference with the shooting.

Relocating

Smart young dogs and experienced old timers may relocate on their own when a bird moves out on them and this can be a highly valued trait. But until the youngster has proved his stanchness it is better to require him to remain stanch until you order him on to relocate bird or birds that have sneaked away from him.

When you can't get them up, walk back to your dog, pat him lightly on the head and say "All Right!" and caution him to "Be careful!" if he moves out too recklessly.

Should your dog start to move once you've started your flushing effort in front of him, do one of two things. "Whoa!" him and continue your efforts. Or stand still and let him relocate on his own.

You cannot blame the dog for being in motion when the birds get out if you are thrashing around at the same time. The rule of thumb is when the dog is relocating or making game, the hunter should stand still until the dog establishes point. Once the point is established, the dog should remain still while the hunter moves about trying to flush.

Planted Versus Natural Birds

Some dogs are high and hard on wild game, but soften and flag on planted birds, probably because they recognize the scent of man on a hand-planted bird and associate it with training sessions where discipline and restraint was applied.

Dogs that have been worked virtually exclusively on hand-planted game usually show it by an inability to properly handle native birds. To become a really great gun dog, whether pointer or flusher, the hunting dog prospect must have lots of experience on real game.

In the absence of this opportunity, the best thing an owner/trainer can do is join a hunting club where pen-raised birds are random released and the dog can gain experience hunting in the most natural manner possible. Shortly after release, pen-raised Pheasant can become nearly as wily as their wild counterparts. A gun dog can learn his trade well on these released birds.

Quail, Chukars and some of the other game bird species that may be hunted in the wild or on shooting preserves are something else again. It takes proving on wild, shot over quail to develop a real gun dog on that species and others, for the released birds are less wary and easily disturbed than wild game. A dog worked too frequently on them can develop the habit of trying to get too close before pointing, resulting in a flush of spooky native birds.

216

Handling

Too many men seem to think handling a dog in the field consists largely of blowing a whistle and waving their arms. Most important is the exercise of judgement regarding when to blow and wave. It's unfortunate that so few dogs are really handled.

Incessant shouts, whistles and gestures are worthless. They should be resorted to at the proper time and mean something. Otherwise your dog will either ignore the commands if he's independent and thinks he knows what he is doing or will become dependent upon them if he is less bold and very eager to please. Either way, it's a bad deal.

Furthermore, nothing spooks game more than a human's voice. So don't continually hack your dog with voice and whistle. But there will be times when you'll have to pin his ears back verbally. Do it, get it over with and when you've got him back on the track, let him do his thing.

A dog that handles well requires a minimum of noise, but when that shout, whistle or gesture is given, responds to it with alacrity. If you have instilled the proper responses as outlined in this book, that's just what he'll do. Then you can relax and save your vocal cords.

Easy Does It

Some men are totally unfit to train a dog properly because of their drive and temperament. They are impatient and herky-jerky in everything they do. Such attitudes are transmitted to dogs and can drive the animals batty. Around animals, a man must move sure and easy. It is no coincidence that the old time stereotype of a dog trainer depicted a less-than-ambitious country boy who didn't shake up easily.

I have with good reason cautioned my kennel help to adopt a relaxed, easy attitude around the dogs and sometimes must check myself when I get in too much of a rush. When cleaning up in the mornings, I often have 15 to 20 dogs running loose together in the exercise yard. If I'm in a hurry, strapped for time, or upset about something, I can fully expect some difficulties from the dogs as they cavort and frisk around, either in the form of fights or questioning orders I may give them. Human tension is transmitted to canines. So develop an easy, sure and casual attitude around your dog or dogs if it doesn't come natural to you.

Dock Tails

The Versatile pointing breeds and some of the spaniels have their tails cut off at an early age. Some may question why. For one thing, it has become a breed standard and be looked upon as a matter of acceptable appearance, particularly if a long tail seems out of proportion.

But the major reason is practical. Worked in thick cover, the merry tail of a stylish hunting dog can be beat bloody and remain raw through most of the season. The dock-tailed dog has no such problem. It is true, however, that in certain situations a hunter can locate a dog pointing with long tail erect in the air and the merry tail whip when the dog is working and its high style erectness are pleasing to the eye. But there is also something cute or enchanting about the eager wiggle of a stub tail. You suit yourself, short or long tail. Tail length is no criteria of a dog's ability any more than color.

Picking a Pup

If you pick out your pup and take him home at the proper time, seven to ten weeks of age, you are making your choice at a stage where cursory examination of a litter will tell you very little about the individual pups. So picking a good pup is largely a matter of luck.

The owner of a litter, if he pays close attention to the pups, may get some line on the individuals at that age. But even then, it's no sure thing. When I have a litter of pups, I usually spot a couple I favor. But if the pups are for sale, I don't withhold any from prospective buyers. The pup or pups I keep are often those passed up by others and as often as not they turn out just as well as the choice picks.

Environment and training are very important. Get your pup young and raise and train him your way. You may be lucky and get "Superdog, Jr." or you may wind up with the dunce of the litter. There are extremes in every well-bred litter. But chances are you'll get something between the extremes and he will be what you make him.

But just so you have something to go on, look for strong, straight bone, clear eyes, a good coat and an alert and interested expression. I like a pup that looks *up* at me and follows the gestures I may make or seems to study my facial expression. Play with the pups in the litter you are looking at to ascertain which ones perk up when you clap your hands, chase a thrown object or jump up on you for attention. Pick an alert, bold pup. But young pups are unpredictable. The real goer today may be a sleepy-time guy tomorrow and vice-versa. So it's pretty much a gamble.

Look in the pup's mouth to see that the upper front teeth close over the lower front teeth when his mouth is shut, neither undershot nor greatly overshot. Check the navel to make sure he's not ruptured. Avoid either a very small or a very large pup, unless you are seeking a giant or a runt. But again, growth rates of pups differ and this is only a rule of thumb.

The most practical thing you can do is to reject any pup that is kept in dirty, run-down surroundings. Be reasonable. There'll be some mess and smell around a kennel and a mess or two in the kitchen if the pups are being house-raised. But runny eyes, poor coat, bent bones or emaciation with a bloated belly are indicative of lack of concern, poor care, nutrition, sanitation and parasitic control. Such a pup is off to a poor start and it means added veterinarian bills for his purchaser.

Let Him Alone

Every now and then a dog is encountered who not only learns things well on his own, but insists that is the only way it should be done. He may balk at formal training and have nothing to do with anything artificial.

If he does a good job in the hunting field, it may be that the proper course is simply to bend with the wind and accept him for what he is. Routine discipline which keeps dogs that accept it on their toes may spoil everything for you.

An example that comes immediately to mind is a Springer male I have in the kennel now. He's lived up to his name, Ding-A-Ling. He fights a leash, cowers when made to heel, usually refuses to fetch a dummy and has been known to swim a ditch, crawl up on the opposite side and sit looking away and refuse to obey or look at me when forced to go after the dummy.

But when we're gunning afield he is something else. Hunts hard but handles beautifully and is a superlative retriever of pheasant whether they splash or thump down, getting the bird and delivering with gusto and sitting to put it in your hand.

I cite the personal example to point out that while most dogs should and can be formally trained, there are always exceptions.

Papers

Most purebred dogs are covered by two "papers", a form showing the dog has been registered with an official registry and another form called a pedigree. Actually every dog has a pedigree—if you can run it down. So do you. It is nothing but a listing, usually in chart form, of an individual's ancestors. The registration form is much more important.

A dog may be purebred but unregistered. It is up to the man or kennel from whom you acquire your pup to make sure that the pup is *eligible* for individual registration. Then it is up to you to register your particular pup. The owner of the litter should have it listed with an official registry and furnish you with a form, which filled out and mailed with a fee by you to the registry, should be accepted and certified and a form returned to you offering proof that your pup *is* purebred. Without this registration, no puppies that may be produced if you use your dog as a sire or dam will be eligible for registration and this of course diminishes your dog's value.

The two registries gun dog owners are concerned with are the American Kennel Club, 51 Madison Ave. New York, N.Y. and the Field Dog Stud Book, 222 W. Adams St., Chicago, Ill. Both accept registration of all the gun dog breeds and conduct field activities for them. The AKC has the field activities for retrievers and spaniels sewed up while the FDSB is dominant as far as the traditional pointing breeds are concerned. Versatile pointing dog activities are conducted through both registries.

If the person from whom you purchase a dog does not give you a filled out pedigree form, you may obtain one of these from the agency with which you register your dog for a small fee.

If you are interested in a study of your pup's ancestors, you should learn to read pedigrees, particularly if you plan to do any breeding. This, of course, is somewhat of a science in itself.

To help you get started, if you see the letters "Ch." preceeding an FDSB-registered dog's name, this is good. It means he has won a major championship event and is designated a champion among field dogs, since the FDSB conducts only field trials, no confirmation shows. You will also see three numbers following the individual registration number of certain dogs listed on the pedigree. This is a valuable indicator for breeders and braggers. It indicates how many wins the dog has in field trial competition, how many winning dogs that particular dog has produced and how many wins the progeny have amassed up to the time the pedigree was issued.

For example: Ch. Titanup (dog's name and indication he has won one or more field trials officially designated as championships) 442280 (individual registration number) 64-132-792 (these three numbers delineate his record as a performer and producer, 64 placements in field trials, 132 progeny sired which placed in trials 792 times).

If your dog is registered with the AKC, his pedigree may be sprinkled with such designations as "F. Ch." or "F. T. Ch." or "A. F. Ch." This indicates that a dog has undergone training and is proficient enough at field work to win the honor of "Field Trial Champion" in an open stake or "Amateur Field Trial Champion" in a stake restricted to amateur handlers. You may also see the designation "Ch." Since the AKC conducts both shows and field trials, this championship title applies to a dog judged on physical appearance and not field ability. It has little meaning for a gun dog man.

Blood and Breeding

Because a particular dog is an outstanding performer is no guarantee of his ability to transmit his qualities to his puppies. When one dog has this ability, as obviously Ch. Titanup referred to in the example above had, the dog is called "prepotent" and is in great demand as a sire.

Blood will tell. A man would be an idiot to knock good breeding practices which are vital in the preservation of top-notch field dogs. But everything must be kept in its perspective and in the matter of producing field trial winners, money, prestige and reputation are as much responsible for the development of outstanding performers as bloodlines and breeding programs.

So I am going to voice a heretical opinion. The average hunter will probably be happier with a gun dog a bit deficient in "hot blood" than one loaded with it. I'll argue the ramifications some other time, but sufficient exertion and money can go a long way toward making a dog with a mastery of field trial mechanics. Just don't let a flock of titles blind you. They were acquired as much by the sweat and ability of diligent trainers, and the financial backing of determined owners, as by any inherited abilities.

It seems very likely to me that if we took two litters of pups, one from hot, field trial breeding, the other from just good hunting dog ancestry (which may or may not have some trial winning ancestors a few generations back) and gave both litters *an equal chance with the same trainer who was unapprised of their backgrounds* we would get darn near an equal number of pups from each litter that turn out to be good hunters—even field trial winners.

Furthermore the top pup or pups out of really hot breeding will be just too much dog for most hunters to train and handle and hunt over. They tread a thin line between being outstanding or outlaw. It takes talented training to do right by them. Just handling such a dog afield is a full time job and a hunter is more comfortable with a bit less or a good deal less "quality".

However, *do not* knock the man who is devoted to and produces from hot lines. It is much easier to breed down than up and a reservoir of good field performers is furnished by the "reject" progeny of champion dogs who have not the temperament, ability or opportunity to succeed in competition under judgement.

The most practical attitude for you to take is to make sure you select a pup whose pappy and mammy were both satisfactory gun dogs and if there are some field trial winners in his background, accept this fact happily. If not, don't let it bother you. What you do with your dog and how you do it will be more important than the record of his great-grandpappy.

Prices

There is really no set price that you can expect to pay for a puppy. There are all kinds of qualifications which determine price. But as a very flexible guideline, I'll lay it out for you based on the 1974 economy. If inflation continues, expect to pay more. If a depression hits, expect a bargain.

If you get a purebred, eligible for registration, pup out of good hunting stock for less than $100 you've made a good buy. For less than $50 you've made a steal—with some danger that you may be buying something inferior. At the same time, I wouldn't pay more than $150 to $200 for a puppy regardless of its highly touted ancestry. Pups are really "pigs in a poke", real gambles, between the ages of six and twelve weeks.

House Dogs and Kids' Dogs

A home environment and children for playmates are good for gun dogs. In fact, most breeds respond best to this sort of treatment and develop a rapport through close association with the man who is to hunt with them. It is a rare individual among the gun dog breeds who does *not* make a fine companion and kids' buddy. Get double duty out of your dog by sharing your home and fireside with him.

Help From the Old Dog

You may be tempted to start your gun dog in the field with an older dog. If the older dog is well trained and a good performer, yield to the temptation. But if the dog available to you, a hunting buddy's or your own, is some kind of a double-dyed son of a bitch, you are better off to introduce your youngster by himself.

The main reason for using a good older dog is not that some of his qualities will rub off on the pup. They won't. But he should show the pup some game and what it's all about. Once this has been done, work the puppy on his own. You do not want him to become dependent

Children and pups are good for each other, Kathleen Duffey, then five, and a Pointer pup display mutal affection and enjoyment of each other while the pup's somewhat apprehensive dam, Twist, makes sure all is well.

Children should be encouraged to work with dogs and here the author's daughter, Debbie at age ten, trains her eight-month old American Water Spaniel, McGurk.

upon his more capable and experienced "mentor", or discouraged because he can't keep up.

Diversions and Temptations

Your gun dog should be exposed to everything he's likely to encounter in normal living. Depending upon his reaction to strange things, he should be encouraged if he's frightened and scolded if he's aggressive.

You can't isolate your young dog and then get upset when something strange provokes misbehavior. If livestock, for example, should spook him, walk him through barnyards and pastured herds at heel or on leash to give him confidence. If he wants to chase stock, call him off and punish severely.

Anticipate he may be interested in domestic fowl and walk him through a flock of chickens, just as you did through the decoys, jerking him and swatting if he indicates any interest in the tame birds, telling him "No!" It will save you embarrassment, a bill and getting booted off good hunting land.

All Work, No Play

Some dogs are discerning enough to know the difference between work and play. But don't count on it, particularly with a young dog in training. Therefore, caution the kids about throwing balls, sticks and stones, letting the pup run off with such objects, or chasing the pup to recover them.

If this sort of thing is allowed, the dog is very likely to try this game with a dummy or bird and the training you gave him at an early age regarding proper retrieving can go down the drain. Throwing sticks out in the water for a dog to swim after and then letting him drop them on the shoreline as he emerges, picking up and tossing for him again, can cause great difficulty in obtaining proper delivery on water retrieves.

Have your children play with the dog, romp with him, take him for walks etc. but make sure they *don't* use the commands you are teaching or have taught without demanding obedience. Don't allow game playing that can confuse the dog or will encourage the development of habits contrary to the goal to which you are working.

But never forget that kids and dogs have an affinity for each other and there are all kinds of things a kid will accidentally get a dog to accept that you'd have to consciously work at doing. So allow the kids some leeway but exercise good judgement regarding what they can and can't do.

By all means encourage their participation in your training sessions and they'll quickly pick up what they should and shouldn't do around dogs. A responsible youngster, 10 years or older, can eventually be entrusted to do some unsupervised training and brushing up work as well as shoot guns, throw birds and do legwork that are all part of training.

Kids are great help and as they get older it may be feasible to get them dogs of their own to train if their interest holds. You can work together, sharing the problems and their solutions and the joys of developing good gun dogs. Good dog trainers, amateur or professional, aren't born. They are made.

Dog Care

You assume a considerable responsibility when you take up ownership of a dog. It is a living, breathing, feeling animal, not a mechanical device that can be gassed up, started up, used, shut off and forgotten about until the next time you are ready to go.

But careful studies and concern over the welfare of dogs has today given any dog owner who exercises a modicum of common sense the assurance that he can properly take care of a dog's needs with a minimum of fuss or worry. It will take a bit of time and consideration on your part, but you shouldn't begrudge that to a hobby and your dog's gratefulness will be most rewarding.

There are a number of good books on the market that will go into great detail to tell you what's best for your dog. Get one and read it, absorb the basics and then modify these considerations as your common sense dictates.

To stay happy and healthy a gun dog's essential requirements are:

1. Nourishing food and fresh water daily.
2. Dry, draft free sleeping quarters.
3. Sufficient exercise.
4. Human attention, including training, play and conversation.
5. Occasional grooming.
6. Veterinary attention as required.

The best indicators of how well you are caring for your dog are what he looks and acts like. You should be able to see and judge this in your daily contacts with your dog. As you train and play with your dog, you will observe his attitude and his physical condition. As you pet him, you will detect coat condition and the presence of clumps that need untangling, burrs that should be removed, nails that need trimming.

The very best method of feeding is to utilize the dry dog foods that are commercially manufactured and to supplement them with table-scrap treats. It is simple, time saving and economical. House dogs can have food in their bowl all the time, eat when they choose. Kennel dogs can be fed out of a hopper. But I suggest feeding a measured ration each day, no more than a dog will clean up in a 24 hour period. This not only allows you to control the amount given in relation to the dog's condition (if thin, feed more; if fat, reduce the amount) but requires you to spend some time in contact with the dog even on those days when you are busy and don't give him the desired attention, training and exercise.

Up to about six months of age, puppies should have food in front of them at all times so they can eat what they need, when they need it. If you insist on mixing food with some liquid, feed a pup small amounts three or four times daily rather than one big meal.

From the age of four to six months pups can be fed as adult dogs, once a day if food is prepared or a measured ration in the feed pan every 24 hours, the amount depending upon the dog's appearance and condition. Water must always be available and is particularly important when dry feeding since the dog, in effect, must do his own mixing and requires more water. Crunching the dry food also stimulates the salivary glands aiding digestion and proper utilization of the food.

During hunting season, if your dog is being worked hard more than once or twice a week, increase the ration and/or supplement all you can with fat and meat scrap. He won't get fat and can use the added energy provided. If kenneled out of doors, you will also find that he'll need more food to keep warm in severe winter climates.

Outwitting the Rascal

Prevention is always superior to curing. As you work with your dog and get to know him, you'll find you can often anticipate what he's going to do before he does it. Once you've developed this knack, try to cut him off at the pass whenever possible. You are much better off to stop something before it ever gets started than being forced into correcting some act after it's been committed. Correctly guessing what your dog's action or reaction may be will save a deal of hard work.

Turning to the Pro

It could very well happen that you undertake to train your own dog but the exigencies of earning a living or a quirk you can't cope with turns up and you despair of getting the job done properly. If you want to keep your dog and still want him developed into a good hunter, a professional trainer may turn out to be your best friend.

Pick a man of good reputation with clean kennels and adequate facilities. Pay his price and give him and yourself a break by telling him as honestly as you know how what the trouble is and what you want done with the dog—even the mistakes you've made if you recognize them. Don't conceal anything. The trainer will find out in a short time anyway.

If you level with him it will take less training time, he can avoid duplication and won't use a procedure that may worsen a problem you may have caused or been unable to solve.

If a dog trainer had $100 for every man who's come in and said, "This is a real good dog. All he needs is a few birds shot over him" only to discover that the dog is gun-shy, a bolter, afraid of water, hardmouthed or just a plain knuckle-head he wouldn't have to train dogs for a living. He could retire.

So if you have to turn to a pro, treat him honestly as a professional who deserves your confidence and knows what he's doing and you

226

will be repaid with a trained dog, good advice and at considerably less cost than if you try to con him.

Dog and Man Age Comparisons

Self-centered man has, for many years, made correlations between the life-span allotted to him on this earth with the years of life normally accruing to his boon companion, the dog.

Comparing ages of dogs and men during the various stages of their development and decline is more than just an academic exercise. Since men are more familiar with other humans than dogs and presumably understand their own kind better, matching a dog's years to those of a man can lead to better understanding and appreciation of a dog by his owner and give some idea of what can be expected of a dog during the various stages of his development.

The comparison of age factors comes in when it becomes obvious that expecting from a puppy the same ability and work desired on the part of an adult dog is as ridiculous as sending a boy to do a man's job.

But when do "baby" dogs become the equivelant of boys and girls? When do these canine boys and girls become men and women? What are the prime years for a dog? Comparatively speaking, how old is a 12 year old dog?

The scale of comparison used by most laymen seems to be that one year of a dog's life is equal to seven years of a human's. Based on personal observation and experience, regarding the prime years of a man's and a dog's life, there isn't too much to argue with that easy to remember scale. A dog is in his prime from three to six years of age. If men will concede that their prime years are between the ages of 25 and 40 the figuring isn't too far off.

But I have always been bothered by the youth and old age comparisons. In my observation the 1 to 7 formula just does not work out there.

For example, much much more can be expected of a one-year old male or female dog than can be hoped for from a seven-year old boy or girl. Furthermore, few men or women attain the ripe old age of 84, much less go beyond it. But a common age for natural causes to strike down a dog is between 11 and 13 years, so might not those years have more in common with the end of man's normal life span, ages 65–75?

With such things in mind I've set up my own scale regarding the rough comparisons in the approximately 11 or 12 years of a dog's life to the actuarial statistics that indicate 65 to 70 is normal man's life expectancy. The table is strictly my own. It should be easy to remember or you can cut it out and carry it around in your wallet or paste it on your wall. I'll give reasons for my conclusions a little further on. If you disagree with the age comparisons don't throw them out before you've read why I've arrived at them. If you don't think my reasoning is valid, make up your own Dog and Man Age Comparison chart.

There is general agreement that the lives of men are shaped during their childhood and adolescence. Learning is literally soaked up and a great many things informally acquired through chance happenings and experiences make an indelible impression. It is no different with dogs. They are ready, able and willing to learn at about two months of age. They form habits, attachments and quirks and they learn from their environmental surroundings. Their development and reaction to their experiences can be guided through play and informal education which will decide whether they will be open, trusting and well-balanced individuals rather than neurotic spooks.

At four-months of age formal schooling can begin for most normal pups just as most normal kids start their book learning in the five to seven year bracket. The physical similarities are there as well. Kids can play hard endlessly, then tire suddenly and fall sound asleep. So do puppies in that age bracket. Neither is ready for hard work.

At six months of age most of a pup's behavioral patterns will be set, based on the treatment he received, instilling the proper attitude toward and responses to further training during the formative months. At eight months of age, most pups should have learned there are some rules they'll have to live by. If they haven't, they can take the discipline that will impress that fact upon them. They are on the verge of adolescence.

Males have become confirmed leg-lifters when urinating, following considerable experimentation. Some, when kept in the company of other male dogs, start this much earlier in seeming mimicry of the "big boys" while others, secluded from contact with other dogs, will continue to squat for months longer. Coinciding with the three-point stance when voiding comes a sexual awakening, again stimulated or retarded by the presence or absence of other dogs of both sexes.

Female dogs are likely to experience their first heat period from seven months on and the precocious males and females are capable of siring and conceiving puppies even though no serious dog breeder would consider using them for that purpose at such an early age. Some pups also simply remain puppies for longer.

At 10 months of age, the pup is ready for high school. He is a teen-ager, an adolescent. He needs plenty of attention and hard mental and physical training, well planned and controlled so as not to tax his still developing brain and muscles to the point of fatigue, but to pre-

Dog and Man Age Chart

Infancy

Dog	Man
Birth to 7 weeks	Birth to 1½ years

Childhood

2 months	2 to 3 years
4 months	5 to 7 years
6 months	9 to 10 years
8 months	11 to 12 years

Adolescence

10 months	13 to 14 years
1 year	15 to 16 years

Maturity

2 years	21 years
3 years	25 years
4 years	30 years
5 years	35 years
6 years	40 years
7 years	45 years
8 years	50 years
9 years	55 years
10 years	60 years

Old Age

11 years	65 years
12 years	70 years
13 years	80 years
14 years	90 years
15 years	100 plus years

Given consideration an elderly dog, like Dave Duffey's Clinker Dhu shown at 11 years of age, can still furnish hunting satisfaction.

pare him for the rigorous and demanding life of a good gun dog.

Again, this coincides with the athletic development and academic pressures that increase as youths leave grade school and enter high school.

And at the age of one year, dogs like mid-teen youths are just a shade off of full maturity. They are physically and mentally capable of doing just about anything adults can do, they are sexually capable although often a bit confused about the whole bit. Much can be expected of young dogs and teen-agers. But both require a certain tolerance and latitude if they are to develop into adults worth their feed.

The two year old dog must be compared to the young man and young lady of 21, the general statute age for assessing adult responsibilities. In comparison to their elders, they still may be a bit wet behind the ears. But their enthusiasm, endurance and recuperative powers are out of this world.

The prime years of a gun dog are between three and six, just as those of a man are between 25 and 40. Lessons have been learned, experience has taught what does and does not work and the physical development, toughness and confidence is there to handle the most arduous tasks and accomplish great things. Thus it seems reasonable to equate three years in a dog with age 25 in man, four dog years with 30, five with 35 and six with 40.

When buying a dog, a properly trained three year old is a prime prospect. The six year old, a seasoned campaigner, may be prized for his experience and polish. But his remaining productive years will affect a possible reduction in purchase price.

At seven years of age, most gun dogs are "over the hump." At age eight the decline has set in. They remain vigorous and capable of a hard day's work, but have learned how to pace themselves and happily sieze the opportunity for a recuperative break when one is presented. They start getting set in their ways, they've run the gauntlet, they know the score and they may even be stubbornly resistant to change and variation. Despite the grey on their muzzles they may do puppyish things when faced with competition or antics of younger dogs. Yet, when the chips are down they can be relied upon to come through. This seems also a fair appraisal of most men and women of 45 or 50.

Nine and 10 year old dogs show the greatest individual variance of any age class, just as do 55 to 60 year old men and women. Some appear and act years younger than their calendar time indicates. Others are old before their time. But everything is generally done at a slower pace as old age approaches.

Special consideration should be given the 11- and 12-year-old dog that is still capable of and willing to hunt just as it is due the 65- and 70-year-old man or woman who carries on beyond the normal retirement years.

When a dog gets past 12, he is truly an old dog. Just as many humans, some remain alert and comparatively active in old age. I knew one old Labrador of going on 15 who was still going hard at the end of a day that wore out prime-age dogs. But this is phenomenal, whether in dogs or among 80- to 100-year-old citizens who are up and at it daily. Most dogs and people are then simply living out their time.

There you have the reasons for the simple and, in my opinion, accurate comparison chart of canine and human age periods. It is not offered with any claim being made for scientific objectivity or on the basis of any special qualification in the academic orders, genetic or social specialties.

A framework quickly and easily comprehensible to the man in the field for assessing the performance of his gun dogs and giving them the consideration due them has some importance.

A father, in the prime of life, would not expect his 10-year-old son to keep up with him or display his talent with a shotgun while on a hunting trip. An athletic young man in his prime, who tagged along with a sportsman father since boyhood and has watched him slow down as the years piled up, might kid the "old man" but would unobtrusively show him certain considerations.

A good gun dog, prospective or well-seasoned, deserves no less.

14

Training Devices and Accessories

VARIOUS devices used in the training of gun dogs range from pure and simple to ingenious and complicated, whether reference is to the training aid itself or methods used in applying it. Some, like a collar and lead, are essential and universal in use. Others are rather esoteric and will have only limited use.

Any training device, however, is merely a tool. It can be a valuable aid when used wisely by the trainer. But in today's situation it appears that more and more trainers will have to acquaint themselves with various devices which dog trainers of yesteryear might have scoffed at if they'd heard of them.

So use training aids extensively or sparingly as your personal situation dictates but always look upon them as a supplement to your own knowledge of training.

Because it is the one device most commonly associated with dogs, let's start off with what goes around a dog's neck to exercise control over him.

Collars

Everyone knows what a collar is. But they come in different designs and for different purposes. A small pup should be started with a slim leather or nylon collar to accustom him to wearing it. It will also serve to get him used to restraint as he is tugged from time to time while being walked and this in turn will condition him to prevent fighting a collar should he have to be tied out.

Keep close tabs on any collar you put on a pup so that his rapid growth doesn't make it uncomfortably tight. You should be able to run your little finger between the collar and the pup or dog's throat without the collar tightening appreciably. Take the collar off and put it on frequently.

Larger dogs, of course, need collars to fit, and different sizes can be obtained. For the gun dog, I think the most practicable collar in the field is a one-inch leather collar with a metal ring opposite the buckle which is called a "safety collar." Should a dog get caught by the collar the ring aids in preventing strangulation, it is readily available for snapping on a lead, leash or check cord, and it snugs up when a dog pulls against a lead.

A collar of this type or of the regular style without the ring (flat collars are generally preferred for shortcoated dogs, rolled collars for long coated dogs) is mainly used for controlling a trained dog and as an identification carrier, although it can be used as a training collar. It is important that a dog used in the field be identified if he should run off or get away. This is best done by riveting a brass plate imprinted with the owner's name, address and phone number onto the leather collar.

Training Collars

Depending upon the degree of severity necessary to punish the dog to obtain compliance there are three types of training collars available —the slip chain (or choke) collar, the obedience collar and the force training collar.

The mildest and most generally useful is the slip chain collar, featuring a ring on each end of the links. Such collars are available in different lengths and chain weight. The links are dropped through one of the rings and a noose is formed. This is slipped over the dog's head and a leash attached to the other ring. The correct size is one that slips snugly but easily over the dog's head when being removed. The collar rides free until the protruding ring is pulled by hooked finger or attached leash. This tightens the collar. Release of the tension loosens it.

Proper use of this collar involves a quick jerk which squeezes the dog's neck, an unpleasant experience but neither cruel nor harmful. It is superior to the regular leather collar because the pressure is applied evenly and the dog can tense his neck muscles against it, in contrast to all the pressure exerted by a leather collar on the soft throat. It can be used in training all dogs.

Many people leave slip chain collars on their dogs just as they do

234

a leather collar, but this carries some slight risk of a dog getting hung up and strangling around the kennel and home. The collar should always be removed when the dog is used afield.

It is an essential tool in the training of any gun dog to comply quickly with such commands as "Heel," "Sit" and "Stay," It also provides better control over the dog than a leather collar should something tempt him to chase or bolt when he is being walked.

A properly started puppy will require only the slip chain collar to break properly. The other two types of training collars are best used only on extremely recalcitrant adult dogs that require severe measures to overcome a lack of training in their formative months or for a specialized purpose.

The obedience training collar is all metal with blunt spikes to the inside which press against the dog's neck when the collar is tightened. The force training collar is of leather with brass spikes on the inside which poke the dog's neck when the collar is pulled on. They may be used in the same manner and for the same purpose as the slip chain collar but are much more severe and, in some cases, can cause panic or snapping by a timid dog, particularly if they jam, or if enough slack in the leash can not quickly be given a struggling dog.

Some trainers use them to stanch and steady particularly tough bird dogs but the most practical use by an amateur is for force-breaking a dog to retrieve, the jab of the tightened collar being substituted for the ear or toe pinch. The collar then should be manipulated by hand with no leash attached so the pressure can immediately be released when the dog complies.

Leashes, Leads and Check Cords

Leashes are short (one to two feet in length) leads are long (about six to ten feet) and check cords are very lengthy (25 to 50 feet). To be completely equipped a trainer should have at least one of each. The lead is for starting the youngster in the yard, allowing for slack and leeway when accustoming him to restraint and calling him to you. The leash is for control of the older dog when walking him at heel or steadying him to shot in retrieving work. The slender check cord is allowed to drag after the dog in the field and can be picked up by the handler as he approaches a dog on point or held as he guides a dog into birds, permitting some control from some distances off. All have snaps to attach to the collar and a loop for the hand when made of leather or nylon. Cotton and nylon rope is also used for check cords.

Leather is the traditional material used in leads and leashes but nylon is stronger and rot and mildew proof. However, whenever a nylon lead or check cord is used gloves should be worn to prevent possible friction burns. A short leash can be hooked on a belt loop or a lead can be folded and carried in the game pocket when afield. They are useful for chastising as well as controlling a dog.

Flushing whips, which are stiff leather bats with fringed tips on one end and wrist and belt loop on the other, are used primarily by field trialers to beat the brush in their flushing efforts but can also double as dog chastisers, quirts or short leads.

Dummies

The training dummies used primarily to teach retrieving are canvas-covered and kapok-filled. They, and the other aids mentioned here, are available at good supply houses like Sporting Dog Specialties, Inc. in Spencerport, N.Y. Plastic dummies are also available, are heavier and can be thrown farther than the canvas ones. But since some dogs don't seem to like the smooth, hard texture they should be used only with older trained dogs who will pick up anything they are expected to.

A piece of rope approximately the length of the dummy can be attached to the eyelet on the end of the dummy allowing you to sling it farther when throwing it during retrieving practice. The dragging length of cord also helps condition a dog to carrying with high head to make a more stylish delivery. If you use a bright color it will aid you in spotting a dummy in dense cover should the dog not manage to find it.

Besides being thrown to retrieve, dummies can also be hidden in cover to teach a dog to seek game and, when bird wings are taped to them, aid in the transition from dummy to actual bird finding and retrieving.

Training Scents

A few drops of concentrated scent prepared from game bird glandular extractions applied to a training dummy will attract a gun dog and serve to accustom him to finding and picking up game birds of similar odor. They will help in the transition from dummies to the real thing. Scents of a number of different birds are available commercially.

But once a dog has actually hunted game, application of scent to a dummy is of questionable value and may even be confusing to a dog unless feathers in the form of bird skins and wings are attached to the dummy. I have had dogs that were good hunters and retrievers home in on a scented dummy, pounce, stop, leave the dummy and go off seeking the real thing.

It proved to me the scent works. But is also indicated the dog knew better than to pick up an inanimate object just because it smelled like a bird and sought to locate something with feathers on it. Also once a dog has learned to work on dummies, particularly if they are carried around in the game bag of a hunting vest where they pick up plenty of scent, he will smell them and work them without the application of scent.

If you have been unable to use any real pheasant or duck during your training sessions, you may find it valuable to sprinkle some of the scent of those birds on the pigeons or other available training birds you are using in traps or for retrieving. When taken afield the dog will hunt that scent and make the proper correlations.

Bottled scent of animals you do not want your bird dog to have anything to do with, such as deer, are also available to use in breaking a dog of his interest in off-game. Attach a scent pad or wind a rag around a dog's collar, saturate it with scent and smear some on his muzzle. The idea is to make him so sick of that particular odor he'll avoid it afield.

Dummy Launchers

For the man who wants to save his throwing arm, a launching device that will propel specially designed dummies with a blank cartridge charge are available for training dogs to retrieve on water or land. In essence it provides the sound of gunfire and arcs a flying dummy some 40 to 70 yards from the firing point, depending on the type of blank cartridge used.

It has all kinds of uses, but is essentially a gadget to do the job of shooting and throwing and it requires both hands to operate. Care should be taken in loading and firing. If used without a glove on the hand gripping the launcher handle, or too frequently with the high power loads, the launcher can do a good job of bunging up the hand which must absorb the not inconsiderable recoil.

Guns

In addition to his shotgun, a dog trainer ought to have a blank pistol. A .22 blank starter's pistol is sufficient when starting puppies or working dogs on being stanch or steady. The idea is to have an easily portable gun with you at all times when training so you can pop off a shot when required, but no killing is necessary. Blanks can be

A dummy launcher can really fling an object for a dog like this black Labrador to retrieve.

fired in regular handguns, but you are above question by the law if you tote around a starter's pistol.

Slingshots and Marbles

A pocketful of marbles and a slingshot is the poor man's electric shocker, a great deal simpler, more readily available and handled, and very effective to as far as you can shoot a marble accurately—not much over 20 yards for most of us.

A marble propelled by a slingshot is a great attention getter, easily carried in a coat pocket and available when needed and has a most salutary effect on any dog who chooses to ignore you.

A live pigeon is inserted in this release trap which will propel the bird into the air, assuring flight at the proper time. Unless ejected from the trap, some captive birds will refuse to fly.

A few plinks in the ribs or flanks with a well-aimed marble quickly teaches a dog to pay attention when you speak to him and, once you've gotten to him just the threat of the slingshot, whether by sight or the sound of snapping bands will remind a dog of his duties and bring him to attention.

Use only light glass or clay marbles, never stones or "steelies" and aim only for the dog's back half. Don't stretch the rubbers to full power and never align the slingshot along your face lest a rubber snap you in the eye.

Release Traps

When using live birds in training, keeping them in the place you want them can pose problems. Dizzy them too much and a young dog may catch them. Dizzy them not enough and they will run off or fly off. To save time when training you want to be assured of a bird being right where you want it when you want it there. Small traps that hold unfettered birds, released by springing open the trap solve this difficulty.

There are various styles in these devices but the basic job they do is the same—keep a bird in one place until the proper time to have it fly and release to fly at that time. My personal preference is the type that snaps open, actually popping the bird up into the air, over those that require the confined bird to furnish his own spring and momentum of getting underway. Sometimes confined birds just won't get out of the trap and fly unless they are boosted by the trap's operation.

These gadgets are very useful, but like anything else must be used with judgement. For example, they are of no value in training a flushing dog unless you have a version that is sprung by a long trip wire, allowing the trap to be sprung before the dog pounces on it. If the flushing dog makes it to the trap he will either catch the bird, catch both bird and trap or be frightened and hurt when the trap springs.

While useful with pointing breeds, traps shouldn't be used except with a dog that is already reliably stanch or, if used with a youngster who is not stanch, should be used only when you can restrain or control the dog, as on the end of a check cord. The release traps are very helpful when the dog is being "corded in" to a bird to stanch him, steady him or teach him to back.

Use it with a free running dog who is not stanch at your peril. The unstanch, unrestrained dog will invariably work in too close, see or hear the bird rustle in the trap and pounce on the trap. You then develop a flusher or a blinker depending upon his reaction to contact with trap and bird.

Unless there is a decent breeze blowing, most dogs will point very close to release-trapped birds. Since it is set down in one spot and concealed with grass or brush there is only one spot from which the bird scent can emanate, in contrast to normal free movement of a bird.

Wetting a bird slightly (not so much that flight is impaired) will aid in making the scent stronger. If you use dizzied birds it is good practice to rub them lightly through some of the cover in the area you plant them. The faint scent will caution the dog and he will work more naturally as he would on a normal, unplanted bird.

Wild Bird Corollary

There will be instance when you are actually hunting wild birds when your dog will pass a bird or have difficulty finding one that is knocked down. A tight sitting bird gives off little scent. One that is stone cold dead when it hits the ground and never flutters will be hard

A dead bird is used here to demonstrate that this type of release trap does indeed propel a bird into the air affording a shot.

to find. Activity and, in the latter case, what old timers used to call "air washing" affects the amount of scent given off. Just as a steamy locker room smells more of man than a classroom, so does an active bird give off more scent. So don't fault your dog if he has difficulty under such circumstances.

And if you train in the spring or hunt on a preserve that furnishes spring shooting, expect your dog to have some difficulty handling birds properly. The vegetation is strong and rank (early fall hunts may present the same condition) and, during the breeding and nesting season, birds give off less scent and are more inclined to stay on the ground and sneak off than to flush properly.

Clothing

I'm not about to suggest a uniform for dog trainers. Anything that is comfortable and suitable for the conditions you are working under in the line of boots, shirts, pants and jackets is fine. If you are really serious you will find yourself training (and hunting) in all kinds of weather and you know best what suits you.

I do suggest, however, that you utilize your hunting vest or any jacket with a lot of pockets in it and a game bag attached as a *training coat.* Keep all the miscellaneous things you need—leash, collar, pistol, blanks, slingshot, etc. stashed in that vest. The game pocket holds a number of dummies. Shrug into it when you take your dog out. Then you will have at hand and for immediate use just about everything you might need. Nothing breaks up a training session like having to run back to the car or house to get something you forgot.

I suggest a vest because it is cooler in the summer and can be slipped over raingear or heavy clothing making everything easily available.

An item you might not have hanging in your closet but which you'll find very useful is a pair of naugahyde chaps. You can pull them off and on quickly and they will save wear and tear, wetting and mud on good clothing if an opportunity affords itself to train or hunt when you can't change clothes. They are also effective when you are fooling with an exhuberant puppy who can mess up your good trousers by rubbing against you, jumping up or shaking on you.

Whistles

A dog whistle should be plastic or bakelite, small and sharp in tone. No doubt there are others manufactured, but the two most satisfactory whistles I've used, by brand name, are the Roy Gonia and the Acme Thunderer. You can fiddle with a "silent" whistle if you like. But I like a whistle with a bit of authority when I blast on it and if I can hear it I know damn well the dog can and he has no excuse for not paying attention.

There are commercial lanyards available for suspending the whistle from your neck. Don't leave them too long or each time you bend over the whistle will get in your way. Keep the lanyard short and you won't know you are wearing a whistle except when you want to use it.

I haven't yet found a whistle that won't freeze up frequently in bitter cold weather. There's nothing you can do about that. But your lips will be too stiff and chapped to emit a decent natural whistle. So in virtually every instance an artificial whistle does the job better than your natural lip whistle—unless you can't resist letting an attractive girl know how much she impresses you.

Just don't get a metal whistle. It will stick to your lips and pull off skin in bitter weather and is tougher on teeth. Never shoot with a whistle in your mouth, unless you enjoy visiting the orthodontist.

Shock Collars

These clever electronic devices are often advertized as "electronic trainers" which implies that a remote control gadget can train your dog. It can't. And the instruments should be called just what they are, electric shock collars. They are training tools just like other less expensive and more reliable accoutrements.

Just as with a whip, a check cord, a force collar or any of the other time-honored tools of the trade, the shock collar is effective only if properly used. It is not a cure-all and, while it can obtain startlingly fast results in breaking a dog of bad habits, if used injudiciously and for the wrong thing it can do just as rapid a ruination job on a dog.

It has a great deal of practical application in the hands of a professional, a man who through experience, trial and error has learned to analyze individual dogs and is expected to train problem dogs who are near mature or mature, lack introductory training or have been goofed up by their owners.

But the one-dog hunter-trainer who introduces his dog to the field, game and guns properly and makes a hunting buddy of him should have no call to resort to this expensive gadget. If he does, he would be better off to invest the $100 to $200 he'd pay for a shock collar in a new beginning with a puppy or started dog who is of better temperament and gets off on the right paw.

I equate the shock collar with the old time desperation measure of "let him get out aways and then tickle his ass with fine shot" except that the electric jolt can do no permanent physical harm as clumped shot pellets might. Peppering an outlaw dog with shot and buzzing him with electricity have both proven effective. But they are both last ditch measures to be resorted to in dire straits.

The device should not be used as an aid in handling or stanching a dog unless the dog is already trained and is not likely to associate the unpleasantness with birds. But juicing a neophyte when he's around birds can develop a blinker and hitting him with a charge in an effort to *teach* handling response can confuse and cow a pup.

As far as amateur use is concerned, the shock collar is a fine investment in disciplining a dog to break him of a fault or habit when he is out of your reach. Thus, if you have a dog who is good otherwise, but chases deer, kills chickens, fights, barks excessively, jumps fences, bites the postman or just can't be broke of some other fault, by all means get you a shock collar, put it on him and when he engages in the undesirable act, push the transmitter button. If he's up to a quarter

243

mile from you he can be quickly brought to realize such activities are no-no's.

Reactions to shocking vary with individual dogs. Whatever you do, refrain from becoming "button happy" and zapping the dog at the slightest provocation, or giving a test push "just to see if she's working."

It has been argued that the beauty of using a shock collar is the "fact" that the dog doesn't associate the punishment with you. Hell, I want my dog to associate the punishment (along with the praise) with me. How else is he to know what displeases me?

And I'm not so sure about the disassociation. I've known of at least one case when an extremely intelligent, but not overly docile, dog was given a jolt for misbehavior, spun around, homed right in on the trainer and took a healthy chew of him. He knew from whence that particular "blessing" flew.

Generally if you decide to use a shock collar to "train" your dog, you may expect one of three things to happen.

1.) With certain dogs it will work just as you desire it to.

2.) With others you will have a cowed, hesitant animal who will leave your side only with the utmost urging and which you may or may not be able to retrain to run and hunt like he ought to.

3.) The very smart dog will behave himself as long as the shock collar or the dummy collar (which is used to fool the dog into thinking the real thing is hung on him) is around his neck. But take it off and he reverts to his old wild-running self.

Summed up, the shock collar when properly used is a wonderful device for breaking a dog of something you want him to have nothing to do with, and is very effective in re-enforcing his response to a command he knows but is disobeying. But it is not a teaching instrument, except in the most negative way.

Books

Obviously if you are reading this you have decided a book or books can be a training aid. I can only suggest that you not confine your reading to a single book on dogs or on training dogs. Pick one for your "Bible" if you are a beginner and follow the procedures outlined therein. Steps and repetition in an organized program are important and you should have one mentor for the training you undertake.

244

Skipping around using divergent methods usually doesn't work too well.

But no trainer or author has a mortal lock on *the* method for training a gun dog. And let no one tell you that if you try his "magic formula" it will produce "instant gun dog" from your easy chair. It takes actual doing with a dog to train one properly. The man who goes out and tries to train and who hunts with his dog may make all kinds of mistakes but produce a better gun dog than the man who memorizes sentences and can glibly quote the experts but does little or nothing with his dog.

So, when you aren't working with your dog, pick up and read as many new, old and different books about dogs and their training you can get your hands on. The basics are pretty much the same, but every individual who has trained dogs successfully will come up with some peculiar gimmick that another hasn't developed or has forgotten to mention. I've waded through some very dull books on dogs, but never failed to find something of which I was previously unaware.

Talk dogs all you can with knowledgeable dog people. But fall back on your book or books as a ready reference, a source of information and an authoritative check on some procedure you may have forgotten.

So, I hope you've found this particular book good reading and practically informative. Good luck with your training efforts.

245